ALSO BY GREG STEINMETZ

The Richest Man Who Ever Lived:
The Life and Times of Jacob Fugger

AMERICAN RASCAL

—◆—

HOW JAY GOULD BUILT
WALL STREET'S BIGGEST FORTUNE

GREG STEINMETZ

SIMON & SCHUSTER

New York   London   Toronto   Sydney   New Delhi

Simon & Schuster
1230 Avenue of the Americas
New York, NY 10020

First Simon & Schuster hardcover edition August 2022

SIMON & SCHUSTER and colophon are registered trademarks of Simon & Schuster, Inc.

For information about special discounts for bulk purchases, please contact Simon & Schuster Special Sales at 1-866-506-1949 or business@simonandschuster.com.

The Simon & Schuster Speakers Bureau can bring authors to your live event. For more information or to book an event, contact the Simon & Schuster Speakers Bureau at 1-866-248-3049 or visit our website at www.simonspeakers.com.

Interior design by Carly Loman

Manufactured in China

10   9   8   7   6   5   4   3   2   1

Library of Congress Cataloging-in-Publication Data

Names: Steinmetz, Greg, author.
Title: American rascal : how Jay Gould built Wall Street's biggest fortune / Greg Steinmetz.
Description: First Simon & Schuster hardcover edition | New York, NY : Simon & Schuster, [2022] | Includes index.
Identifiers: LCCN 2021042306 | ISBN 9781982107406 (hardcover) | ISBN 9781982107437 (ebook)
Subjects: LCSH: Gould, Jay, 1836–1892. | Capitalists and financiers—United States—Biography. | Businessmen—United States—Biography. | Wall Street (New York, N.Y.).
Classification: LCC HG172.G65 S77 2022 | DDC 332.6092 [B]—dc23/eng/20211208
LC record available at https://lccn.loc.gov/2021042306

ISBN 978-1-9821-0740-6
ISBN 978-1-9821-0743-7 (ebook)

For our children: Axel, Anya, Jasper, and Alta

CONTENTS

————⋅▸•◂⋅————

Introduction   xi

PART ONE

PART TWO

INTRODUCTION

O n a warm April afternoon in 1873, the financier Jay Gould took time off from counting his money to have lunch at Delmonico's, the fanciest restaurant in town. While he was eating, a lawyer walked over to his table, cocked his fist, and punched him in the face.

A series of spectacular financial triumphs—some said swindles—had made Gould fabulously rich. Now, at age thirty-six, he was the most notorious businessperson in the country. Like others who tried to claw back money from Gould, the lawyer was getting nowhere in court. The laws were too weak, enforcement too lax, and the judges too crooked. Gould had them in his pocket.

Oysters and Veuve Cliquot were the rule at Delmonico's. The *biftek* was served *au naturel*. For most people, a meal cost a week's wages. For the rich, it was a place to enjoy their wealth, not pick fights. Joseph Marrin, the lawyer, didn't care. Frustrated to the point of rage, he took justice into his own hands and clocked Gould in front of the lunch crowd. In a piece called "Gould's Nose," *The New York Times* declared Marrin a hero and worried about a pileup if others followed his lead. "The flattening of Gould's nose," it wrote, "would be an incidence of hourly occurrence."[1]

This book seeks to explain Jay Gould and his underappreciated—and aggressively maligned—role in the country's transformative economic expansion of the nineteenth century. But it is just as much an exploration of Wall Street during its Wild West era after the Civil War when, by the rough means on display at Delmonico's, the seeds of our current financial system were planted. Stock and bond markets were hitting their stride. Only the strictures of conscience, rather than law and regulation, governed the participants. That left the unscrupulous free to self-deal, fix prices, trade on inside information, lie to investors, and manipulate stock prices. Out west, Jesse James and other train robbers stole your wallet. In New York, men in top hats, abetted by corrupt politicians, snatched your life savings.

The state of play was tolerated. It was an objectionable by-product of progress. Sure, there were cunning moneymen who abused the system. But that was a side effect, the price of opportunity. After all, it was Wall Street that raised the money to build railroads, to settle the plains, to create jobs, and to elevate living standards. The bankers and investors at the corner of Wall and Broad had their faults, but they were making America the most powerful nation on earth and its people the most prosperous.

A few people, the men the writer Matthew Josephson condemned as Robber Barons, amassed spectacular wealth. Cornelius Vanderbilt, John D. Rockefeller, and Andrew Carnegie come to mind. But they aren't the focus of this book because they made their money in industry, not in finance. Vanderbilt toiled in steamships and railroads, Rockefeller in oil, and Carnegie in steel. Only the lesser-known figure of Jay Gould, as rich as any of them and another of Josephson's "scoundrels," was foremost a creature of Wall Street.

To the extent Gould is remembered, it is for Black Friday, the day he blew up the gold market and paralyzed the financial system.

For this and other bold and sometimes undeniably felonious acts, lawyers swamped him with suits, prosecutors hit him with subpoenas, and Congress hauled him in for hearings. This was as far as things got. Arrested three times, Gould never spent a day in jail. In a better world, he would have. But these were raw times. Frustrated opponents, like the lawyer at Delmonico's, turned to vigilante justice. One victim tossed Gould down a stairwell. Another pulled a gun on him. During the contested presidential election of 1884—an election in which Gould was believed to have interfered—a lynch mob marched on his Broadway office. As they waited in hope of spotting their prey, they riffed on the "Battle Hymn of the Republic." Out went "Glory, Glory Hallelujah." In came "I Hang Jay Gould on the sour apple tree." For them there was no doubt. Gould deserved the noose. "Jay Gould was the mightiest disaster which has ever befallen this country," wrote Mark Twain. "The people had desired money before his day, but he taught them to fall down and worship it."[2]

For Twain, Gould was the biggest robber of the barons. It was one thing to clean up at the poker table when you played by the rules. It was another to cheat. Gould, he argued, was a champion cheater. Even worse, he was an inspiration for others inclined to cheat. He showed that no act of financial villainy was too bold. The publisher Joseph Pulitzer saw Gould the same way as Twain. "Convicts will wonder," wrote Pulitzer, "what mental defect robbed them of such a career as Gould's."[3]

Gould's peers were more charitable. Gould stood not much over five feet tall. But to those who appreciated his gifts, the Little Wizard, as the newspapers called him, was a giant. Vanderbilt told a Syracuse newspaper that Gould was "the smartest man in America."[4] Rockefeller, when asked who he thought had the best head for business, answered "Jay Gould" without pausing to think.[5] They recognized Gould as a master of his craft. Ruthless? Yes. A liar? Maybe. It depended on the definition. But no one disputed that he was an extraordinary problem solver, an unparalleled negotiator, an expert communicator, a lightning-fast thinker, and a masterful tactician with a staggering memory. He knew the numbers better than his accountants. He knew the law as well his lawyers. When it came to business, Gould had it all.

Gould complemented his natural endowments with nerves of iron and a work ethic, even as a teenager, so strong that it damaged his health and, quite possibly, shortened his life. With his mix of brains and single-mindedness, he was suited to make the most of the moment. Gould's friends thought he got attention for the wrong reasons. They cited his talents and wondered why he never seemed to win praise. "Why is Rockefeller held in so much higher esteem than Gould in the public mind?" asked the banker Jesse Seligman.[6]

Gould, of course, didn't see himself as a crook. He bribed politicians because his competitors bribed politicians. Equally, he made his money not at gunpoint but by manipulating others to make bad decisions. They would pay him too much when he was selling or accept too little when he was buying. Gould would say his victims—those on the other side of his trades—had only themselves to blame. If someone was too lazy to read the fine print, too greedy to consider the downside, and too dumb to watch what Gould did rather than what he said, they deserved their fate. Gould feasted on other Wall Street professionals. They were trying to do to him what he did to them. Did that make him a crook?

GOULD WAS ONE of the most famous people of his time. During an 1886 labor dispute, his name appeared on the front page of *The New York Times* every day for a month. Such was Gould's reputation that the public assumed, wrongly, that he could single-handedly move the market. Such was Gould's notoriety that once, after a train robber picked clean every passenger on a Texas train, the crook told the onboard postal clerk that he would leave him alone, saying he wasn't after the government's money, "only Jay Gould's." [7]

These days, Gould is all but forgotten. In 2019, *USA Today* published a ranking of rich Americans. Gould was there, smack between Marshall Field and Warren Buffett at No. 14. "Jay Gould 1836–1892."[8] The paper got that right. But it muffed the picture. It didn't show Gould. It showed his grandson, Jay Gould II. Jay Gould II was prominent, too. He won a gold medal in tennis at the 1908 London Olympics. But he wasn't the shadowy buccaneer who ransacked Wall Street.

Gould would have enjoyed the error. Obsessively secret, he talked to the press for strategic reasons, but never sat for a magazine profile nor gave thought to an autobiography. Like a camper determined to leave no trace behind, he ordered his papers burned upon his death and that his name appear nowhere on his burial site. Still, it is tantalizing to think how the Gould name would resonate if he had lived longer. Gould died when he was fifty-six and before he could decide how his money might build enduring institutions in his name. Rockefeller was sixty-two when he endowed Rockefeller University. He lived long enough to see his son build Rockefeller Center. Vanderbilt was seventy-nine when he financed Vanderbilt University. Gould gave some money to New York University and was negotiating a bigger gift and possible naming rights when he died. If the academic establishment sprawled over lower Manhattan was called Gould University instead of NYU, we'd see the name Gould on baseball caps and bumper stickers. Instead, about all he gets is the Florence Gould auditorium, a small concert venue in a 59th Street basement named for his daughter-in-law. It pales besides Carnegie Hall.

Why does Gould matter? There is an easy answer. While he made his money on Wall Street, he did as much as anyone, through his work with railroads, to build the country. Railroads changed America in the nineteenth century much as automobiles changed the country in the twentieth century and the internet has changed the twenty-first century. Gould built as much track as anyone, laying down the "thin lines of rust" that crossed the country's interior and let Americans tap the economic potential of the country and make it the richest nation on earth. Gould's contributions elevated St. Louis, Kansas City, Dallas, Denver, Omaha, and Memphis, not to mention the countless smaller settlements he literally put on the map. He was among the biggest employers, if not the biggest employer, in the country. The money he spent to stay competitive made the nation's rail network faster, safer, and more comfortable. He reinvested his profits in a way that created more jobs and economic growth. America would have developed without Gould, only not as fast or efficiently.

Gould also changed the way we think about markets. America was founded on the idea that the best government was the one that governed least. Europeans crossed the Atlantic for freedom, to get away from kings, secret police, and censors. The freedom America offered to get rich went hand in hand with freedom to worship one's own god and the freedom to march against the government. In business, laissez-faire was best. When it came to consumer protection, caveat emptor—buyer beware—sufficed. The invisible hand, the unseen power that governed the economy, was a benign force of good.

For decades, the approach worked miracles. It fostered rapid economic growth and, remarkably, a relatively even division of wealth. There were few rich people and few beggars at the time of the American Revolution. Benjamin Franklin saw wealth disparity up close as ambassador to France. He delighted in the social and economic equality back home. America wasn't a place of rich and poor, he wrote. "It is, rather, a general happy mediocrity that prevails."[9]

Faith in markets remained strong at the time of the Civil War when Gould started his Wall Street career. The "self-adjusting meter of supply and demand," wrote the philosopher Ralph Waldo Emerson in 1860, solved for all. "Do not legislate," he wrote. "Meddle and you snap the sinews."[10]

By the time Gould died in 1892, everything had changed. The best-selling book in America after the Bible wasn't one that celebrated liberty but *Progress and Poverty* by Henry George. *Progress and Poverty* ranks among the most influential works in American history. It served as the manifesto of the Progressive movement and was translated into dozens of languages. In muscular prose, George argued the rich received all the benefits of economic expansion while the poor, despite that growth, stayed poor. Unchecked capitalism lifted supremely gifted men like Gould and caused misery, despair, and hardship for everyone else. The market gave rise to "the shocking contrast between monstrous wealth and debasing want."[11] It was the job of government, George wrote, to correct the wrongs.

Gould, as much as anyone, catalyzed the call for change. His first great coup was the capture of the Erie Railroad in 1868. He did it with deception and bribery. A year later, Massachusetts, partly in reaction to Gould, created the Massachusetts Railroad Commission. It was the country's first regulatory commission. Henry George himself made an example of Gould. Gould was his poster boy for economic inequality. "So boldly, so skillfully, so unscrupulously has he played the great game," George wrote, "that he is likely to die the richest man in the country, probably the richest man in the world."[12]

George didn't have all the answers, but he was right about one thing: Gould knew how to play the game.

❖ PART ONE ❖

ONE

SCHOOL DAYS

In 1853 when Jay Gould was seventeen, he made an announcement to his friend Abel Crosby. "Crosby," he declared, "I'm going to be rich. I've seen enough to realize what can be accomplished by means of riches, and I tell you I'm going to be rich."[1]

Young men talk big. But Gould wasn't one for loose talk. When he said something, he meant it. There was no doubt. He would succeed. Where did he get the confidence? And the impulse?

In a bit of delightful prefiguring, the first Gould in America was named Gold. Major Nathan Gold, a Puritan, came to Connecticut in search of religious freedom and lucre. He found both, practicing his nonconformist belief while striking it rich shipping beaver hides and deerskin back to England. His grandson Abraham served in the Revolutionary War as a lieutenant in George Washington's Continental Army and died in the Battle of Ridgefield. Abraham's son, another Abraham, preferred the name Gould to Gold. No one knows why. The Goulds went west to take up dairy farming in New York's Catskill Mountains, settling in the town of Roxbury. They had ten children. The oldest was Jay Gould's father, John Burr Gould. Burr was a family name. Aaron Burr, who killed Alexander Hamilton in a duel, was a distant cousin.

John Gould took over the farm from his father. He made cheese to sell in Albany and New York City. A "churn dog," hitched to a wheel to make butter, pitched in. John married a local woman named Mary More. After having six girls, Mary gave birth to a seventh child on May 27, 1836. The baby was premature. Not wanting to tempt fate, the Goulds waited before giving their small and ailing baby—a son they had longed for—a name. Several agonizing weeks later, they named him Jason. Jason gave way to Jay.

Another child of the backwoods, Andrew Jackson, was president. Ninety percent of the country's population—a population that doubled every quarter century during this age of staggering growth—lived on farms. Westward migration was in swing. Saltbox houses were replacing log cabins in Ohio and Michigan. Illinois and Missouri were already states. Just weeks before Gould's birth, Sam Houston's army captured the prideful Mexican general Santa Anna and won freedom for Texas. The Catskills were hardly the frontier. But the roads were poor and travel was slow. New York City, already the biggest city in the country, was 150 miles away from Roxbury. It took a day to reach it.

The nation's economy was healthy and its growth the envy of other countries. Trading on the New York Stock Exchange came to fewer than eight thousand shares a day, but volume grew every year and flag bearers stood atop hills, manning a semaphore line that sent price quotes from Manhattan to Boston. While most Americans were farmers, the biggest businesses in the country were banks. Railroads, the industry that would eventually consume Gould as well as dominate trading on the exchange, were just getting started. There was no income tax and, for the last time, the government was free of debt.

On a January morning when Jay was four, the girls were in

school when their teacher dismissed them early. Mary was sick and wanted to see her children. Jay went with the girls to Mary's room. He pulled himself up on her bed, bracing his feet on the frame, and kissed her lips. They were cold. Mary Gould was dead at age thirty-five, a victim of typhoid fever. At the funeral, Jay held sister Anna's hand as the family buried Mary in the snowy ground of the Roxbury Baptist Church. Gould later said the only thing he remembered about his mother were her cold lips.

Mary was survived by her family and a legacy in the form of a magnificent garden. When she wasn't cooking meals, milking cows, or making clothes, she tended to a fine collection of roses and hyacinths. As they bloomed anew each spring, they served as a beautiful reminder of the mother Gould barely knew. Mary was said to have a head for money along with an even temper. Gould inherited those traits. A more tangible link could be drawn to the flowers. After Gould made it big, he bought a country estate that came with the largest glass-enclosed conservatory in the country. He filled it with roses and hyacinths.

Family tragedy didn't end there. John Gould, now fifty-one, immediately remarried. The new wife died less than a year later. Understandably anxious about raising the family on his own, he married a third time. The woman died within two years. Jay's sister Nancy, age eleven, also fell ill and died. That made four deaths in four years. The Goulds seemed cursed. John Gould took to drink. The family cringed at a church picnic when he toppled over drunk.

John Gould could be cruel. Jay was once sent home from school for misbehaving. John locked him in the cellar. The girls returned from class and asked Jay's whereabouts. John, who might have been drunk, said he didn't know. Only later did he remember Jay was in the cellar. The girls hurried to liberate their brother. They found him in tears.

Jay had an impish streak, but not at the expense of his studies. He worked on math problems as long as it took to get an answer. He read whatever he could get his hands on. When John needed him for chores, Jay was often nowhere to be found. He was off hiding somewhere with his books. Jay left home when he was thirteen, explaining that the local school was too easy. He later said that his father, who had given up on his dream of Jay taking over the farm, didn't care and told him, "I was not worth much at home and I might go ahead."[2]

Gould was short—almost elfin—and frail. But when he wrestled with friends, he surprised them with his determination. One friend was John Burroughs, who grew up to become a famous nature writer. "He was very plucky and hard to beat," Burroughs wrote. "He was made of steel and rubber."[3] Gould was bright, articulate, and thoughtful. His most remarkable quality was precocity. To pay tuition and board at his new school, Hobart Academy, he taught himself basic accounting and kept the books for a blacksmith. A year after leaving for Hobart, his old school in Roxbury hired a new teacher. Jay heard good things about the teacher and, perhaps feeling homesick, came home. In an assignment for the new instructor, Jay wrote an essay that detractors later mocked for its irony, but was more noteworthy for its deft use of language. He called it "Honesty Is the Best Policy." Gould warned readers that "we should not acquaint ourselves too much with the world" and observed that "conscience is not the voice of thunder, but a voice gentle and impressive."[4]

Two years later, Gould was rising at three to study by firelight. His area of interest was surveying. He hated the drudgery of farming and believed surveying was his way out. He got on with a draftsman who planned to make and sell a map of Ulster County, one of the counties in the Catskills. The draftsman told Jay not to worry about food and shelter because his credit was good. He assured that farmers along the way would provide for him; he would pay them later. On Jay's third day on the road, he was turned down everywhere he went. The draftsman had exhausted his credit. Jay was hungry, miles from home and alone. He walked into the woods, sat by a tree, and fell into sobs. "It seemed to me as though the world had come to an end," he said later.[5]

The tears restored him. He approached another farmer and asked what he could do to earn a night's stay. The farmer offered him 50 cents to use his surveying tools to make a noon mark, a simple sundial that indicated midday. With that, Jay was in business. Sustaining himself with noon marks, he traipsed the roads of Ulster County, surveyed the whole thing, and sold the maps himself. He earned a few hundred dollars. "That was the first money I made in business," he said.[6]

He agreed to map other counties and soon had a modest but thriving business. He gathered surveys from correspondents in three states, drew up maps, made copies, and sold them to farmers, road contractors, and schools. "Look at Gould," marveled the father of one of his friends. "Isn't he a driver."[7]

Gould's shortcoming was an inability to slow down. While other farm children mended fences and threshed hay, Gould filled his teenage years with deadlines, sales calls, and personnel decisions. Consumed by work, he ate poorly and slept little. His friends were hardly astonished when, during the summer of 1854, he collapsed into bed with chills and stomach pains.

The doctor diagnosed typhoid fever. After the fever passed, Gould rushed back to work. Like an injured ballplayer who returns too soon, he fell ill with a bowel infection. He took morphine to numb the pain. His sisters feared for his life. "You know this disease terminates one way or the other, soon," wrote his sister Polly to their sister Sarah.[8] He couldn't keep down food and lost weight. When he recovered, he attended Sarah's wedding looking like death.

The doctor told him to lay off work. He tried but couldn't stop thinking about his neglected projects. Polly complained that relaxing "seemed to make him even worse."[9] After spending months in bed, he grew impossibly restless. Winter was approaching and frost already covered the mountains. He dragged himself up on a horse and rode off on one of his map ventures. He was on the road only a few days when pneumonia struck. He recovered, but, at the about the same time, his sister Polly took ill and died of tuberculosis.

Her death was a wake-up call. He resolved to stay at home until he was back at full strength. Not that he was idle. He took the time to finish another piece of work. At the behest of a local agricultural organization, he wrote a history of his home county of Delaware. He sent it to a printer shop in Philadelphia that picked that time to burn down. From his notes, Gould rewrote the 426 pages. "As you know," he said to a friend, "I'm not in the habit of backing out of what I undertake, and I shall write night and day until it is completed."[10] Years later, in an otherwise scathing profile of Gould, *The New York Times* grudgingly conceded that his opus, *History of Delaware County and Border Wars of New York*, was "admirable," and not just because it was written by an eighteen-year-old.

About this time, Gould hopped on the Hudson River Railway for a visit to Manhattan. He was heading to the Crystal Palace in Bryant Park for the Exhibition of Industry. He had work to do. His grandfather had invented a rat trap and asked Jay to display the device at the show and sell the license. President Franklin Pierce opened the event. Walt Whitman supplied a poem. Elisha Otis debuted his new elevator. The crowd gasped when Otis boarded his contraption and ordered the cables slashed in confidence that his new safety brake would stop his fall. Jay sold the rat trap and earned a few dollars but not before an encounter with a pickpocket who stole the trap. Jay grabbed the thief by the leg and held on until the police came. *The New York Herald* devoted half a column to "the plucky visitor's" apprehension of the thief.[11]

Gould toyed with the idea of college and took prep courses in Albany. He visited Rutgers, Yale, Harvard, and Brown. After seeing the students darting to class and the professors sauntering the commons in their gowns, he concluded college was an expensive indulgence. Why bother with college when he could teach himself from books?

Back home, Gould joined a reading circle that explored spirituality. Gould wasn't religious but he searched for answers after the loss of his sister Polly. Contemplation of the afterlife served to drive him harder. "As regards the future world, except what the Bible reveals, I am unable to fathom its mysteries," he wrote to a friend, "but, as to the present, I am determined to use all my best energies to accomplish this life's highest possibilities."[12]

There is another story from Gould's youth worth noting. During his long convalescence from the bowel infection, Gould worked in a store owned by the most successful merchant in town, Edward Burhans. Gould took a liking to Burhans's daughter Maria. One day, a farmer walked into the store and told Gould he wanted to talk to Burhans about some land he had to sell. Gould knew the property and a good idea of its worth. He offered to buy the parcel on the spot and closed the deal before Burhans had a chance. Gould flipped it for a $5,000 profit, an amount equal to about $100,000 in current dollars. Burhans was enraged. He fired Gould and made sure Maria had nothing more to do with him. When it came to love or money, Gould chose money.

TWO

────◆─◆─◆────

THE SEDUCTION OF ZADOCK PRATT

On a rainy spring morning in 1856, the famous gentleman rose early and rode an hour through the mountains, tied up his horse, and walked into the Roxbury Hotel. An onlooker recalled his appearance. The visitor was an "old, gray haired man—tall, erect, booted and spurred."[1] He announced himself as Colonel Zadock Pratt. He had a question. Where could he find Jay Gould?

Pratt didn't need to introduce himself. Everyone knew Zadock Pratt. *Merchant's Magazine*, the *Fortune* magazine of the day, once compiled some biographical sketches to inspire the young. It included chapters on Henry Clay, John Quincy Adams, and Washington Irving. More ink was spilled for Zadock Pratt. Pratt was an inspiration. Born in 1790, Pratt began his career traveling town to town as a saddle maker. Then he ran a country store, worked fourteen-hour days, and saved money by sleeping under the counter at night. He had his first big commercial success selling oars to the military in the War of 1812. Looking for a bigger opportunity after the war, he was riding through the countryside when he happened upon a site along the Schoharie River, not far from Roxbury. He instantly recognized it as a perfect location for a tannery. From the moment he signed the deed, his fortune was secure.

Leather was big business. The country needed shoes, boots, machine belts, leather breeches, and, as Pratt well knew, saddles. Tanners made the leather by soaking cowhides in the tannic acid found in tree bark. No tree produced more tannin than hemlock. No place in America had more hemlock than the Catskills. Tanneries were popping up all over the mountains. It was a dirty business. The stench of hides filled the air. Rotting remains fouled the rivers. The tanners themselves were rough, drinking men despised by the locals, and notorious for leaving behind shantytowns, unpaid bills, and acres of decaying logs and tree stumps.

Pratt vowed to do it better. Promising to "live with the local people and not on them," he said he would build a sustainable community and stay after the hemlock was gone.[2] Upon finding his site, it took him less than three months to build the biggest tannery in the country. Pratt was soon buying hides from as far away as Buenos Aires and turning them into high-quality leather that he mostly shipped to New York City. Pratt ate meals with his men. To minimize employee turnover, he encouraged them to bring their families upstate. Instead of letting the felled trees go to waste, he cut it into lumber. He built schools, houses, and churches. He removed tree stumps to ready the land for planting. Other Catskills communities were unorganized collections of farms united only by a church, a store, and places like the Roxbury Hotel. Pratt's community, which he dubbed Prattsville, was a fully formed, economically diverse city with a neatly arranged center of shops and homes. New Yorkers called it "the gem of the Catskills."

If Pratt had a business card, it might have said something like "data scientist." He doubled his leather output by experimenting with different boiling times, tannin concentrations, and hide size while recording every data point in a book. He vertically integrated with an in-house blacksmith and used his own men to fell trees instead of the usual contract laborers. Other tanners guarded their secrets. Pratt, eager to advance best practices, published his.

Pratt was drawn to politics. He ran for Congress as a Democrat in 1836 and won by an impressive three thousand votes. During his two terms, he never missed a day on the House floor. His bills cut postage rates, advanced the transcontinental railroad, and created the federal Bureau of Statistics. He commissioned the Washington Monument.

Pratt was eccentric. On the Fourth of July, he'd put on a fur coat and drive a sleigh through town. He liked playing soldier. With real gunpowder, he reenacted famous battles. More than once, he blew up a barn and reimbursed the owners. A phrenologist, a practitioner of the quackery then in vogue, examined Pratt's skull in 1848. The phrenologist pronounced the skull's occupant "peculiar, isolated and detached from the species."[3]

Pratt's life was marked by sadness. His son George was the youngest person ever elected to the state legislature. An army colonel, he was shot dead in the Second Battle of Bull Run. Pratt buried four wives—one more than John Gould. His fifth wife was a young writer with *Leather and Shoe Reporter.* He was seventy-nine and she was twenty. She survived him.

Pratt had a weakness: pride. Calling his little tanning community Prattsville was defensible. There were plenty of villages named after their founders. Nor was it unusual when he started a bank and called it Prattsville National. It got strange with the banknotes. Banks issued their own notes in those days, backed by their own credit. They adorned the notes with images of milk maids, schooners, and beehives. For his bank, Pratt used a portrait of a middle-aged gentleman with a calm gaze, a firm jaw, a chinstrap beard, and a bow tie. There was a good reason for that, he'd say. Who wouldn't accept a banknote graced with an image of Zadock Pratt?

His portrait shows him with three medals around his neck. He commissioned a stone cutter to sculpt his likeness on the rocks overlooking Prattsville. Pratt Rocks stand to this day as a Catskills Mount Rushmore. He commissioned another reporter from *Leather and Shoe* to ghostwrite his autobiography. In it we learn that Pratt was the best marksman, the fastest runner, and the strongest horseman around. We discover that lesser men have neither the skill nor stomach for big business, thus it was Pratt's obligation, like it was for "the founders of the House of Medici," to assume the burden himself.[4]

Some years before Pratt rode into Roxbury, Gould, then sixteen, had tried to sell Pratt a map. Pratt didn't need a map. But he liked Gould's spirit and promised to keep him in mind. Gould made sure of it by sending him letters and telling him about his maps and other projects. Then came the rainy morning when Pratt went looking for Gould.

Gould rushed to the hotel. Pratt asked Gould to survey his farm. By now Gould was sick of surveying. He instead told Pratt about an idea he had. Gould's brother-in-law operated a tannery in Pennsylvania and knew about a hemlock forest near the Lehigh River. It was the ideal spot for a tannery. Not only was it on a river but a crew was building a train line nearby to haul coal. Once the railroad opened, New York would only be a day away from the hemlocks. Gould wanted to build a tannery there and asked Pratt to back him.

Pratt had retired from tanning. After clearing all the hemlocks within ten miles of Prattsville, he had switched to farming. He was now grazing cattle. Gould's idea struck him as fishy. Although he had once owned a Pennsylvania tannery, he had never heard of the El Dorado Gould described. Pratt wanted to see it. Gould promised to take him but first he had to find it himself.

Gould grabbed his compass and surveying tools, and rode over the mountains through wild country. Bears and wolves roamed the hills. Mountain lions screamed for their mates. Gould saw plenty of oak and pine in eastern Pennsylvania but little hemlock. He eventually came to what seemed like a promising area not far from Wilkes-Barre. He looked up a mountainside. There they were, hemlocks as far as the eye could see. They stretched across the mountain and down into the valley. They bounded over streams and rocks. There was enough hemlock to keep a tanner busy for years. He returned with Pratt. They rode together, the slight young man with no money and a tall, rich, sixty-five-year-old with money to burn. Pratt saw the hemlocks. He and Gould became partners.

Just like that, Gould was an industrialist. After choosing a spot by the river, he hired a crew, picked up an axe, and joined the men to fell trees. Vats for boiling tanning solution arrived along with the two-handled knives for shaving bark. Gould and his men built a dormitory in two days, then a tannery. They dubbed their little encampment Gouldsboro. Gould wrote to Pratt about the dedication ceremony sounding like a kid sending his parents a note from camp. "I have moved into a new boarding house," he wrote. "It is small but commodious affair." He slipped in some flattery. "Three hearty cheers were then proposed for Hon. Zadock Pratt," he wrote. "A more hearty response I am certain this valley has never before witnessed."[5]

A happy pattern developed between Pratt and his acolyte. Pratt offered an idea. Gould praised its brilliance. Pratt sent a check. Gould acted on the idea. Pratt suggested building a church and a school for workers and their families. Gould replied, "Pride in community will encourage and inspire our men."[6] Pratt suggested maintaining detailed records. Gould replied: "The most successful men are invariably the most careful about small things."[7] Pratt told Gould where to buy cowhides. Gould replied: "I am under many obligations for your good advice." Pratt offered an idea for shipping tanned hides to New York. Gould replied: "I am much obliged."[8]

If Pratt noticed insincerity, he never said so. Gould showed no concern about crossing the line. If anything, he became more of a sycophant. When Pratt told Gould about his idea for an autobiography, Gould recommended that the introduction declare Pratt a model for mankind. Wrote Gould, "Col. Pratt has arisen by his own untiring industry from comparative obscurity to become the most eminent and most useful man in the world."[9] Pratt loved it. And the more flattery Gould delivered, the more money flowed from Prattsville. By and by, Pratt sank $120,000 into the tanning venture. For his part, Gould contributed no cash, only labor.

One day a wagon rolled up to the tannery carrying a large crate. Inside the crate was a metal contraption with a wheel on the side. Gould and his colleagues unloaded the thing and gave it a look. It was a steam engine. Pratt had read in *Leather and Shoe* about a new way to make tanning fluid. The key ingredient was hemlock bark ground into small pieces for boiling in water. The article advocated a steam engine for grinding the bark instead of a water wheel. The benefit was year-round production. Whether or not the river was frozen, it could keep on grinding. And it was powered not by expensive kerosene but by setting fire to the boiled tree bark after it dried. It sounded good on paper.

After some fiddling, Gould's men attached the engine to the grinding mill, fed the fuel bin with bark, and started it up. The bark didn't catch fire so much as it smoldered. They let the bark dry some more and tried again. This time the engine wouldn't turn over. The engine was junk. Gould sent it back. While waiting for a new one, he learned that the manufacturer had gone out of business. He'd have to find another one.

One of Gould's remarkable characteristics was an ability to project good cheer in dark hours. But he was in a hurry because every lost day was another day without a profit. He let his frustration slip in a letter to Pratt. "I am inclined to think that my original suggestion—building a water-wheel as a backup to the more modern plan—may have saved us time, expense and frustration."[10]

Gould made up for lost time by driving himself and his men harder. Once the new engine arrived, he worked nonstop. The tannery was soon up to capacity and shipping as much leather each month as Pratt had shipped from Prattsville. For Gould, it had been a year of furious effort punctuated by maddening delays. As the cash rolled in, he had reason to cheer. He had a half interest in a profitable tanning operation supplied with enough hemlock to last for years. He was twenty-two years old. He could see the day when he would be rich just like he had predicted.

Still, he felt unsatisfied. He had not forgotten the mansions and carriages he had seen in Manhattan during his rat-trap adventure. He wasn't sure what the people along Fifth Avenue did to afford such luxuries. But he knew it wasn't tanning cowhides. The letters from Pratt suggested another way, that the real money in leather came from doing what Gould himself had done years back when he flipped the farmer's land in Roxbury. The secret was to buy low and sell high. He had noticed that leather prices were as mercurial as land prices, and that powerful and sometimes hidden forces drove prices. Leather production wasn't itself a bad business: he could work his tail off, expand the factory, hire more workers, and tan twice as many hides as Pratt ever did. But it occurred to Gould he could make even more money by understanding the forces that moved prices and then trading on that knowledge. Gould had taught himself bookkeeping. He had taught himself surveying. He had taught himself about Shakespeare, Milton, and Pope. Now he would teach himself everything about how leather was bought and sold. "I want to gain a grasp of the bartering," he wrote to a friend.[11]

THERE USED TO be a wet patch of land covered with cattails and sawgrass on Manhattan's East Side, a few blocks north of Wall Street, where tanners made leather from hemlocks that grew on the island. The area reeked of putrefying cowhides. Locals called it the Swamp. Production could only last as long as Manhattan had hemlocks. After the trees were gone, the tanners moved to places like Prattsville and the wetlands were filled in to expand the city's boundaries. Production had fled the city, but trading stayed in the Swamp. Tanners shipped their hides to New York for sale and the Swamp thrived as a marketplace.

Pratt's son George, the one who later died at Bull Run, worked for his father as a leather broker in the Swamp before the war. He made a living buying and selling Gould's hides. Gould occasionally tagged along with George. The visits confirmed something he suspected. Not only could he make money buying low and selling high. He could also make money as a broker, buying and selling for someone else. The best part was he didn't have to put up his own money. He could pocket handsome commissions as a go-between. Gould pummeled George with questions. "I'm not sure Mr. Pratt enjoys my shadow," Gould wrote.[12]

Back at the tannery, Gould's mind returned to the Swamp.

What a place, he thought. No crews to supervise, no steaming vats of boiling hides, no broken steam engines, no odor so vile that it made the eyes water. The Swamp was moneymaking distilled to its essence. The tannery made things. The activity was physical. In the Swamp, the value came not from making things but by making decisions. Brains and information won the day. Gould decided New York, not the backwoods, was the place for him. "I've come to realize," he wrote to his father, "that it is the merchants who command the true power. The brokers take what seems the smallest share but is in fact the largest. Theirs is nearly pure profit made on the backs of the shippers and the tanners, never their hands dirtied."[13]

The more Gould visited New York, the more opportunities he saw. He learned something else, too. He discovered that others would pay more for his leather than George Pratt did. Risking a confrontation with Zadock, Gould took his hides to George's competitors. He didn't care about the consequences. By this time, he had gotten all he needed from the Pratts. It was time to make a break.

In September 1857, a large bank in Ohio collapsed amid allegations of fraud. Its depositors and investors lost everything. Panic engulfed Wall Street as investors worried their own bank would be next. European investors pulled out of the American market. Jacob Little, a fabulously wealthy trader and a board member of the New York Stock Exchange, went under and would die penniless a few years later. Half of the Street's brokers went bankrupt in the ensuing recession.

Leather prices sank along with everything else, and Gould's tannery went from making money to burning cash. Gould couldn't pay the workers. Pratt proposed buying him out for $10,000. The figure was laughable. Pratt and Gould each owned 50 percent of the stock. Pratt had invested $120,000 in cash and Gould had put up his labor. Gould's half wasn't worth $120,000 anymore, not with leather prices in the tank. But it wasn't worth $10,000 either. People still wore shoes. When the economy recovered, leather prices would recover. Gould told Pratt to stuff it. He'd take $60,000 for his stake but not a penny less.

Pratt turned Gould's logic back on him. If Gould really thought a half share was worth $60,000, Pratt should be willing to sell his own half share to Gould for that amount. Otherwise, his original offer to buy out Gould for $10,000 was the best he could do. Confident that Gould could not conjure the money, Pratt gave him ten days to decide.

With the deadline approaching, Gould rushed to the Swamp and met with the biggest leather broker in town. Charles Leupp had been trading leather for forty years. He lived in a Madison Avenue mansion where he hosted writers and artists including the beloved Hudson River School landscape painter Jasper Cropsey. Gould said if Leupp gave him $60,000 to buy out Pratt, he'd give him two thirds of the business. Gould didn't like watering down his ownership, but his back was to the wall.

Leupp thought for a minute. Gould was young but he was producing a lot of leather. Leupp himself had bought some of it and knew the quality was good. Besides, if Pratt was interested in the tannery, it had to be worth something. They came to terms and shook hands. Gould took Leupp's money and paid Pratt.

A few years earlier, Gould had known nothing about tanning, manufacturing, and trading hides. Zadock Pratt, on the other hand, was a seasoned veteran. He was one of the richest men in New York.

It was Pratt's face that adorned banknotes, not Jay Gould's. But Pratt's pockets, not Jay Gould's, were the ones picked that day. Pratt had invested $120,000 of cash in the tannery. Gould had invested nothing but his labor. When the market recovered, Gould, not Pratt, stood to clean up.

THREE

TANNERS WAR

When Charles Leupp signed the agreement with Gould in January 1859, he was fifty-two years old and losing his mind. Gould's new partner saw elephants in the living room and bats on his shoulder. He thought detectives hid in his rafters. He demanded someone check his pulse every ten minutes to prove he still lived.

Leupp's mental state may explain why he did the deal. How else to account for it? Leupp had no business owning a tannery. He was a trader, not a manufacturer. The manufacturers counted on him to look out for them. If word got around that he was making leather himself, other tanners would regard him as a competitor and take their business elsewhere. He'd be finished. In his reduced, delusional condition, he gambled that he could keep the deal secret and have it both ways. To cover his tracks, he instructed Gould to leave his name off the documents. Gould filed papers with the state listing himself as sole proprietor. Leupp's name was nowhere to be found.

Leupp came home one afternoon and had dinner with his daughters and one of her friends. As they sat at the kitchen table, Leupp seemed confused, looking at the others with a blank stare. He left the table, paced the floor, and darted back and forth between different rooms. A friend who thought Leupp had been acting erratically that day came over to check on him. He remembered his friend storming into the kitchen looking "wild-eyed." Leupp kissed his daughter with unusual fervor and fled the kitchen through a back door. As the others tried to make sense of it, they heard a gunshot. They ran to Leupp's dressing room to find blood gushing from his chest. "The community was shocked yesterday morning by the intelligence that Mr. Chas M. Leupp, a leading leather merchant in the Swamp, had committed self-destruction," wrote the *Herald.* In describing his suicide, it recounted how Leupp grabbed his double-barreled revolver, opened his vest, placed the gun muzzle to his chest and "blew his heart to atoms."[1]

Leupp's heart atomization led to another ownership shuffle for Gould's tannery. The heirs wanted out. So did Leupp's partner, David Lee. Gould scraped together funds and proposed buying their interest for the same $60,000 Leupp had paid Gould. In March 1860, Lee invited Gould to New York to finalize the deal. When Gould arrived in the Swamp, Lee's assistant told him Lee was out but would be back the next day. When Lee failed to show up, Gould became suspicious. He asked around and discovered Lee was on his way to Gouldsboro. Lee didn't want to sell his stake after all. He had only said that to buy time. He was going to Pennsylvania to seize the tannery by force.

Gould went to his lawyer. The lawyer told him something useful. Even though Lee and the estate owned more stock in the tannery than Gould, Gould could throw Lee off the property for trespassing. That's because, thanks to Leupp's attempt to hide his ownership, Gould was registered as the sole proprietor. When Gould got to Gouldsboro, he found Lee and a goon squad of about forty-five men—men Lee paid with whiskey—inside the tannery, daring Gould to fight.

Gould was more a diplomat than a soldier. In hopes of a negotiated peace, he slowly approached the tannery, unarmed and alone.

Lee's men poured out of the building. They surrounded Gould and threatened to kill him if he didn't leave Gouldsboro. Gould backed off. Back in town, he gathered the community to muster an attack force. Lee had fifty men. That left another 250 men available to fight. Gould easily found recruits. The people of Gouldsboro knew their boss as someone who had worked alongside them and paid them without interruption. Lee was a stranger. Gould was delighted by the show of support. "I was surprised to see so large a body of volunteers collected," Gould later told the *Wilkes-Barre Union.*

Gould had never before fired nor loaded a gun. His only experience as a fighter was his grade school wrestling matches. But the prospect of economic annihilation was motivating. It overwhelmed his fear of death. "I quietly selected fifty men," he said, "commanding the reserve to keep aloof."[2] He and his force marched to the tannery, surrounded the building, and demanded Lee's surrender.

Gould showed flair as a military commander. Because he had built the tannery himself, he knew the layout and its vulnerabilities. He sent half his team to the far end of the building where they could tear down a flimsy side wall. While they were doing that, he and the others would create a diversion in front. They'd ram through the front door and, with the power of superior numbers, root out the enemy.

Gould gave the order. The battle was under way. He and his fighters burst in. As Gould later recalled, he was "immediately showered by a salute of balls." After a brief retreat, Gould mounted a second charge. Shots rang. The smell of sulfur filled the air. The wall on the far side crashed to the ground and the full force of Gould's army raced into the building. Lee was outnumbered. Some of his men fled by jumping from second floor windows. Others scurried out the back of the building. Lee suffered a buckshot wound to his hand. Abandoned by his troops, he surrendered.

The battle of Gouldsboro made good copy. "Quite an excitement pervaded our community last week," wrote the *Wilkes-Barre Union*. It described how a "fierce riot was raging in the village." Lee said Gould's men had "rushed through the building yelling like wild Indians."[3] He insisted that if his mercenaries had stayed with him, he would have throttled Gould.

Gould relished his victory. Asked how he overcame the enemy, he credited superior force. But that wasn't the whole story. There was something else at work, he said, something that made a difference in all aspects of life, not just in armed conflicts. It was temperance. While Lee promoted drunkenness by paying his men with whiskey, Gould insisted on sobriety for his own. Lee's men were drunk. Gould's were not. That tipped the balance. "I used the most vigilant care to prevent the use of a single drop of liquor," Gould said, "for it is a well-known fact that I neither use it myself or countenance its use in others."[4] The temperance movement was gaining steam. Gould, the son of an alcoholic, was an advocate. This wouldn't be the last time he preached sobriety.

The experience soured Gould on tanning. He turned the operations over to others, earning little on the sale, and, in a momentous step, embarked on a new chapter in his life that had nothing to do with tree bark and cowhides. A man could make a good living in leather. Leather wasn't going away. But Gould was convinced the big money wasn't in the wilds of Pennsylvania. It was on a narrow street in New York wedged between Broadway and the East River, a place where men went to work in woolen suits, not leather breeches. "I am trying to start myself in the smoky world of stocks and bonds," he wrote to a friend in November 1860. "There are magicians' skills to be learned on Wall Street, and I mean to learn them."[5]

FOUR

THIS THING AMBITION

Gould left Pennsylvania and, with money earned selling lumber in Gouldsboro, took a room at the Everett House on Union Square. New Yorkers didn't have apartments in the 1860s. Young men on the make roomed in boardinghouses or hotels. The Everett was one of the grandest hotels in the city. President Buchanan stayed there when in New York. Gould found a city divided over slavery. On one side were the merchants and bankers made rich by the slave economy. New York supplied the South with everything from loans to insurance to hoop skirts. New York shipbuilders fitted out southern ships. A New York sheet music publisher collected royalties on "Dixie," the unofficial anthem of the Confederacy. Poor whites, among them recent immigrants, also supported slavery, fearing they'd lose work to freed slaves. Benjamin Wood was the editor of the New York *Daily News* and brother of Mayor Fernando Wood. He warned about having to compete with "the labor of four million emancipated negroes."[1]

On the other side were abolitionists. From the pulpit and in newspaper editorials, they railed against the peculiar institution. Brooklyn preacher Henry Ward Beecher held mock slave auctions to publicize southern atrocities. Horace Greeley, the owlish editor of the *New York Tribune*, warned against putting money ahead of compassion. "In order to line our pockets," he asked, "must we utterly stifle our souls?" [2]

Offered the choice between money and morality in the 1860 election, the city went with money. While Beecher and Greeley voted for Lincoln, New York as a whole went with the Democrat Stephen Douglas. New Orleans publisher James Dunwoody De Bow explained the outcome. "Where would New York be without slavery?" he said. "Ships would rot in her docks. Grass would grow on Wall Street and Broadway."[3]

Sentiment changed after Fort Sumter and Confederate secession. Embracing the Union cause, volunteers marched down Broadway on their way to defend Washington. The business class grew concerned that the South would forge commercial ties with Europe and bypass New York. It swung to the Union cause and discovered it could make even more money in war than in peace. Old notions of government parsimony went out the window as Washington spent what it took to crush the enemy. The Lincoln administration issued oceans of Treasury bonds, paying investors more than 7 percent at a time when corporate borrowers paid less than 5. Steel mills, garment factories, and gunmakers worked around the clock to feed the demands of the military.

Railroads raced to keep up. A one-factory operation like a textile mill was small. It could finance itself out of profits. It was self-financing. Not so with railroads. Railroads needed outside capital. They needed it in staggering quantities. They needed it to pay for land, rails, and rolling stock. An organization like the Pennsylvania Railroad would eventually employ more people than a small state. New York financiers, with their ability to tap deep-pocketed investors at home and abroad, found the money. Along the way, Wall Street went from being an interesting, at times exciting, corner of the nation's economic landscape to an essential part of it. Wall Street put the country on an industrial footing.

Trading in railroad stocks dominated the New York Stock Exchange and Wall Street itself became crowded for the first time. At one end of the street stood Trinity Church with its slender spire and graveyard. To the east, ship chandlers catered to schooners launching for New Orleans, Baltimore, and Liverpool. In between were eight blocks of brick buildings, fronted at street level by coal chutes. The buildings were four stories high; their floors divided into tiny offices to accommodate demand for proximity to the stock exchange. Rents were as steep as anywhere in the city. Lunch counters—an innovation—sprung up to offer slabs of meat and bread to harried traders. To feed their information needs, newspapers expanded their business coverage. Robert Dun and John Bradstreet hired reporters to ask nosy questions about creditor solvency. Anyone stepping outside to the street to buy one of their publications would have smelled burnt coal, tobacco, and horses.

The general public wanted in on the action. As stories flew about the mechanic or the store clerk who made a quick killing, money came out of mattresses and into securities. "The mania seemed to possess everybody." wrote *Fraser's Magazine*. "Professional men, tired of their slow gains; clerks, sick of starvation salaries; clergymen, dissatisfied with their niggardly stipends followed fast in the same course. Even the fair sex dabbled."[4]

Gould set himself up as a stockbroker and private investor. He got ideas by reading the papers and measuring the reports against rumors gleaned on the Street. Gould didn't invest on hunches. He dug deep to discover whatever was knowable, separating the nonsensical from the plausible. This in itself didn't make Gould special. Most investors would claim they did the same. The difference was Gould's diligence. He was more methodical, more voracious in search of insights, and more patient with minutiae. These qualities served him well in the hand labor of surveying and tanning. They served him better in the brain labor of Wall Street.

Gould connected with the right people. John Church Cruger, a wealthy landowner in Westchester County, took an interest in the young stock trader and invited Gould to join him and his family for a Sunday sail on the Hudson. As the hours passed, Gould fretted about making his train back to the city. He urged his host to go faster. Irritated by the pestering, Cruger toyed with Gould by secretly removing the centerboard and "accidentally" beaching the boat short of the dock. Gould stripped down to his red shorts and jumped overboard. Holding his clothes above his head, he dog-paddled to shore. The Crugers were still laughing as they watched a conductor pull Gould onto a moving train.

Gould also made the acquaintance of Daniel S. Miller. Miller was the sort of person Gould aspired to be. Before retiring to invest for his own account, Miller was one of the leading merchants in New York, having made a fortune as a produce wholesaler by selling eggs, Chinese tea, and Midwest corn and wheat. Robert Dun once described him as "more than ordinarily bent on making money."[5]

Miller and his family lived in Murray Hill, a fashionable East Side neighborhood of quiet brownstones not far from the Everett House. Miller had a daughter with a round face, a sweet smile, and a shy manner named Helen. She was twenty-three and went by Ellie. Like others in her social set, she watched her posture, took pains to appear sunny, and, when conversing with men, let the men do the talking. She expected to marry someone from her class.

Gould didn't fit the bill. He had prospects but came from nothing and had no inheritance or guaranteed income to fall back on. Despite Gould's modest background, Miller was probably the one who introduced him to Ellie, but only after concluding Gould was sober, hardworking, and would do right by his daughter. Gould's prior experience with women, excluding the flirtation with Maria Burhans, was vicarious. When he was in Roxbury, illiterate acquaintances called on him to pen love letters. Gould's florid writing style fit the task. His verbal kisses, remembered a relative, would "exhaust the list of adjectives."[6] For his own part, Gould rarely talked about women or marriage. When he did, he despaired he would ever find someone. He called marriage a "strange uneven sea of human experience upon which I never expect to embark myself."[7] Now, at age twenty-five, he was ready. He courted Ellie for two years, taking her to the theater and on walks in the park. On January 22, 1863, with Burnside's army stuck in the mud and pinned down by Lee in Fredericksburg, Gould said his vows. Accounts vary but as many as four hundred people may have attended. The Millers had a large house. After the wedding Gould moved in.

About this time, an acquaintance from the Swamp offered Gould a large block of bonds in a troubled railroad, the Rutland & Washington. Its locomotives, with balloon stacks and cow catchers, hauled quarry stone from Rutland, Vermont, to Troy, New York, where freight handlers transferred the cargo to barges for the journey down the Hudson. Stone volumes hadn't materialized as expected and the price of the railroad's bonds came to only 10 cents on the dollar, a value that suggested the railroad would fail.

Gould liked the price. He judged the Rutland's assets as solid and believed the railroad, in the right hands, could turn a profit. Plus, the bonds could be converted into enough stock for him to take control. Gould bought the bonds for $5,000, converted them to stock, and named himself president. Gould had never worked for a railroad other than as a surveyor. He counted on his general knowledge of business to see him through. Spending his weekdays in Vermont and commuting home on the weekends, he invested in track, cut costs, and pitched customers on the railroad's services. He also pinched pennies. An office boy named Charles Frost worked for Gould in Vermont, earning 50 cents a day to run errands. Frost once accompanied Gould on a trip to buy wood for the locomotives. After a morning spent measuring logs, they broke for lunch. Gould offered to share some of the food he brought. He was a man of means and Frost expected a feast. Gould pulled from his satchel nothing but dried prunes and crackers.

Rutland & Washington had western Vermont to itself. Once it reached New York, it ran into a challenge that Gould battled the rest of his career: too many railroads and not enough freight. That convinced him the Rutland wasn't a keeper. Eighteen months after buying it, he got out by selling it to a New York rival and earning a bundle. His $5,000 dollar investment—an investment that others on Wall Street thought a sure loser—brought him $100,000, an amount equal to $2.5 million in current dollars.

While Gould was in Vermont, Ellie was pregnant with their first child. Gould was elated about becoming a father. "I am missing my fond wife terribly," he wrote. "I am hoping she is not feeling too delicate or indisposed. I know she is as brave as she is beautiful and I know the great gift she is about to bestow."[8] Ellie gave birth to George Gould, the person destined to inherit Gould's business empire, on February 6, 1864.

Family life agreed with Gould. He proved a devoted husband and father, making sure Ellie was pampered. When George was a year and a half old, Gould wrote a remarkable letter to his former teacher, James Oliver. Gould, still in his twenties, had not yet become the secretive, guarded recluse of his later years. He was open, introspective, and sincere. In the letter, he seems all but overcome by excitement for the future. In lyrical prose, he wanders down a spiritual path and confronts his ambition. His drive to succeed, he says, is the manifestation of divine will.

"Now that I am at this place, it is a puzzlement to me how I endured before. Everything prior seems to have been boxing in the dark, scraping without reason. Now I have my road to walk and my reason for walking it. Now the pieces fit, and this thing ambition is no longer blind but divine, a true and noble and necessary path. I see things very, very clearly. I feel inspired with an artist's conception. Divine inspiration? I cannot say. But my road is laid out before me in the plainest of ways."[9]

FIVE

INFLUENCERS

The Forty Thieves ran an extortion ring on the Lower East Side. They took a skim from every storekeeper, shoemaker, and carriage operator transacting on their turf. The Thieves considered themselves a cut above the usual crooks. They dressed in top hats and frock coats. They smoked fine cigars. When they entered their imposing hideout on Centre Street, doormen ran to assist. Most of all, they had class. Let the tenement gangs—the Pug Uglies, the Bowery Boys, and the Dead Rabbits—crack skulls. The Thieves had a better way to steal. They had power, the power of elected office.

The Forty Thieves was a nickname. Their official name was the Common Council of the City of New York. Nowadays, the New York City Council is packed with lawyers. Then it was tavern owners. The joke went like this: A guy walks into City Hall council chambers. He yells, "Your saloon is on fire!" The room empties.

On an afternoon in April 1863, with the war in its third year and Joe Hooker poised to attack Richmond, the council convened. A clerk hustled out reporters as the members filed in. There was important work to do. Hours passed. An attendant lit the gas lights and brought food. When the meeting broke near midnight, the clerk handed out a press release. It said the city had awarded the Harlem

Railroad the right to dig up the roads south of 23rd Street and build a streetcar line to the Battery. The public was incensed. Tree-lined Broadway was the most beautiful road in the city. On weekends, it filled with people out for a stroll. But the Harlem belonged to Cornelius Vanderbilt. He was, at age sixty-eight, the richest man in the country. His money meant more to the council than public sentiment.

Thus began one of the most fabled and exciting chapters in the history of Wall Street, the Harlem Corner. The episode would cement Vanderbilt's reputation for nerve and alert the public to the dangerous alliance between big business and politics. Gould, who had just arrived in New York, was not involved. But he watched with the avidity he showed as a student in the schoolhouse. Gould learned the lessons of the Harlem Corner, absorbed its subtleties, and, soon enough, employed his learnings to more powerful effect.

In a way, Vanderbilt served as an instructor for Gould in a master's class. Known as the Commodore, Vanderbilt hoed potatoes as a youth on Staten Island. After buying a boat with a loan from his mother, he paid her back by ferrying passengers around New York Harbor. He won customers with his reliability and attention to safety. He had good hands and made boats himself. He had good fists, too. Tall as Gould was short, he once leveled the bare-knuckle heavyweight champion Yankee Sullivan. He took his tea with ten lumps of sugar. When crossed, he retaliated with ferocity. "I don't care half so much about making money as I do about making my point," he said.[1]

Early in his career, Vanderbilt switched from sailboats to steamships. The wind was fickle, making steam an easy choice. Railroads carried even more promise. Trains were faster than ships, hauled more freight, and could go anywhere there was track. But they were dangerous. In 1833, a curious Vanderbilt tried out the rails by taking a ride with the Camden & Amboy Railroad in New Jersey. Outside of Hightstown, an axle snapped, the train derailed, and the car carrying Vanderbilt flipped. Vanderbilt flew from his seat and broke a leg. Two passengers died, becoming among the country's first railroad fatalities. Vanderbilt was done with trains. "I'm a steamboat man, a competitor of these steam contrivances you tell us will run on dry land," he said. "I shall never have anything to do with them."[2]

It took the Civil War to change his mind. The North had more track than the South, giving it an edge in transporting troops and supplies. Awokened to the advantages of rail, Vanderbilt backtracked and decided never was a long time. He sold most of his ships and went all in with steam contrivances.

In 1863, three decades after his rail accident, many of his most colorful triumphs were behind him. He had made a fortune operating the Staten Island Ferry and some steamship lines out of New York. He had already created a water route between the Atlantic and the Pacific by taking the helm of a steamer and charging full throttle over the cataracts of Nicaragua's San Juan River. When he sold the Nicaragua business, the buyers stiffed him and he vowed revenge. "Gentleman," he wrote, "you have undertaken to cheat me. I won't sue you, for law is too slow. I will ruin you."[3] He was as good as his word.

Stocks in that era went public, like bonds, at a price of $100 a share. Through mismanagement, neglect, and looting, stock in the Harlem Railroad, which traveled north from 42nd Street to upstate New York farm country, had fallen from 100 to 9. Vanderbilt bought control and, to use his word, "overhauled" the Harlem with the same sound business practices he had brought to shipping. The railroad was soon profitable, and Vanderbilt made money on the stock.

Now it was the turn of the Forty Thieves to make money. After receiving their bribes, they bought stock in Harlem before announcing the extension.

The stock soared after the mayor, who was in on the insider trading, signed the bill. The council members were ecstatic. They had nearly doubled their money just by moving their lips and saying aye. This was magical. They might as well have said abracadabra.

Vanderbilt's crews began ripping up paving stones on 14th Street. They didn't get far. Inspired by their success as investors, the council decided to run the play in reverse. They'd take away Vanderbilt's charter, crush the stock, and make money by betting against it in a short sale.

The concept of a short sale couldn't be simpler. You make money by betting that the price of a stock goes down. The mechanics, however, are devilish. To short a stock, you borrow the stock from an owner and, without ever owning the stock yourself, you sell it. If you bet right and the price falls, you buy the shares back at the lower price, return them to the owner, and profit on the difference. You lose if the stock goes up. Short a stock at 100 and it goes to 0? The profit is $100. If the stock goes to 200? It's a $100 loss. There is no upper bound. In theory, the stock could go to 300, 400, or even to a price high enough to destroy you. Of course, you don't expect destruction. You expect to profit on a fall or to get out ahead of disaster. The idea of profiting from misfortune rubs some the wrong way. It's unpatriotic to bet on decline. Defenders note that it pricks bubbles, unmasks unrealistic expectations, and contributes to a healthy, functioning market.

The councilmen had no interest in a policy debate about short selling. They were interested in profit. To them, it was plain to all that the Harlem was worth less without the Broadway extension than with it. What could go wrong?

* * *

HARLEM WAS TRADING at 83 when the conspirators borrowed shares and sold them. At the next council meeting, they revoked the charter and, just as anticipated, the stock "fell like a shot partridge," wrote the stockbroker William Worthington Fowler.[4] To cash in, the lawmakers only had to buy back the borrowed stock and return the shares to the lenders.

They met with a surprise. When they went to cover, they found no stock available. Vanderbilt had bought all the shares. "He who sells what isn't his'in, must buy it back or go to prison," went an old Wall Street adage. To save themselves from prison, or at least bankruptcy (the New York debtor's prison closed in the 1830s), the council sent a negotiating party to Vanderbilt's office to beg. When the men arrived at 5 Bowling Green near the Staten Island Ferry terminal, Vanderbilt turned them away.

He awoke the next day feeling more charitable. When the negotiating party returned, he made an offer. "Let matters be placed in the status quo," he said. "And then I will see what I can do with the outstanding contracts."[5] The council returned matters to the status quo. They reinstated the charter and Vanderbilt sold them the Harlem shares they needed at a greatly marked-up price. "They ate the leak," wrote *Harper's*.[6]

A year passed. The Civil War raged. Gould was shuttling between New York and Vermont, investing on the exchange as a speculator and operating a railroad as an industrialist. Vanderbilt moved his master's class to Albany. The state legislature was seething over the Harlem project. The way it saw it, New York City had no authority to grant a railroad charter. Only Albany could do that. If anyone should be shaking down the Commodore, it was the state legislature.

Shares in Harlem fell on concern that Albany would intervene. Vanderbilt himself was unconcerned. He could just pay off the legislature like he paid off the council. He bought more shares in Harlem and encouraged associates to follow. He sent a lieutenant to Albany to negotiate. Daniel Drew, a Harlem board member, tagged along.

If Vanderbilt led the master's class, Drew served as guest lecturer. Vanderbilt taught the section about corners and short squeezes. Drew taught market manipulation. He and Vanderbilt went way back. In the old days, they competed in the steamboat business. Now friends, they talked about horses and played whist together at the Manhattan Club. Drew was a farmer's son from New York's Putnam County who, as a cattle driver, became infamous for fattening up cows before auction by feeding them salt and letting them gorge on water. He moved downstate in 1830 and kept a tavern in an unsettled area of 24th Street. With his profit, he bought a steamship, the *Water Witch*, to carry freight down the Hudson. He fought so aggressively against Vanderbilt that the Commodore bought him out. Now in his seventies, Drew's days of binge drinking were over. But he still played the market during the week, gambled at the track on Saturday, and, for penance, sang with the Methodists on Sunday.

His specialty was the bear raid. He'd sell a company's stock short, spread lies about the company's supposedly wretched condition, and close the position at a profit after the stock crashed on rumors of collapse. His talent was stirring up fright. He commemorated this by naming his favorite horse Panic. With his drover hat, furled umbrella, cadaverous frame, and full-length black coat made of sealskin, he resembled a skeleton dressed for Halloween. Fowler, the stockbroker, had literary flair. Commenting on the nature of Drew's intelligence, he wrote, "The word subtle doesn't altogether express it. It should be vulpine."[7]

In Albany, Vanderbilt's aide doled out bribes. When word leaked that Vanderbilt would get his charter, the stock leapt and Drew, whose wealth rivaled Vanderbilt's, sold his Harlem stock at a gain. Then he went behind Vanderbilt's back, shorted the stock, and persuaded the lawmakers to do the same. Just revoke the permit, he said, and the stock will fall. He promised there would be no second corner of Harlem. This time the math was against Vanderbilt. Harlem was selling at too high a price for him to buy all the shares. The legislature, swayed by Drew's logic, shorted the shares in anticipation of a windfall.

The Senate banking committee voted down the charter. Shares in Harlem again fell like a shot partridge. Vanderbilt fought back, bought more stock, and advanced the price to 200. Confident in their math, Drew and his Albany friends sold more stock short. But the math was wrong. Vanderbilt had more reserves than Drew thought. The Commodore bought more and advanced the stock to 300, breaking the backs of the plotters.

Drew went whimpering to Vanderbilt, insisting he'd be ruined if the Commodore didn't show mercy. Drew reminded him that he once gave a job to Vanderbilt's son. He reminisced about the adventures of their steamboat days. Vanderbilt was a hard man but had a soft spot for his whist partner. He let Drew settle at 165, a fantastic discount to the market price but one that still left Vanderbilt with a profit. Drew, teary-eyed, thanked him. He lost $1 million on the adventure but he was still in business.

The second Harlem Corner was a masterpiece. "There can hardly be a doubt," wrote Henry Clews, another broker and Wall Street commentator, "that the Commodore was a genius, probably without equal in the financial world."[8]

The Commodore didn't know it but another genius was emerging, one who was studying his methods, taking in the lessons, and sizing up Vanderbilt's character and vulnerabilities. This was another self-made man who grew up on a farm with nothing to his name, another railroad operator with a brilliant and cunning mind, a man who would soon prompt Vanderbilt to look upon him with grudging respect and call him "the smartest man in America."

Vanderbilt had not yet heard of Gould. Gould was just another face in the crowd. The introduction would come later. For now, Vanderbilt would enjoy his coup, winning a permit for his streetcar line and, above all, having made a point. He shared a laugh with a friend. "We busted the whole Legislature," he said.[9]

SIX

ERIE

Murray Hill suited Gould. After moving in with Ellie's parents, he easily settled in. The area was quiet, especially compared to the chaos downtown. It was also well-to-do. It improved his image to say he lived down the street from a Civil War admiral, a prominent heiress, and a hobbled but still wealthy Daniel Drew. The writer Edith Wharton hated Murray Hill's stuffy culture and its Victorian primness. She held a special contempt for the area's mud-colored houses, calling brownstone "the most hideous stone ever quarried" and complained how it coated neighborhoods like "warm chocolate sauce."[1]

Gould was good with Murray Hill and good with brownstone. Even as he and Ellie filled the house with children—George, Edwin, Helen, and Howard were born in the house—he saw no reason to leave. He and Ellie preferred simplicity and domestic pleasures. They were not social. Whether in Vermont or New York, Gould stuck to business and minimized his interactions outside the office. Ellie busied herself with the children. She was happy and, if she was happy, Gould was happy.

In 1866, three years after Gould got married, his hard-drinking father, John Gould, died at age seventy-four. Gould rarely spoke about his father. Maybe it was out of anger over the alcoholism or the childhood punishments that included being locked in the cellar. When asked about John Gould, Jay Gould fell back on trite expressions as if to say more would prove overwhelming. "He walked a hard road," Gould said. "He drank from a bitter cup."[2]

In a room full of businesspeople, Jay Gould was no longer the youngest. He had a beard now, not the bushy beard of his later years, but one kept neatly in check. He was haggard and painfully thin. "I saw him take a plunge in the Turkish bath at Saratoga," wrote the journalist William Croffut. "I never saw such a prominent bull with such insignificant calves. Perhaps—perhaps you could not put a napkin ring over his foot and push it to his knees. I am not certain."[3]

Gould had been CEO of a railroad. Now he was back on Wall Street trading stocks. What did that make him? Was he a railroad man or an investor? He didn't know himself. Then opportunity struck in the form of the one of the largest enterprises in the country, the Erie Railroad. The story of how Gould seized Erie shows his brilliance as a financial strategist, his deep understanding of law, a surprising grasp of human nature, and a mastery of political reality. The Erie episode also linked his name, for the first time, with treachery. Gould's life of crime, said his enemies, began with Erie.

Seventeen years earlier, when Erie opened a station west of Buffalo in Dunkirk, New York, the town partied with banners, bands, and windy speeches. President Millard Fillmore, his thick white hair blowing in the breeze, boarded the first train. Why not celebrate? The Erie created an incalculable economic advantage. Blessed with a railroad, Dunkirk was sure to become a crossroads where Midwest grain and cattle began the journey to the big cities of the coast. The Erie wasn't just any railroad. It launched the country into the steam age as the first railroad to connect the Great Lakes with the Atlantic Ocean.

Or at least almost to the Atlantic. Because of complications of getting into Manhattan, it stopped short of the city, ending its journey twenty-eight miles upriver in Piermont, New York. To make matters worse, it terminated on the New Jersey side—that is, the wrong side—of the Hudson River. The railroad's gauge was another challenge. At six feet it was wider than the standard gauge of four feet eight and a half inches. The width enhanced the stability, but made it impossible to transfer cars from Erie to other lines. Then there was the horrifying safety record. Derailments were common. In 1864, a switchman's error diverted a train carrying Confederate prisoners into an oncoming coal train. The head-on collision near Shohola, Pennsylvania, left seventy-two passengers dead.

Despite all this, ridership and cargo volumes were soaring. Much came at the expense of the Erie Canal. The canal had revolutionized transportation by cutting the travel time from Buffalo to New York from three weeks to eight days. Now here was a railroad that covered the same ground in a single day. The canal, the onetime disruptor, was itself doomed. A contemporary writer, with only slight exaggeration, called the Erie Railroad the Appian Way of America.

The Erie was busy but high construction costs and debt made it vulnerable. The Panic of 1857, the one that trashed Gould's tannery prospects, swept Erie into bankruptcy. When it emerged, it had a new set of stockholders led by the wily Daniel Drew. Drew joined the board and became the railroad's treasurer and guiding force. With the ascension of Drew, Erie kept its day job as a railroad but freelanced as a financial plaything for Drew and its other executives who, over the next several years, treated other shareholders with stupefying contempt.

Being an insider was a dream come true for Drew. As an outsider, he had to make up stories to manipulate stock prices. As an insider, he didn't have to make up anything. He just had to buy or sell ahead of corporate news. Even better, he could determine the news. He could raise the dividend or slash it on a whim. He could cut freight rates and scare investors. Or he could raise rates and whip up prospects for higher profits. Eric's share price was a yo-yo in his hands. For extra cash, he could have Erie award contracts to businesses he owned on the side.

These days, Drew's manipulations would put him behind bars. Back then, they were perfectly legal. Drew's fellow board members merrily rode along and shared in the profits. Drew lost no sleep over fleecing the public. If professional men, clerks, clergymen, and the fair sex got burned investing in Erie, it was their own fault. Buyer beware. The press called Drew the Speculative Director. "No title was ever more justly given," wrote *Fraser's Magazine*.[4] After a spectacular manipulation in 1867, Drew's Methodist friends seized the moment and persuaded him to bankroll a seminary in Madison, New Jersey. The Drew Theological Seminary, now Drew University, opened that same year.

While the Methodists rejoiced, Vanderbilt cast his gaze on Erie's competitor, the New York Central. The railroad ran across the Mohawk Valley from Buffalo to Albany. From Albany, it connected with Vanderbilt's Hudson River Railroad to bring passengers and freight to New York City. The arrangement worked well and both sides made money. The relationship changed after Vanderbilt became interested in Central. In a ploy to smash Central's stock price so he could buy it cheap, he ordered the Hudson, without warning, to refuse Central's traffic. Freight and passengers were left stranded outside Albany, sitting on their suitcases. Nervous investors sold their Central shares. Vanderbilt snatched them at close-out prices and took control. Summoned by the legislature to testify about his high-handed tactics, Vanderbilt was asked two questions. Where was he when the passengers were stuck outside Albany? And why

Erie

hadn't he done something? "I was at home gentlemen, playing a rubber at whist," he said, "and I never allow anything to interfere with me when I'm playing that game. It requires, as you know, undivided attention."[5]

Once Vanderbilt had the Central, he moved to blunt Erie as a competitor. A simple, still legal price-fixing deal should have been enough. But that was out of the question because of Drew. Cartels rise and fall on trust. If one side undermines the deal to win business, the cartel falls apart. For Vanderbilt, it was one thing to be Drew's friend. It was another thing to trust him. He bought Erie shares in a bid to gain control.

Then Gould entered the picture. Gould spotted the struggle developing between the two titans and angled to put himself in the middle. If managed deftly, he could profit regardless of which side won. The annual meeting of Erie was coming up. To get himself elected to the board, Gould bought voting rights, known as proxies, from English shareholders too oblivious to care about the outcome. By voting for himself, Gould gained a seat. As for Drew, he promised Vanderbilt to behave. The Commodore was not inclined to clemency. But softened by Drew's pleas, he let Drew stay on the board.

With the election out of the way, it was back to business. Vanderbilt acted on his cartel plan. He proposed not a two-way deal between his New York Central and the Erie, but a three-way with another railroad, the Pennsylvania. A price-fixing scheme would propel Central's profits and its share price. The Commodore advised his friends to buy the stock before it went up. His friends tipped their own friends. "Vanderbilt advises his horse companions to buy Central," wrote one of them.[6]

Drew, meanwhile, set up an investment club, known as a pool, to profit from the cartel news. Vanderbilt, Gould, and other Erie insiders chipped in. Erie was selling for 71. Drew announced the cartel to the public and sent the stock to 79. He took profits. Then he shorted the stock and spread word that Erie wanted nothing to do with cartels. The stock fell. He gave Erie another kick by issuing new shares and diluting the value of the Erie shares already on the market. The share price fell back to where it started.

The failure of the cartel hurt Central, too. Vanderbilt was furious. "Damn the face of that old hypocrite," he said. "I'll whip him if it costs me a leg."[7] Thus began the Erie War, a gigantic struggle that revealed Wall Street at its worst, rattled faith in unfettered capitalism, and triggered the country's first calls for progressive reform. The Erie War also introduced Jay Gould to a national audience.

WALL STREET WISDOM said if you went to court, you hired a lawyer but first you hired a judge. Vanderbilt hired Judge George Barnard, a Yale man whose qualification was a willingness to do the Commodore's bidding. Clarence Stedman, a stockbroker and writer, said the judge "numbered among the Vanderbilt properties." A man who appreciated fashion, Barnard dressed like a riverboat gambler. His shirts were ruffled, his bow ties white, and he wore a Stetson at a rakish angle atop his head. He completed the picture with a droopy mustache that ran to the bottom of his cheeks. In court, he put his feet on the bench, slurped brandy, and whittled with a pocketknife while insulting lawyers who came before him. He had failed as a prospector in California and was serving as the New York City recorder when William Magear Tweed, the boss of New York politics, put him on the bench. The appointment shocked Barnard's brother, who said, "George knows as much about law as a yellow dog."[8]

Canine proficiency was enough. That's because he had Vanderbilt's lawyers to write his rulings. Vanderbilt couldn't immediately oust Drew. He'd have to wait until the next board election for that. But he could stop him from flooding the market with shares. The judge froze the Erie share count at 250,000 shares, the share count from two years before. The order assured that Vanderbilt could buy a majority of Erie's shares without fear of Drew fabricating more stock and diluting his ownership.

Vanderbilt went to his stockbroker, satisfied that justice had been served. Buy more Erie, he said, and keep buying until he had a majority. Vanderbilt was done with Drew. He'd drop Drew on the curb and leave him there.

There were two ways to operate a railroad in the 1860s. There was the Vanderbilt way of running the trains on time, keeping the rolling stock in top condition, charging a fair price, winning customers with good service, and paying a steady dividend to shareholders. That approach won the trust of shareholders and made it easy to raise money for new projects.

Then there was the Drew way. For him, transporting freight and passengers was ancillary to the main activity of insider trading. He wasn't interested in building a sustainable commercial enterprise. He only wanted to manipulate stock prices and profit from the moves. Smart investors looked away from Erie. But Drew didn't need them. There were plenty of dumb ones to sucker. So what if the moralists on Wall Street condemned him as a "stock jobber"? Stock jobbing, the term contemporaries used to describe stock price manipulation, had paid for his Murray Hill mansion. Stock jobbing had paid for his horse farm in Putnam County. Stock jobbing had paid for Drew University. Stock jobbing had made him, after Vanderbilt, the most successful businessman in the country.

When Jay Gould joined the Erie board, he had a choice. He could back Vanderbilt and be a builder. Or he could back Drew and be a speculative director. He could join Vanderbilt and "overhaul" the railroad by plowing the profits into making it bigger, better, and more useful to the community. Or he could spend his energies on fooling with the stock price. He could be on the side of the angels or on the side of darkness. In the Great Erie War, he chose darkness.

SEVEN

SARDINES

There is a fourth character in the Erie drama who needs introduction. This character is the one who gave the Erie War its sizzle, its absurdity and vitality. He didn't determine the outcome, but as a sidekick to the hyperrational Gould, he made the conflict human. He was a vulgar, bottom-pinching, cigar-chomping cotton smuggler with a weight problem named Jim Fisk.

Fisk's first job set the tone for his career. He sold tickets for a circus. Dressed in striped pants, he learned the arts of hyperbole, phony conviction, and persuasion. When Fisk took over his father's peddling business, traveling around Vermont selling linens door-to-door, he doubled sales by painting his cart like a circus wagon and wearing a ringmaster's outfit. Fisk's voice was shrill. When the overworked farm wives of New England heard his shouts, they ran outside, happy to let him brighten their day with a story. "He talked a blue streak," said Robert Fuller, a childhood friend.[1] The literary stockbroker Fowler, who knew Fisk professionally, said Fisk was "continuously boiling over with jokes, good, bad, and indifferent."[2]

Fisk's success won him a job in Boston with the retailer Jordan & Marsh. He became a top buyer. During the Civil War, he snuck over enemy lines to buy Confederate cotton for Union army uniforms.

Daniel Drew got to know him and hired him to sell a steamboat. Fisk got a good price. Impressed by Fisk's promotional skills, Drew invited him to New York and set him up as a stockbroker.

Fisk dressed for success, fitting himself out with the best suits from Brooks Brothers. He accessorized with a silk handkerchief, a bejeweled cane, and a dazzling diamond stickpin visible from a block away. A person had to be crazy to flaunt their wealth in those days. Just a few blocks from Wall Street was the Five Points, a slum where hoodlums dragged victims into back alleys, cracked open their skulls, stole their money, and tossed the corpses into the river. But Fisk couldn't help himself. He filled his Broad Street office with French furniture and stocked a bar with fine wines and whiskey.

On Wall Street, Fisk was the fool at the poker table. The veterans licked him clean. He made some money shorting Confederate bonds on the eve of Appomattox. He lost it betting on crops. Broke but unbroken, he left for Boston to raise cash. "I'll be back in Wall Street inside of twenty days," he said. "And if I don't make things squirm I'll eat nothing but bone button soup until Judgment Day."[3]

Drew put Fisk on the Erie board where he became friends with Gould. Gould and Fisk were about the same age but had little in common. Fisk was loud, charismatic, emotional, and tubby. The pint-sized Gould was a prude and so soft-spoken that he often went unnoticed. "The difference between Jay and me is I have more trouble to get my dinner than to digest it, and Jay has more trouble to digest it than to get it."[4] Despite the differences, they were so close that one associate described them as "Siamese Twins." Vanderbilt and Drew were role models for Gould. Jim Fisk wasn't a role model. He was a bad influence, the kid down the block who encouraged friends to cut class and go shoplifting.

Fisk admired Gould's brains. No one could think through a problem like Jay Gould, Fisk would say. Gould valued Fisk's energy and willingness for dirty work. Fisk had another quality Gould appreciated. Fisk was loyal, at least to Gould. Gould never had a truer friend. Gould, wrote Fowler, "is the engineer while Fisk is the roar of the wheels."[5]

WITH THE INJUNCTION from Judge Barnard that blocked Erie from issuing more shares, Vanderbilt snapped up the stock on the open market, trying to gain a majority. Drew fought back with injunctions. Amid uncertainty, investors dumped the stock. "The Street is afraid to hold Erie," reported the *Herald*.[6] If investors had recognized Vanderbilt's determination, they would have held. He was so fixated on taking Erie away from Drew that he broke his own commandment and borrowed money to buy more shares. The banks were happy to give it to him if he put up shares of New York Central as collateral. But they refused to loan it on Erie, rejecting the shares as too risky. Vanderbilt sent his lieutenant Richard Schell to Wall Street to play chicken with the banks. Schell told them that if they didn't loan on Erie, Vanderbilt would sell all his shares in Central, pouring more shares on the market than buyers could absorb. The price would crash. And when Central crashed, the banks that had it as collateral would go down with it. "If you don't lend the Commodore half a million on Erie," Schell said, "he will put Central at 50 tomorrow and break half the houses on the street. You know whether you will be among them."[7]

After the banks gave in, Vanderbilt commanded his brokers to buy Erie. "For ten minutes bedlam seemed to have broken loose," wrote Fowler.[8] Vanderbilt's men grabbed every share they could. Not knowing when they would stop, sellers fought to offer up their lots. A giant blackboard behind the trading pit, known as the Big Board, noted prices. Erie sold for 68 at the beginning of the week. Vanderbilt pushed it to 80.

Gould was making money but the profit offered no comfort. If Vanderbilt took over the railroad, ousted Drew, and brought in his own people, he'd be out of a job. Unwilling to leave the privileged and lucrative life of an insider, Gould joined the fray on Drew's side.

Hamilton Harris was an upstate lawyer who crowned his career by serving in the U.S. Senate. He liked to tell a story from Gould's days as a surveyor. Developers of a small railroad near Albany had hired Gould to survey the route and act as a subcontractor. It was a big assignment for a seventeen-year-old. The project looked doomed when a group of affected landowners threatened to sue and block construction. Harris sat his clients down to tell them all was lost. Then a small voice piped up with a question. The voice was Gould's. Harris looked in astonishment. He thought Gould was a kid who had come with his dad to work. What if, Gould asked, they built the disputed section of road before the court had a chance to rule. Would that make it legal? Harris thought about it. Yes, he concluded. The theory was sound. Gould hired a crew on the spot and got the job done before the landowners could stop him.

At Erie, Gould was once more the small voice that piped up. He noticed that Barnard's injunction against new share issuance enjoined the Erie board and only the board. What if another entity, say, Erie's executive committee—a group composed of Drew, Gould, and Fisk—issued the stock instead of the board? Would that work? The Erie lawyers liked the idea and followed up by finding a judge who signed an order expressly empowering the executive committee to issue shares.

Before Vanderbilt knew about the order, printing presses began to roll and spit out fresh Erie share certificates. Clerks stacked them in neat bundles and handed them to a messenger. Fisk wanted the job done right. He grabbed the shares and headed to Wall Street to deliver them to brokers personally. Soon, Erie shares were readily available but Vanderbilt, believing the share count was fixed, kept buying. "If this printing press don't break down, I'll be damned if I don't give the old hog all he wants of Erie," Fisk said.[9]

Vanderbilt became suspicious when he noticed that his buying wasn't affecting the share price. The price should have skyrocketed as shares became scarce. Instead, the price held steady. Vanderbilt looked at the certificates. What was this? The certificates looked new. They felt new. They smelled new. Then it hit him. Erie had thumbed its nose at Barnard's order and issued more shares. After presumably muttering some curses, Vanderbilt stopped buying. If the supply of shares was infinite, there was no point. He'd never get a majority.

The morning after Vanderbilt's discovery, Fowler stopped by Erie headquarters at the corner of West 10th and Duane Street. He found the directors in a giddy mood. "Uncle Daniel's corrugated visage was set into a chronic chuckle," he wrote. "Jay Gould's financial eye beamed and glittered, and the blonde bulk of James Fisk Jr. was unctuous with jokes."[10]

The executive committee had reason to celebrate. They had just tricked America's richest man into giving the Erie treasury $7 million and he was no closer to controlling the railroad than before he bought the shares. As they lifted toasts, a messenger came with news. Judge Barnard, ignoring the ruling of the other judge, had cited them for contempt. They knew what that meant. The sheriff was on his way to Erie headquarters to put them in handcuffs.

EIGHT

THE FLIGHT

A beat cop happened to be walking down Duane Street a few minutes later. He saw men running in and out of the Erie building hauling boxes from inside and dropping them on the sidewalk. Was Erie being looted? No need for concern, the men said. Boxes in hand, they said they were relocating the Erie's offices. The men were Jay Gould, Jim Fisk, and Daniel Drew, the executive committee of the Erie Railroad. They introduced themselves. The cop moved on, satisfied nothing was amiss.

But something was amiss. With the sheriff presumably closing in, they were preparing an escape. But where to go? The answer was just over the river. New Jersey, only minutes away, wasn't obligated to return fugitives to New York. It might as well have been Switzerland. Anxious to get moving, Drew grabbed a ferry to Jersey City. Gould and Fisk said they'd catch up, but it was dinnertime and exile could wait. The two directors, one skinny and one fat, went to Delmonico's on Chambers Street and pondered what to order.

Fisk ate with gusto. He tore at meat. He shoveled his potatoes. Gould picked at his food. A nervous stomach destroyed for him the pleasure of eating. He sipped sherry when obliged but believed liquor came from the devil. At Delmonico's, in full view of New

York's rich and powerful, they discussed the week's adventures. Gould had at his feet a bag of cash, cash from selling new Erie shares to Vanderbilt. Fisk, aware their meal could be interrupted, had a lookout at the door and an escape plan in his head. If the cops came, they'd dash through the kitchen, run out the back, jump in a cab, and race to the pier where they'd grab a boat to Jersey City. The plan didn't call for diving over tables but, if it came to it, dive they would.

Sure enough, someone had tipped off the cops. Before dessert arrived, officers crashed through the front door, handcuffs and billy clubs in hand. The lookout sounded the alarm. Gould and Fisk ran out the back, found a cab, and made it to the Chambers Street pier. Complications developed. The sun had already set. Gaslights lit up the docks as a defense against the river pirates then active in the waters. As Gould's anxious eyes darted up and down the pier, Fisk hired transportation. The captain of the steamboat *St. John* was tucking his boat in for the night. The *St. John* hauled freight. It was not a water taxi. No matter. Fisk had cash. Fisk persuaded the captain to release two crewmates to take him and Gould to Jersey City in a lifeboat. They hopped aboard.

New York Harbor didn't rest. Ships plied the inky waters around the clock. Deaths from collisions were routine. On this night, fog covered the river. A lantern was little help. The oarsmen got lost and rowed in circles. As they foundered on the icy water, a ferry burst through the fog, heading toward their bow. Gould clutched the money. The crew rowed with all their strength. The ferry roared by.

Suddenly, another ferry, faster and more menacing than the first, came at them, its giant paddlewheel churning the water. They'd be crushed unless they steered clear. Fisk shouted. Gould shouted. The oarsmen put their backs into it. The boat was nearly atop them when the ferry captain heard the shouts and slowed his craft. Fisk pleaded to let them board. He was soon hoisting his belly over the rail with Gould, clutching his bag of cash, on his tail.

Gould and Fisk arrived in Jersey City looking like drenched spaniels. They wondered if they would ever get back to New York. In the days that followed, couriers crisscrossed the river as the fugitives ran the railroad from an upper floor of the Taylor's Hotel. The Taylor was a waterfront establishment popular with salesmen who couldn't afford New York prices. It had the strategic benefit of being near Erie's Jersey City terminal. Reporters from New York came in search of copy. The story of the Erie War, a cliffhanger they could unfold in serial form, moved from the business page to the front page.

New Jersey was thrilled to have the Erie, a jewel of American commerce, relocate to its shores. Authorities promised to help any way they could. When a rumor spread that Vanderbilt put a bounty on Drew's head, the governor sent a police unit to defend Jersey City from amphibious assault. Heeding a suggestion from Fisk, the police put guards and cannons on the roof and the Taylor's Hotel, in the words of the press, became Fort Taylor. Fisk hired a New York street thug named Tommy Lynch to patrol the lobby. Just as feared, a pair of New York gang leaders came looking for Drew. Lynch intercepted them at the docks.

The New Jersey excursion came at a bad time for Gould. Ellie was expecting again. It killed him to be away from home. Fortunately, the New York law covering fugitives was merciful. The police and the courts needed occasional breaks. The law let fugitives come home on Sundays. During what came to be a nine-week sojourn in New Jersey, Gould ferried back on Sundays to see his family.

Fisk was married, too. Lucy Fisk lived in Boston with her girl-friend and he rarely saw her. "She is no hair-lifting beauty," Fisk told a friend. "Just a plump, wholesome, big-hearted commonplace woman such as a man meets once in a lifetime."[1] He prized her willingness to leave him alone. "Never, never does Lucy surprise me with a visit. God bless her." Fisk made New Jersey tolerable by bringing along a friend. Josie Mansfield was a self-described actress from Boston. Divorced and ready to start fresh, Mansfield came to New York to begin life anew. She found her way to a brothel on 34th Street. The sex trade paid especially well at the time; Victorian prohibitions against premarital intimacy crimped supply. Fisk was twelve years older than Mansfield. Stately and upright, she was, in the words of a *New York Herald* reporter, "shaped like a duchess."[2] Her curves, her pearly skin, and her doe eyes overwhelmed the peddler's son. Upon meeting her, Fisk's reaction, wrote the reporter, was the same as Oliver Cromwell's when he first saw Ireland: "This is a country worth fighting for."[3] Fisk wrote her touching letters and spoiled her with gifts. He called her "Dollie." She called him "Sardines." Unable to separate from her while on the run, he installed her in a suite at the Taylor where she pretended to love him back.

Drew hid in his room trying to fathom just having taken $7 million from Vanderbilt under circumstances that a judge ruled criminal. He wanted to make peace. He wanted to go home. Gould and Fisk all but forced him to stay, promising to find a way to keep Vanderbilt's money. "Drew has been kidnapped not by roughs but by the directors," the *Herald* wrote.[4]

Meeting in Mansfield's suite, Gould and Fisk hatched a plan. They'd lobby Albany to sanction their heist with a law to permit the share issuance. It wouldn't be easy; Vanderbilt had friends in the capital. But the Erie men had a policy argument. They had saved the people of New York from becoming thrall to a Vanderbilt monopoly. Vanderbilt had the Central, the Harlem, and the Hudson. If not for Erie, Vanderbilt would control all of the state's rail traffic and could charge whatever he wanted. Like Robin Hood, their interests might be considered criminal, but they aligned with those of the people. Fisk and Gould invited the press to the hotel bar and explained their case. The *Times*, the mouthpiece of Republicanism, wasn't buying it. Gould and Fisk were hoodlums, pure and simple. The *Herald* took the opposite view. Gould and Fisk might be rascals, but Vanderbilt was worse.

Public relations was easy. The hard part was buying votes, especially when there was a rival bidder who was the richest man in the country. Erie sent a lobbyist and a bag of cash to Albany. Vanderbilt sent the state senator who represented Manhattan. He was none other than Boss Tweed, who, in 1868, was near the height of his power.

Tweed knew just what to do. He rented a seven-room suite at the Delavan House, Albany's best hotel. He stocked whiskey in every room and, dashing between them, he bought enough support to win an Assembly committee vote by a wide margin. He paid a rumored $3,000 per vote. The *Herald* ridiculed Erie for being cheap. It mocked its "unsophisticalness."[5]

The State Senate came next. For Gould, it was all or nothing. Erie was his chance for the big time, the opportunity that would elevate him above the brokers on the curb and justify all those hours of study back in Roxbury, the lonely months surveying the countryside, and the dreary nights in Gouldsboro gagging from tannery stench.

Gould fired the lobbyist and went to Albany himself. He was young but he knew the capital. Back when he was a surveyor, he had gone there to lobby for a law requiring schools to buy maps. The bill failed, but Gould had seen how money made legislators dance. He boarded a train in Jersey City and, in less than an hour, was over the New Jersey frontier and back in New York where an officer could cuff him and stick him in jail for contempt.

The Erie had extracted millions from Vanderbilt. If forced, Gould would spend all of it on bribes. This was no time for frugality, no time for half measures. He'd be generous, more generous than Vanderbilt and Tweed. The *Herald*'s man on the scene reported that Gould arrived at the Delavan House with a trunk "literally stuffed with thousand dollar bills."[6]

Hearing that Gould was in New York, Judge Barnard wired Albany with an arrest order. Gould was ready. He had prearranged bail. When the trial date for the contempt charge came two weeks later, he won a delay by faking illness. The *Herald* could not accuse Gould of being "unsophistical." He knew his way around the court system. He nursed his "cold" by staying in Albany, pouring champagne and passing out cigars at the Delavan House.

Loose laws facilitated Gould's exertions. New York had an impossible evidence standard for bribery. To establish guilt, a third party had to witness the payoff. As long as Gould closed the door when he handed over cash, he was safe. The proceedings were an auction. Whatever Tweed offered, Gould offered more. If Tweed bought a vote, Gould bought it back. His trunk of cash seemed bottomless.

The Senate voted with Gould and the bill went back to the Assembly for final approval. Hearings were held. Witnesses testified. Then, before bidding commenced for the final stretch, Vanderbilt bowed out. He'd pay no more. He was done with bribery. Furious lawmakers expressed their wrath with a 106-to-6 vote for Erie. They gave the Commodore another kick by making it illegal for him to ever own Erie. The governor signed the measure the next day. Shares in Vanderbilt's New York Central, the stock he pledged as collateral to buy his Erie shares, plunged 20 percent. Bankers fretted that he was finished. "The market was full of rumors about the solvency of Vanderbilt," wrote Fowler.[7]

Vanderbilt wasn't finished. He was only changing tactics. Vanderbilt knew this about Drew. Drew, as he told friends, had "no backbone."[8] While Gould was in Albany, Vanderbilt commanded Drew back to New York for peace talks. The great bear was desperate to come home. When he met the Commodore, he offered unconditional surrender. If Vanderbilt dropped the criminal charges, he'd make sure Erie would buy back the shares and the Commodore would come out whole. Vanderbilt attached two conditions. First, Drew, Gould, and Fisk had to leave the Erie board. And to make sure they would never trouble him again, they could never, absolutely never, have anything more to do with the railroad.

When Gould heard about the deal, he was flabbergasted. "Jehoshaphat!" cried Fisk. What was Drew thinking? The New York governor had just signed a law legalizing what they had done. Maybe they couldn't keep all of Vanderbilt's loot but, at minimum, the law gave them a way to tangle their adversary in court for years. Didn't Drew understand that? How could he be so dumb?

The following Sunday, another holiday for exiles, Gould and Fisk went to Vanderbilt's mansion to seek a better deal. They arrived so early that Gould felt embarrassed about ringing the bell. A servant opened the door. Fisk brushed by the man and went straight for Vanderbilt's bedroom. Gould waited in the parlor. Fisk found Vanderbilt sitting in bed with one shoe on and one off. Vanderbilt's shoes had a stylish four-buckle arrangement that Fisk paused to admire. When he got over the shoes, he demanded that Vanderbilt let Erie keep some of the money. Vanderbilt refused. He demanded the plotters return every penny or else, recalled Fisk, he'd keep his "bloodhounds on our tracks." Fisk told him "it was an almighty robbery."[9] He left the mansion wondering where he could get the shoes.

A week later, Drew met Vanderbilt in the home of a Vanderbilt judge. Gould and Fisk got wind of the meeting and ran to the judge's house. Fisk burst through the door. Gould shuffled in be-hind. Gould made an offer. Erie would give Vanderbilt his money back and Drew would leave the board, but—and this was an im-portant "but"—he and Fisk could stay. Vanderbilt had nothing to lose, he explained. There'd be a board election in October. That was just seven short months away. If Vanderbilt had the votes and still wanted them out, he could kick them out then. In the meantime, he'd get his money back right away, without having to go to court. Vanderbilt took the offer.

NINE

PECULIAR AFFAIRS

One evening shortly after the peace accord, Vanderbilt and Drew were shooting the breeze at the Manhattan Club when Drew told Vanderbilt he was better off without Erie. Erie was an empty shell, he said. There was nothing left to plunder. Bankruptcy was inevitable. "There ain't nothing in Erie no more," Drew said.

Vanderbilt thought otherwise. In the hands of someone capable, someone who knew how to overhaul a railroad, someone, that is, like himself, it could mint gold. He considered Erie's four hundred miles of track, its route from Dunkirk to Jersey City and how Erie still offered the most economical way to move freight from lake to ocean. An empty shell? Hardly. "Don't you believe it," Vanderbilt said.[1]

Gould saw it the same way. When he walked through the doors of New York's 127 West Street in his first day as president of the railroad, he wasn't thinking about empty shells. He was thinking about how he now could buy Erie stock before he made it go up and how he could short Erie stock before he made it go down. He also thought about expansion. At that moment, a group of Boston investors were building the Union Pacific, laying track across the plains to connect with the Central Pacific for the rest of the journey to San Francisco. The Golden Spike that would join the two railroads a mile above sea level would soon be pounded into the ground in Utah. Lake-to-ocean was exciting. Ocean-to-ocean more so. Gould's head swirled with plans. Vanderbilt had already created a seamless connection from New York to Chicago. Gould wanted to match him. And once he got to Chicago, the West would lay before him.

The first order of business was keeping Erie afloat. Erie wasn't earning enough to cover its interest payments. Although it had bought back Vanderbilt's stock and promptly resold the shares to raise money, it still fell short and, if it missed an interest payment, bankruptcy wouldn't be far off. Where to get more money? Banks were out of the question because Erie had already pledged all its assets. Wall Street was out, too, because Drew had burned too many bridges. Even with Drew sidelined, stockbrokers could not in good conscience recommend Erie securities. There was, however, another possibility.

AUGUSTUS MELMOTTE WAS the richest man in London. An investment banker, he lived in a palace on Grosvenor Square where he hosted a reception for the Chinese emperor. He won election to Parliament. In his most ambitious venture, he raised money to build a railroad from Salt Lake City to Veracruz, Mexico. The project was speculative, but as Melmotte knew, there were rich people in the U.K., France, and Germany with plenty of cash and nowhere to put it at home. America, by comparison, was booming and investment opportunities were plentiful. Aided by endorsements from aristocratic friends, Melmotte raised the money. It quickly became clear there was no railroad and the venture was a fraud. Investors lost everything. As for Melmotte, he went bankrupt and shot himself.

Melmotte was fictitious, a character in Anthony Trollope's 1875 novel *The Way We Live Now.* Although the story was made up, the part about indiscriminate European investors was true. They were suckers for anything American, especially railroads. New York Central. Union Pacific. Atchison Topeka & Santa Fe. Erie. Didn't they all have locomotives, tracks, and rights of way? Didn't they all ferry passengers into the booming interior and bring back cattle, grain, and coal? An inspiration for Melmotte was August Belmont, a London investment banker sent to New York by the Rothschilds. Belmont had a love of wine, French art, and horses. The creator of the Belmont Stakes, the third and most grueling leg of the Triple Crown, Belmont made a fortune supplying Europeans with American investments. So did Junius Morgan and his son John Pierpont, better known as J.P. Another immigrant, the German banker Joseph Seligman, represented Erie. With Seligman's help, Gould raised $10 million in London and filled the Erie treasury.

Next for Gould was the matter of keeping himself in office. Like Vanderbilt, Gould watched the calendar. As the months sped by and spring turned to summer, Vanderbilt went to Saratoga, relaxed in the fresh mountain air, and raced the trotters. He had yet to amass enough Erie shares to oust Gould but there was still time. As per the Erie bylaws, anyone with stock on the day of the board election could vote. One share, one vote. Gould's hold on power was tenuous.

Then Gould stumbled on an idea. He read about an Indiana railroad that changed its bylaws and advanced the cut-off date for voter eligibility. Gould took the idea to the Erie board on August 19. The board accelerated the cut-off date to that same day, making it impossible for Vanderbilt to vote shares bought later. Gould followed up by getting the legislature to let Erie directors keep their jobs for five years instead of having to face annual reelection. The moves blindsided the Commodore.

When the board election came two months later, Gould kept an eye out for process servers. Vanderbilt couldn't vote him out of office but he could try to block the vote with another of his court orders. Despite these concerns, everything proceeded swimmingly. Gould and his slate swept the polls. He could keep his job as Erie's president. Fisk could remain treasurer. After the ballots were counted, Fisk sent a note to his girlfriend using language appropriate to announce a successful but turbulent Atlantic crossing. "My dear Josie," it read. "We are all safe."[2]

Mansfield was now living in Fisk's pleasure grotto, a house he bought for his lover. Fisk sent a note to tell her he was bringing over two fellow board members to celebrate. One was Frederick Lane, the Erie's general counsel. The other was a well-known politician. "Mr. Tweed and Mr. Lane will dine with us at half-past six," he wrote.[3]

Tweed joined forces with Erie's young masters after having a lunch with Fisk at Delmonico's. The restaurant's signature dishes of Lobster Newburg and Baked Alaska hadn't been conceived yet but even a simple meal of steak, potatoes, and oysters cost a bundle. Fisk considered it money well spent. Tweed, by delivering the two things politicians cared about most—money and votes—ruled New York politics. His power was unchallenged. He could do things for Erie.

Tweed grew up poor on the Lower East Side. After making a name for himself as a political operative, he spotted the opportunity that came with immigration. In return for small favors, the new arrivals, mostly from Ireland, would vote however Tweed instructed, often multiple times. Tweed climbed the political ladder. Once at the top, he awarded city contracts to carpenters, plumbers, painters who he told to pad their bills. He took the extra for himself and his friends at Tammany Hall, the Democratic organization that controlled New York politics. A new courthouse that should have cost $3 million ultimately cost $13 million. "If we get you a contract for

$450,000," Tweed asked an electrical contractor, "will you give us $225,000?"[4] The money came from the sale of city bonds. Between 1868 and 1871, the city's debts tripled. Tweed kept the press quiet with advertising and printing contracts.

Tweed flaunted his wealth, splitting his time between a Fifth Avenue mansion and an estate in Greenwich, Connecticut. Vanderbilt was the richest man in New York. Tweed might have been second. Estimates go as high as $50 million. Good government groups forced an investigation. John Jacob Astor, one of the city's most respected businessmen, led a committee to inspect the books. Unbeknownst to Astor, Tweed showed him phony books. Astor proclaimed no signs of wrongdoing.

To Fisk's delight, he and Tweed clicked. Like Fisk, Tweed appreciated conversation, cigars, women, and, most of all, food. Fisk was fat. Tweed was even fatter. At three hundred pounds, Tweed could pack it in. Fisk had a mistress. Tweed had two. Tweed saw in Erie the corporate reflection of Tammany Hall. He grasped the synergies. Tammany could pass laws, grant permits, and secure judicial orders for Erie. Erie could benefit Tammany—and make Tweed even richer—by splitting the profits with him. The benefits were mutual.

With his job secure, Gould concentrated on taking Erie to the next level. He was a dervish. He bought an interest in another railroad, leased a second, and talked to several more, all with the aim of getting Erie direct access to Chicago and another city he considered destined for greatness, St. Louis. He bought a steel mill so Erie could make its own rails and replace its dilapidated tracks. He remade decrepit wooden bridges with iron. He bought new locomotives. On the sales front, he signed an agreement with a small Pennsylvania railroad to ship two million tons of coal a year over Erie. There were times when Gould worked three or four days in a row without sleep.

Along the way, he made time for speculative direction. When he raised money by issuing more Erie stock, he shorted the stock ahead of time. He knew the market wouldn't appreciate seeing the value of existing Erie shares sliced even thinner. The New York Stock Exchange demanded details and warned him against raising more. Gould apologized, saying it wouldn't be possible.He was considering further expansion. The stock fell a third from where Gould initiated his short.

Gould wasn't finished. The money he raised—$10 million in all—gave him another club to bash Erie's stock price. To execute the scheme, known as a lockup, he'd deposit the money in a bank and then have Erie write a certified check on it. The bank would have to hold in reserve an equal amount of cash in case the check got cashed. Ten million dollars was a lot of money, comprising a significant share of the ready cash in the city's banking system. By locking it up and making cash scarce, banks would charge higher interest rates for cash they still had to lend. When interest rates go up, stocks go down. Gould was confident share prices would crumble.

Gould was envisioning market manipulation on a grand scale. The fact that he even considered it displayed his capability to think big. He was willing to push the limits like no one else. His audacity was breathtaking. His target was Erie, just one of dozens of stocks on the exchange. To bring it down, he was prepared to hammer the entire market. New York Central, the Pennsylvania Railroad, Western Union, American Express, and every other stock on the exchange would be collateral damage. To make money on just one stock, he'd bring pain to everyone with money in the market. That couldn't be helped. He had spotted an opportunity. He had to take it.

On the exchange floor, traders sensed money was getting tight but believed the banks had it under control. The *Times* reflected their indifferent attitude, describing the lockup as "by no means extensive or formidable." Indeed, the interest rate to buy stocks, known as the margin rate, stayed flat at 6 percent. Erie sold for 48 before the lockup. It barely moved after Erie wrote its certified check.

The traders didn't know that Gould was just getting started. He reached out to Drew and, overlooking their past differences, informed him of his scheme. He persuaded Drew to join his bear pool and take more money out of the circulation. A week later, the interest rate hit 7 percent and Erie sold for 44, down $4 from where they started. Other stocks fell, too, but Erie fell more because it was riskier to begin with. The *Times* was convinced the worst was over. "The locking up process ceased to excite remark," it wrote.[5]

Erie dropped another four points the next day, leading a down market. "Money is extremely close and dear among brokers today. Some of the mercantile houses are said to be needy," wrote the *Times*. Out-of-town banks jumped in to provide cash.[6]

The infusion made no difference. A day later, on November 4, the *Times* said the market was experiencing "a semi-panic."[7] It became a full panic a few days later when interest rates hit 10 percent. Desperation took over. "Banks relieved their wants by throwing their stocks on the market for cash," the newspaper reported. Erie hit 38, down $10 from the start of the lockup. Vanderbilt's New York Central, the bluest of blue chips, fell apace.

By now, everyone knew Gould was behind the rout. The *New York Evening Post* demanded justice. "It is said that frauds were committed within the letter of the law," it wrote. But "a sound public opinion would never stop to quibble upon the letter of the law before overwhelming such men with scorn." By making speculative sales of his own company's stock, Gould had committed the "vilest form of fraud."[8]

Drew had to admit that Gould had talent. Still, he was used to being a ship's captain, not a member of the crew. He quit Gould's pool and bounded back into the market, shorting Erie for his own account. He made a huge bet. A week after Drew's short, Erie fell to 35. Drew was cleaning up. He let his bet ride.

In every bear raid, there comes a time when a stock price becomes so untethered from reality that it can fall no more. Gould decided 35 was as low as Erie should go. It was time to shift gears. November 14, 1868, was a Saturday, a day when banks and the stock exchange had abbreviated hours. The morning dawned clear and crisp with wind blowing from the west. Horses skipped down Broadway with their carriages. Ships tooted whistles in the harbor. Children rolled hoops down the street. Gould was in his office giving orders to brokers. He invested for profit, not for vengeance. But if there was a day to inflict maximum pain on an enemy, Saturday, a day of light trading, was the day. Anyone short a stock would find few shares to cover their positions.

When the banks and the exchange opened, Gould closed his own short position by buying Erie stock to return to lenders. He had to pay up to get the shares, but it was worth it. Then, as if commanding the wind to change direction, he canceled Erie's certified check and terminated the lockup. Everything that had blown north—interest rates, the money supply, the availability of bank credit—instantly blew south toward friendlier waters. The results were instant. "Money was easy," reported the *Times*. Gusts of liquidity powered stocks higher. New York Central left port at 116 and comfortably cruised to 122. Erie roared past the break wall and into the open ocean, moving from 36 to 52, a bracing 44 percent advance. "On the stock exchange, the day has been one of unusual excitement on the railway list, especially so on Erie,"[9] wrote the *Times*. The day was more than exciting for Drew. It was catastrophic.

The next day, Sunday, Drew went to church as usual. He sang the hymns, recited the doxology, and knelt before the cross. He prayed for salvation. Skipping the coffee hour, he went to Erie headquarters. With Vanderbilt, he could appeal to sentiment. Not so with Gould. Gould didn't play whist or raise horses. Drew's only hope was that Gould had a touch of Methodist in him and that he, like the movement's founder, John Wesley, would put love into action. He found Gould in his office with Fisk, and groveled at their feet. "I'm a ruined man," he said. Gould was quiet. Fisk accused Drew of hypocrisy, saying he "should be the last man that should whine."[10]

Back and forth they went, Drew looking for a way out and Gould toying with his prey. At one point, Drew suggested getting the team back together and doing another bear raid on Erie. He'd give his profits to Gould. Gould demurred. Drew offered to pay an enormous interest rate if Gould let him repay over time. Gould held firm.

Drew had one more card to play. With the clock approaching midnight, he said that unless Gould gave him a break, he'd blow the whistle on Gould's deceptions. Drew reached into his pocket and pulled out a sworn statement he had written for the occasion. It detailed every questionable activity Gould had done since joining Erie. The self-dealing, the undisclosed share sales, the looting of the treasury to execute the lockup. Drew had participated alongside Gould in most of it. He'd be incriminating himself if he submitted testimony. But he had a noose around his neck. He had nothing to lose.

"You know that during the whole of our other fights, I objected to ever giving my affidavit," Drew said, "but I swear I will do you all the harm I can do if you do not help me." Drew put on his hat and left Gould to think. "I will bid you goodnight," Drew said.[11]

Something occurred to Gould. In Drew's desperation to save himself, he had unwittingly given away ammunition. If the court accepted Drew's charges, it would deliver Erie to a receiver. Gould was sure of it. No judge could overlook the urgency of the situation, not in the face of testimony from a co-conspirator. The judge would take Erie away from Gould before he could steal again. But two could play that game. What if Erie was already in receivership? And what if Gould himself was named receiver? He could retain his executive privileges and business could go on as usual.

That Gould even considered such a thing showed, yet again, how the legal system was broken. That he acted on the idea, removed any doubt. Early the next morning, Gould, Fisk, and their lawyers rang the doorbell of Judge Barnard, the same judge who, on orders from Vanderbilt, had Gould arrested in Albany for contempt and the same judge who described the Erie shares Gould sold to Vanderbilt as "counterfeit." Barnard was never really a Vanderbilt judge. He was a Tammany judge. He went where Tweed went. When Tweed went to Erie, Barnard followed. Gould and his friends found Barnard in bed. He signed the receivership order while propped on his pillow.

Expecting Drew's judge, Judge Josiah Sutherland, to send his own receiver at any moment, Gould raced to Erie headquarters, barred the doors, and posted guards. He was huddled with Fisk and the lawyers when they spotted an intruder who had penetrated the defenses. The intruder announced himself as retired judge Henry Davies and said he was now receiver of the Erie Railroad. An Erie guard had mistakenly let him in. Disappointed in Erie's security team, Fisk excused himself from the room.

Gould and Davies, the twin receivers, were not alone for long. Fisk returned and directed Davies's attention to the hallway. The retired judge turned to see the brawler Tommy Lynch and his boys. Davies was elderly and frail. Lynch and his men were young, sturdy, and had fists the size of melons. They eyed him with menace. Davies fled. Gould, now the lone receiver of the Erie Railroad, remained in charge.

Drew settled with Gould at a loss of $1.3 million. This was devastating. Drew returned to his farm with his cows and horses. After a few more failed speculations, he took bankruptcy. The Drew Seminary was left to contemplate a stack of worthless promissory notes. Later asked about Gould, Drew gave a short reply. "His touch is death," he said. [12]

TEN

GOOD MORNING, COMMODORE

That same year, there appeared in bookstores a slim volume
about a homeless shoeshine boy who through a combination
of hard work, pluck, and fair play becomes a success. The book
was a sensation, selling thousands of copies in its first week. The
book was *Ragged Dick* and the author was a young Harvard man
named Horatio Alger. Alger published more than a hundred books
with similar story lines. His name became a byword for how to get
ahead.

Ragged Dick sold well because it validated American prejudices.
America was the land of opportunity. It was the land of freedom. It
was a place where a solid work ethic trumped royal privilege. "I'm
a rough customer," said Dick. "But I wouldn't steal. It's mean."
Gould didn't quite embody the Alger persona. Fair play was foreign to him. But he mirrored Dick when it came to hard work and
pluck.

While Gould wasn't Ragged Dick, he was without question
the embodiment of another popular archetype. He was a victor
in the game of what Herbert Spencer and not Charles Darwin was
the first to call "survival of the fittest." Spencer, a British philosopher, applied Darwin's biology concepts to the social sphere. The

fittest was the person who bested his opponents. Gould qualified as fit. And as much as the American mind was sympathetic to Ragged Dick, it also admired men like Gould, men who began with nothing and made themselves rich regardless of their methods. Yale professor William Graham Sumner shed no tears for the victims of capitalism. "Before the tribunal of nature, a man has no more right to life than a rattlesnake," he wrote. "His right to the pursuit of happiness is nothing but a license to maintain the struggle for existence."[1]

The triumph over Drew announced Gould as a master of the game. The *Herald* made it front page news. "However questionable these schemes may be, the skill and success exhibit Napoleonic genius on the part of him who conceived them," it wrote.[2]

Gould's next scheme put Fisk at the center. He gave Fisk a black satchel and sent him on a mission downtown. Fisk secured the bag between his legs for safekeeping. Erie's outside counsel, Thomas Shearman, rode with him. Born in England, Shearman was a reporter for the *Times* who taught himself the law. He became a protégé of the celebrated attorney Dudley Field and later won the trial of the century when he successfully defended the Reverend Henry Ward Beecher in an adultery suit.

Shearman and his partner, John Sterling, founded what is now an 850-member firm that still bears the name Shearman & Sterling. He was a great lawyer but Fisk, as he approached his destination, thought there might be trouble and he regretted that Shearman would be worthless in a fight. "He was such a little fellow," Fisk said. Rain pelted the paving stones on Washington Square as the carriage came to a stop. Fisk rang the bell. Vanderbilt opened the door. "Good morning Commodore," Fisk said.[3]

Gould hated the Erie peace deal with Vanderbilt. He had agreed to it. But he still believed Erie had sold the stock to Vanderbilt fair and square. Erie should never have made Vanderbilt whole. Gould dispatched Fisk to get some of the money back.

Fisk and Shearman shook off the rain and reminded the Commodore that Albany had legalized the share sale and that Judge Barnard was no longer working for Vanderbilt but for Gould. Barnard would order him to pay. Then Fisk revealed the contents of the satchel. It held fifty thousand shares of Erie. Although Erie was selling for 52 on the exchange, Fisk demanded that Vanderbilt buy them at 70. Vanderbilt refused.

Fisk reported Vanderbilt's refusal to the press. Vanderbilt responded with a bizarre letter to the *Times*. "I have had nothing to do with the Erie Railway Company," he wrote. The next day Fisk gave the newspapers copies of the canceled checks Erie had given Vanderbilt. The checks made Vanderbilt look like a liar and a fool.

Fisk never got any money from Vanderbilt. But with each day, Gould came to better appreciate his portly friend. Fisk completed him. Gould was a thinker. Fisk was a doer. While Gould fled confrontation, Fisk sought it. Gould cherished Fisk. Like an indulgent father, he spoiled him by funding his whims. There was a new theater at 23rd Street and Eighth Avenue not far from Fisk's townhouse. Fisk toured Pike's Opera House, gazed upon its twenty-foot mahogany doors and grand foyer staircase, and thought, with a little work, it could make a fine headquarters for a railroad. He bought it with Erie money, transferred the title to himself and Gould, and summoned decorators to bring it up to his standards. In came black walnut panels with gold inlays, wash basins with nymphs, floor-to-ceiling mirrors, and a giant bust of Shakespeare. The letters ER, for Erie Railroad, were cast in bronze and attached to the front door. Telegraph machines were installed in the executive offices along with, according to one newspaper account, "such desks as a coquette might have for her boudoir."

The theater stayed in operation under a new name, the Grand Opera. The press called the place Castle Erie. Fisk personally served as manager. "I'm a prostitute," cried the impresario Bordenave in Émile Zola's 1880 novel *Nana*, lamenting how he used flesh to fill the seats. Fisk had no qualms. He found a hit with the Twelve Temptations. A dozen sequined dancers—blondes one night, brunettes the next—twirled and kicked before a packed house to the sound of thunderous clapping.

Fisk returned Gould's affection with grand gestures. He endowed a militia unit and dubbed the unit's summer retreat Camp Gould. When Erie bought steamships to ferry passengers from Jersey City to Manhattan, Fisk named one of the boats after himself. He named the other one the *Jay Gould*. Out of embarrassment, Gould only rode the *Jim Fisk*.

Gould, meanwhile, bought himself a house. After seven years under the roof of his in-laws, he moved with his growing family to a large brownstone at 578 Fifth Avenue at 47th Street. Fifth Avenue was already in vogue with the rich. August Belmont, the New York agent for the Rothschilds, lived on 18th Street and Fifth. Lady Astor was on 34th Street and Fifth. When Central Park opened in 1859 on the avenue's western edge, fashionable addresses crept uptown. Gould felt himself at home on Millionaire's Row.

ELEVEN

PROPHET OF REGULATION

Charles Francis Adams finished the essay and downed his pen. He was pleased. He believed he had something special. "It is good," he told himself. "Very good."[1] He celebrated over dinner with his wife and parents at the family estate outside Boston. The next day, he bundled up the essay and sent it to *The North American Review*, the most influential magazine in the country. He was sure his piece—the most challenging bit of work he had ever accomplished—would make waves. "The goose hangs high," he said.

Adams was thirty-three, a year older than Gould. He had a ferret face with a little mustache. By his own account, he had a "wheezy way of speaking, more English than American."[2] He was an admitted snob. His grandfather was John Quincy Adams. Charles shared with grandpa an inability to filter his words. He shared with his great-grandfather John Adams a tendency to despair and an impatience with small talk. After finishing Harvard, he failed as a lawyer, then distinguished himself as a soldier at Antietam. He left the army as a brigadier general and returned to civilian life to face his greatest fear—a life without distinction. He dreaded the side glances of others. Given his celebrated lineage, he assumed others were judging him. In his diary, he wrote that he feared going down for posterity as "the last of Adamses."

Adams didn't know what to do with his life. He ruled out the law as too boring, business as too vulgar, and daily journalism, although he enjoyed writing, as too pedestrian. As for the family business of politics, the idea was laughable. He'd be a miserable campaigner. He was blunt and hopeless at chitchat. Then it hit him. The railroads were taking over the country, changing perceptions of distance and time, opening the West, and transforming America in ways good and bad. He saw it at home in Massachusetts, the state where the railroad boom started. Train tracks blighted the countryside. The trains themselves derailed and killed passengers. But they let him leave Quincy in the morning and be on Boylston Street an hour later.

The industry emerged from the Civil War as the most important and powerful in the country. It bothered Adams that there was no oversight. Laissez-faire was so firmly rooted that, once a railroad secured a state charter, it could operate any way the owners saw fit. Nowadays, regulatory agencies, bureaus, and commissions trip over each other. Then there was nothing. Federal or state lawmakers dealt with issues as they came up. Adams thought the industry needed a regulatory commission, like those they already had in Europe, to safeguard the public interest. Like a teen who forms a school club to beef up the college transcript, he decided he should be the one to start it.

Adams launched a presumptuous plan —a plan that only someone with wealth and access could dare. First, he'd announce himself as a railroad expert by writing articles and publishing them in the country's most important journals. Then he'd ask his family friend, the governor of Massachusetts, to start a state railroad commission and appoint him as a commissioner. From that perch, Adams felt he could satisfy his ambition, achieve national prominence, and honor the family name.

Adams wasn't anti-commerce. He appreciated the power of the profit motive and feared an all-powerful state as much as his anti-monarchist ancestors. But he differed from the laissez-faire crowd. Economic liberals were happy to tolerate a few bad apples. Better that than using taxpayer money to pay watchdogs and restrict economic freedom. Adams saw the good in free markets but also believed the country needed technocrats—men like himself—to set ground rules. The railroad industry was the ideal place to start. "I endeavored," he wrote, "to strike out a new path and fastened myself not to a star, as Emerson recommends, but to the locomotive engine."[3]

Adams was careful not to overreach. As he proposed it to the governor, the commission would have no enforcement power. It would quietly collect data, and use the data to make sensible recommendations for legislative action. That was it. The proposal seems modest but, for its time, it was novel, so novel as to be revolutionary.

Adams's first article about railroads relied on ideas cribbed from others. He got better after that, giving momentum to his regulatory scheme. Massachusetts created the commission—the country's first regulatory commission of any sort—just as *The North American Review* published, in two parts, Adam's masterpiece, called "A Chapter of Erie." Using court documents, news reports, hearing transcripts, and interviews, the essay recreated the story of the Erie War. Adams peppered it with observations, commentary, and humor. No one was spared. Vanderbilt, Drew, Fisk, a host of judges and New York politicians—all were guilty of cheating the public. "Freebooters are not extinct," he wrote. "They have only transferred their operations to the land."[4]

With tongue in cheek, he introduced Jay Gould to a national audience as a selfless warrior for the people. He only hinted that Gould was in it for the money and accused him of "unspeakable effrontery." But exercising his literary muscles, he portrayed him as a mission-driven benefactor of railroad customers. Gould selflessly braved snowstorms, sheriff's deputies, and a head cold to visit Albany in his epic quest to keep Erie in responsible hands. "The cry of monopoly was a sure card for Gould," he wrote.[5] Adams's narrative peaks when Vanderbilt, realizing Gould was willing to outspend him, crushes the mood of lawmakers by closing his wallet. "In a moment, the lobby was smitten with despair, and the cheeks of the legislators were blanched."[6]

The essay made a point. The system was so corrupt that democracy risked destruction in the hands of rich capitalists. The government of the people and for the people was yielding to what Adams called "Caesarism," a society where a few rich monopolists set the rules and reaped the benefits. Urgent action was needed because "the community is slowly accustoming itself to look for protection, not to public opinion, but to some man in a high place and armed with great executive powers."[7]

The frightening image of the "man in a high place," born of Adams's blueblood moralism, struck a chord. Newspapers across the country ran excerpts. Some followed with exposés of their own with names like "A Chapter of Wabash" or "A Chapter of Missouri." Historians later called "A Chapter of Erie" one of the most important essays in American history. They credited Adams for launching Ida Tarbell, Upton Sinclair, and other muckrakers of the next generation.

Adams would have objected to the label, but the truth was that he was a nativist. To him, it mattered where a person—a voter—was born. You could trust a person born on American soil but not someone informed by a foreign upbringing. The nativists lived by a Protestant code. It was the code of their forefathers in England and the Netherlands, a code that, they would say, valued moderation and reason. From their ranks came the abolitionists, men like Henry Ward Beecher and the journalist William Lloyd Garrison. But despite those exceptions, the nativists were clear about the pecking order. Blacks were inferior to Eastern Europeans and Eastern Europeans were inferior to Italians who were inferior to Irish who were inferior to Germans. Near the top of the order were the Dutch, like Vanderbilt, provided they were born in America. At the very top were those, like Adams, whose ancestors were British.

Nativists possessed most of the country's wealth. In politics, they had lost New York to Tweed and his immigrant voters but they still held Washington. They ran the universities. They were the ministers at the churches for Episcopalians, Presbyterians, Methodists, and Congregationalists but not for the Catholics. Horace Greeley was a nativist. On the pages of his *New York Tribune*, he condemned New York politics as the victim of "a Catholic conspiracy." Walt Whitman held similar views. He fretted about "these dregs of foreign filth."[8] In the pages of *Harper's*, cartoonist Thomas Nast, although German by birth, took the side of the natives and sketched the Irish as monkeys dressed as leprechauns, whiskey bottles in hand.

The papers were unsure how to classify Gould. Gould was a native. He was born in New York, his family came from England, and his ancestors fought alongside Washington in the Revolutionary War. Gould was as red, white, and blue as Adams and Greeley. And Gould himself agreed with much of the nativist canon. But Gould the Episcopalian didn't fit the narrative of Gould the monster. It did nativist editors no good for Gould to be one of them. He wasn't Irish, Italian, or Bohemian. But he had something his enemies could play with. He had dark skin. That was all they needed to link him to a group even more sinister in the public mind than the others: the Jews. Anti-Semitism ran high. During the Vicksburg campaign, Grant suspected Jews of strengthening the Confederacy by trading with the rebels. Although he later apologized, he ordered them out of areas under his control. In 1868, the same year as the Erie War, the Ku Klux Klan lynched a Jewish store owner in Tennessee.

Look at the facts, said Gould's foes. Gould's skin was as dark as an Israelite. He had a sharp nose, a high forehead, beady black eyes, and a pointed beard. Sure, he went to church with his family. But he had a Jewish name. Wasn't it Gold before it changed to Gould? And didn't Gould, above all else, love money? There was no doubt. Gould must be Jewish. When Nast wasn't drawing the Irish as leprechauns and Tweed as Falstaff, he drew Gould as Shylock, with a long nose, the robe of an Old Testament rabbi, and coins falling from his pockets. John Burroughs wrote of Gould's "Jewish look."[9] Henry Adams, Charles's brother and a writer of growing renown, described Gould as "small and slight in person, dark, sallow, reticent, and stealthy, with a trace of Jewish origin."[10]

The Erie affair marked a turning point for Gould. No more was he the young man on the make, worthy of admiration for his pluck and hard work. He was a battle-scarred celebrity giant killer who stole the country's biggest railroad from the country's richest man. Just about every investor on Wall Street would gladly have traded places with him. Gould was someone who came from nothing and, with individual endeavor, succeeded in doing something unimaginable in countries ruled by kings. What's more, by turning the tables on Vanderbilt, he had prevented the last independent piece of the New York rail network from falling into the hands of a monopolist.

Charles Adams recoiled at Gould's methods and was appalled by his association with Tweed. But he didn't argue with the results.

Gould's defeat of Vanderbilt marked at least a temporary victory over Caesarism. Gould was a venal capitalist, but he wasn't, at least not yet, a threat to democracy like Vanderbilt. Better for Erie to belong to an up-and-comer like Gould than to the Commodore. Adams would find nothing laudable in Gould's next adventure.

TWELVE

───◆◆───

GOLD

Rightly or wrongly, Gould's reputation was cemented by the events of September 24, 1869, a day known to history as Black Friday. The term has since come to refer to other Wall Street crashes and the shopping free-for-all after Thanksgiving. But it was first used to describe how Gould's liquidation of an enormous pile of gold went horribly sideways, froze American financial markets, ruined scores of investors, toppled several banks, prompted a suicide, caused reputational damage for a United States president, and took one trader to the Fifth Avenue Hotel where, after trying to drown his sorrows, propped himself up on a pillar muttering "lost, lost."[1] Because of Black Friday, Joseph Pulitzer called Gould "the most sinister figure to have ever flitted bat-like across the vision of the American people."[2]

In the summer of 1869, Gould was still settling into executive quarters at Erie when he shared an idea with Fisk. Demand for gold always surged at harvest time. They could make money if they bought gold and then persuaded the government to let the gold price rise in line with seasonal demand rather than do what everyone expected, which was to intervene to bring the price down. Fisk heard Gould out and thought for a moment. Then he told him what he thought. "I don't like it," he said. "The country's against you. Everybody wants gold to go down, not up. It's too dangerous."[3]

The issue was this. During the Civil War, the Union ran out of gold to pay soldiers and switched to paper money known as greenbacks. It promised to buy them back after the war at a price of six ounces of gold for one hundred greenbacks. No one quite believed the promise so the price of gold fluctuated depending on the war effort. The government said the price should be 100. But before Gettysburg, when default seemed possible, the gold price rose to 287. After Gettysburg, it fell to 131.

The price shot back to 150 by the end of the war because of a fight over redemption. Farmers lobbied to keep the gold price high. Their loans were in greenbacks, and the more greenbacks gold could buy, the more inflation there would be and the easier it would be for farmers to pay back their loans. Banks would be the losers in this. They took the other side. They couched their interest in patriotism. To redeem greenbacks at less than the promised rate would put the U.S. in the same league as deadbeat Latin American republics and forever impair the country's ability to raise money overseas.

Ulysses S. Grant was president. Elected in 1868, Grant didn't know much about economics. His view about greenbacks was decided when he named George Boutwell as treasury secretary. A formidable, self-taught lawyer, Boutwell had been a Harvard overseer, an Internal Revenue Service commissioner, a Massachusetts governor, and a three-term congressman. As a senator, he was a leader of the Radical Republicans, the abolitionist wing of the party. Grant wanted to make him interior secretary but Boutwell turned it down as beneath him. He only took Treasury after lengthy negotiations. By the time he accepted, he had won so many concessions that he believed he had complete independence. "The President accepted the idea that the management of the Treasury Department was in my hands," he said.[4]

Boutwell was a hard money man. To him, paper money was not real money, and the nation's ability to borrow depended on honoring past obligations. "The currency shall be the value of gold," he declared.[5] Even worse for Gould was that Boutwell had principles. He was a man in possession, according to the *Times*, of "unquestioned integrity."[6] He endured ugly criticism before the war for speaking against slavery. He endured more criticism when he championed civil rights for freed slaves. Boutwell had a long beard like the renegade abolitionist John Brown and shared some of his fiery passion. If Boutwell stuck to his guns on emotional and political issues like slavery and civil rights, good luck getting him to flip on something as mundane as monetary program.

Boutwell's influence over the president became clear when, in his inaugural address, Grant announced his monetary policy. "To protect the national honor, every dollar of Government indebtedness should be paid in gold," he said. "Let it be understood that no repudiator of one farthing of our public debt will be trusted in a public place."[7] He backed his words with action. The first law he signed as president committed the government to redeem greenbacks in gold, at the promised rate, as soon as "practicable."

With that, banks, brokers, and speculators borrowed gold and sold it short, taking the price down to 134 amid consensus around further decline. "It looked as if the finger of a child could have rolled it down to 120," wrote William Worthington Fowler, the Wall Street philosopher. "They stood on their shorts or rather sat incubating them as if they were golden eggs."[8]

Gould, of course, knew the administration's view on gold and understood Fisk's reservations. But the contrary nature of the idea made it compelling as did, perhaps, the sheer complexity of the plan.

"Of all the financial operations, possibly the very hazard and splendor of the attempt were the reasons for its fascination to Mr. Jay Gould," wrote Henry Adams.[9]

The gold caper got its start when Gould made the acquaintance of a Washington insider named Abel Rathbone Corbin.[10] Corbin was a lawyer and onetime St. Louis newspaper editor turned congressional staffer. He had a sharp mind, a charismatic smile, and a willingness to compromise himself to make money. He was caught in 1855 selling votes in Congress. Few seemed to care because, when it came to getting things done in Washington, Corbin was a master. He knew what strings to pull. In 1864, Lincoln needed Senate support for the Thirteenth Amendment that abolished slavery. Corbin delivered him the votes.

Gould knew Corbin from a New Jersey real estate deal. He warmed to Corbin less for his résumé than for his relatives. While attending Grant's inaugural ball, Corbin met the eyes of Virginia Paine Grant, the president's younger sister. Jennie was a flaxen-haired thirty-seven-year-old with dove eyes who had never married. He was a sixty-year-old widower who walked with a stoop. Their love ignored age. Corbin soon became the president's brother-in-law, his confidant, and intimate advisor. "I'm right behind the throne," Corbin said.[11]

Gould asked Corbin to help him persuade Grant to reverse course on greenbacks. If the president flipped and agreed to defy Boutwell, the gold price would soar. Corbin, like Fisk, had doubts. Grant was stubborn and incorruptible, Corbin told Gould. He wouldn't take bribes. Gould told him not to worry. Just get him in front of the president, Gould said. He'd take care of the rest.

The Corbins lived in New York on West 27th Street in an elegant home with French furniture. Gould was soon in Corbin's parlor standing before a dignified gentleman with tired eyes and a neatly trimmed beard. Gould had avoided the draft not by paying $300 to buy his way out but by failing the five-foot-three height requirement. Now here he was standing opposite the "savior of the Union."

Grant had been president less than three months and was still getting used to the job. He was then in New York on his way to Boston for the Peace Jubilee, a mammoth celebration of the Union victory with eleven thousand performers. As it happened, Fisk owned the Narragansett steamship line, a two-ship fleet that ferried goods and passengers up Long Island Sound to Boston. One of the ships, the *Providence*, was leaving for Boston that evening at 6:30. The papers called the *Providence* a "floating palace." It accommodated twelve hundred passengers and the freight of forty railcars. A two-story staircase led from the main deck to a ballroom. Corbin booked a ride for Grant and arranged for Gould to join the president at dinner. Gould would have plenty of time to lobby.

Gould left Corbin's house and followed Grant's carriage to the Chambers Street pier. A military escort followed. They found a festive atmosphere on the waterfront. New Yorkers packed the quay hoping for a glimpse of the president. Hawkers sold sweets. Dodworth's Brass Band played polkas. In the war, Confederate cannons greeted Grant. In New York, it was the blattings of oom-pah bands.

Fisk was there to greet them. He wore an admiral's uniform with three stripes on the sleeves and stars on the shoulders. He accessorized with lavender gloves and a stickpin holding a diamond as big as a grape. He stood ramrod straight by the gangway with one arm stiffly at his side and the other in a crisp salute. If the president was surprised to see his host looking like an overstuffed Horatio Hornblower, he kept it to himself.

Dinner was a star-studded affair by the standards of the New York business community. Corbin, who was not present, had pitched the get-together as a chance for Grant to sound out business leaders on economic policy. Joining Grant, Gould, and Fisk at the table were Cyrus Field and William Marston. Field was famous for laying the first telegraph cable across the Atlantic. Marston was a prominent Wall Street investor known for his corner of the Prairie du Chien Railroad. As waiters brought out food, Gould was bursting to talk about gold but held back. He figured Grant would be more agreeable once supplied with whiskey.

After waiters cleared the plates, Grant surprised Gould by refusing a drink. He was trying to quit. Gould described to the president a plan he called the crop theory. Consider the situation, he said. Britain was a huge buyer of American grain. It paid in gold. So the more expensive gold became in greenback terms, the more greenbacks, and thus the more crops, a British importer could buy with gold. It was like tourism. Foreign travelers love a weak dollar because it reduces the price of an American vacation. Importers love a weak dollar because it reduces the price of American products. The cheaper the greenback, the more grain American farmers could sell. Grant should let market forces do their work and, rather than intervening, let seasonal demand lift the gold price. National honor could wait, Gould said. Let the farmers have their day.

Gould spoke from the heart. Like any good salesperson, he believed passionately in his product. The way he saw it, he wasn't trying to con the president. Sure, he was in it for the money, but he was also fighting for people like his late father and mother.

Grant was quiet. He puffed his cigar. Smoke, not words, came from his mouth. When Gould finished his speech, he was too polite to ask Grant's opinion. Grant was the president. If the president wanted to keep his counsel, he could keep his counsel. Suddenly, a high voice pierced the silence. It was Fisk. How about it, he asked. What did the president think about the crop theory and Gould's plan to stimulate the economy? Grant looked at Fisk. Then he took the cigar from his mouth and threw what Gould later called a "wet blanket" over the evening. "There is a certain amount of fictitiousness about the prosperity of the country," the president said. "This bubble might as well be tapped in one way or another."

Fictitiousness? Bubble? Gould was floored. Farmers were the backbone of the country, and Gould had just rolled out a well-considered program to help them. But Grant, under the spell of Treasury Secretary Boutwell and the hard money crowd, thought the economy, booming again after a postwar slump, was overheated, and that Gould's idea would turn up the temperature. If it came down to a choice between economic stability and farmers, Grant would go with stability. Besides, he had national honor to consider.

Gould tried again. Becoming emotional, he conjured tales of apocalypse. Grant was wrong about the link between a weak gold price and economic stability, he said. If the gold price stayed weak, crops would rot in the fields and the woes on the farm would spread to the general economy. A weak gold price wouldn't deliver the soft economic landing that Grant envisioned. It would ignite the very panic that Grant feared. "It would produce strikes among the workmen, and their workshops, to a great extent, would have to be closed," he said. "The manufactories would have to stop." Grant showed his concern for the manufactories by blowing smoke rings.

Fisk piped in. "You see, General, Gould isn't entirely disinterested in this business," he said. "He and I have got the responsibility of running the Erie railroad. We've got forty thousand wives to look after and we can't do it if our sidetracks are full of empties." It had been a long night. Grant was no longer listening. He said good night and went to his cabin.

Gould left the table convinced the president was, as if characterizing him in the vilest terms imaginable, "a contractionist." Fortunately, it was only June and, in the prairie, the wheat was only two feet high. With the harvest months away, Gould had time left to lobby. Still, with contraction being the will of the government, the immediate outlook for stocks was bleak. Gould went ashore the next morning to wire his broker with orders to sell shares. At the telegraph office, he found Marston, the investor who was at their table, already there with sell orders of his own.

GOULD'S GOLD PLAY was later described as a corner. Fisk himself used the term. But it wasn't a corner. Gould could never have cornered gold because, first, there was too much gold for him to buy all of it, and, second, the government would never have allowed it. In the New York market alone, there was about $18 million worth of gold in private hands and $80 million in government hands. It was stuffed in vaults, in the form of gold coins, beneath the city streets. The government could instantly make gold abundant and destroy a corner by releasing gold into the market. Even if the administration came around to Gould's crop theory about how a high gold price would help farmers, it would never let the price rise to the same degree that Harlem rose in the Vanderbilt's Harlem corner because it would be wildly inflationary.

Gould's plan was at best a mini corner. He would buy enough gold to make it scarce and drive up the price, but not enough to make gold impossible to find and force government intervention. But first he had to win support for the crop theory.

In *The Age of Innocence*, Edith Wharton describes how Victorians went to the theater to see who sat with whom. On the night June 18, three days after Grant's visit to Boston, New Yorkers saw Grant at the Fifth Avenue Theatre in the owner's box with Gould. The Opera wasn't Fisk's only theater. He also owned the Fifth Avenue. As the other theatergoers monitored the owner's box, Grant and

Gould watched a sister act dance a can-can and an opera company perform selections from Offenbach. Between the high kicks and high notes, Gould bent Grant's ear about gold.

Gould worked other angles. The post of assistant treasury secretary was open. The sub-treasurer executed the Treasury Department's activities in New York and, as such, was positioned to leak market-moving information. If Gould could get his own man in the post, he could get early warning of government intentions for gold. Gould and Corbin approached Robert Catherwood, Corbin's son-in-law and a successful New York businessman. In return for information, Gould promised to split the profits. Catherwood later described the offer as "to share and share alike." A man of scruple, Catherwood refused.

Corbin then turned to General Daniel Butterfield. During the war, Butterfield won the Medal of Honor for leading a charge at Fredericksburg. It was after another battle that, in a curious footnote, he composed "Taps." Butterfield's father was a founder of American Express and Butterfield himself was now an executive with the company. Grant appointed him sub-treasurer on Corbin's recommendation. Gould went to Butterfield's new office two days after the appointment and put him on retainer with a check for $10,000. That was $2,000 more than Butterfield's government salary. Was that legal? Maybe not. But who would ever know? Gould now had his man on the inside. Grant was still aligned with the bankers and against the farmers, but the gold scheme was off to a good start.

THIRTEEN

THE PLOT

Grant was homeless that summer amid a White House renovation. In the middle of August, he and his wife, Julia, took a seven-day road trip to Pennsylvania and West Virginia. Corbin and Jennie Grant came along. Grant liked Corbin. He appreciated how he doted on his sister. He respected Corbin's experience and knowledge of Washington. Grant felt lost and friendless in the capital. He regarded Corbin as someone who could keep him out of trouble.

Gold was the talk that summer. Everyone wanted to know if Grant and Boutwell planned to release more gold. When gold came up in conversation, Grant wasn't surprised that Corbin had an opinion. Nor was he surprised that Corbin fought for farmers as vigorously as Gould. All sorts of people shared that view. Grant was wary of Gould, but he assumed Corbin had good intentions. As they traveled over the Appalachians together, Corbin said something that clicked with Grant. The gold question wasn't just about the economy and national honor, he said. Nor was it just about farmers and bankers. No, there was something else. The gold price was about America's place in the world. Russia also depended on grain exports, Corbin reminded the president. If American farmers didn't get the business, the Russians would. Russia would benefit at the expense of America. Is that what Grant wanted?

Grant didn't need a degree in economics to know where to stand on that. Somewhere near the Eastern Continental Divide, the president, an avowed contractionist, went the other way on gold. Corbin had done it. Without paying so much as a penny in bribes, he had turned the president's thinking on a core belief. Boutwell would no doubt resist. He'd fight like mad for a strong greenback and weak gold price. But Boutwell wasn't the president. Grant was the president. The president was ready to defy his headstrong treasury secretary.

Corbin dashed to the Opera when he got back to New York. He couldn't wait to tell Gould. Gould was thrilled. All that strategizing and lobbying had paid off. Fisk was in the room, considering if he should invest alongside his partner. He had never liked the gold idea. But now Corbin was telling him it was in the bag. Fisk said he needed to hear it from Grant himself. If Grant told him he was for gold, he'd invest.

At that moment, Grant was back in New York aboard the *Providence* waiting to take another trip to Boston. Fisk raced to Chambers Street, marched past Grant's aides, and went straight to the president. Fisk wore a business suit. It wasn't the time to play Horatio Hornblower. Fisk said he came with urgent news. Russian ships loaded with grain were speeding toward Liverpool, he said. American crops would go unsold unless Grant let the gold price run. Grant listened. There it was again, the argument about America versus Russia. He failed to connect the dots between Corbin, Gould, and Fisk. In all events, if Fisk thought free boat rides entitled him to insider information, he was mistaken. When Fisk asked Grant where he stood on gold, Grant refused to say. "Giving private tips," the president said, "would not be fair."[1]

Fisk didn't like that answer and stayed out of the gold trade. Gould, meanwhile, found two other traders to join him in a pool to bull the price. Together, they bought $9 million worth of gold at 132, giving them more than half the privately held gold in New York. It only cost them around $500,000 because, instead of buying actual gold, they bought contracts giving them the right to buy the metal at a preset price. Contracts were cheap. But they came with a catch. The owners retained their right to buy gold as long as they compensated for the daily change in the price, with cash, at the end of the trading session. The owner of a contract was even more vulnerable to a falling gold price than someone who owned the metal itself. Even a modest decline could wipe out the entire investment.

Rather than cross his fingers and hope for a rising price, Gould sought to lift the price by reviving a trick from his youth. Back when Gould was surveying the Catskills, he got behind a bill in Albany requiring schools to buy maps. If the bill passed, he'd be busy for years supplying the demand. He persuaded a journalist friend at a local paper, the *Bloomville Mirror*, to write an editorial supporting the legislation. "I want you to give an editorial to this effect," Gould instructed. "You must model the editorial over to suit yourself but it must be as strong as it can be made and come direct from you."[2] The article gave Gould a prop to show lawmakers. The bill failed, but the experience taught Gould something about how to use the press.

Now he would try a similar move, only this time he wouldn't be manipulating the *Bloomville Mirror*. He'd be manipulating one of the most influential newspapers in the country, *The New York Times*. The administration often telegraphed policy by submitting unsigned articles to the *Times*. If Gould could place a bullish article on gold in the paper and make it look like it came from Grant, gold would rally.

With Corbin's help, Gould wrote something and attached a

headline: "Grant's Financial Policy." Gould took it to an acquaintance who knew John Bigelow, the editor of the *Times*. Bigelow was the former ambassador to France. Expert on table manners and aged Bordeaux, he was naive about Wall Street's black arts. Veteran editors smelled a rat, but Bigelow was the boss. On August 25, 1869, the *Times* made the article a lead editorial. The piece flatly stated that the government would stay out of the gold market. "The President will not withdraw currency from the channels of trade and commerce; he will not send gold into the market and sell it for currency," it said. [3]

When trading opened that morning, short covering drove gold higher just as Gould intended. Gold settled the day at 134. Gould's position was now $2 in the money. He could cash out at a profit or let it ride. He let it ride.

Grant was back at Corbin's a few days later. Grant mentioned that he had recently chatted about gold with his friend A. T. Stewart. Stewart was the inventor of the modern department store. His downtown store covered an entire block. It was mobbed because it offered the lowest prices in the city. Stewart wasn't in league with Gould, but he shared Gould's enthusiasm for the crop theory. No sense letting the Russians get the grain business, Stewart told Grant. He advised Grant do the farmers a favor and let gold move higher.

Corbin found that interesting but what Grant told Corbin next was even more interesting. Boutwell wanted to smash the price by unloading government gold and had gone so far as to issue the order. He was about to cable the order to New York when Grant canceled it. Grant was fully committed to the farmers. He was not going to let his treasury secretary enrich a bunch of Russians.

When Corbin relayed this intelligence to Gould, it removed all doubt Gould had about his investment. Being on the long side of gold was the right place to be. He and his partners doubled down.

They bought more gold. A decline would be costly. But why worry? The president was with them.

Next, Gould went to solidify his relationship with Sub-treasurer Butterfield. The No. 2 official in the Treasury Department lived in a brownstone on 23rd Street. On Thursday, September 2, Gould waited to intercept him on his way home from work. Pushcart vendors and cab operators lined the street. Gould watched the foot traffic in search of the writer of "Taps." Suddenly, there he was. Gould had not seen the musical bureaucrat since writing him a check to celebrate his entry into government. Now Gould proposed cutting Butterfield in on the plot. "I will buy some gold for you," Gould said.[4] He'd open an account for Butterfield with $1.5 million worth of gold certificates. If Gould made money, Butterfield would make money. It was share-and-share alike. Asked later why he paid Butterfield, Gould said it was innocent. "I did it as a friendly thing," he said.[5] Butterfield may have done the math. If all went well, Butterfield would be rich. All he had to do was what he already had committed to do, that is, warn Gould if the government planned to sell gold.

Gould stepped up his purchases and, on September 8, gold rose $4 to 138. If not for short sellers, it would have advanced even more. The tug-of-war between the bulls and the bears made gold front page news. Without naming names, the papers wrote about a mysterious "gold clique" and how it seemed inexplicably ignorant of the government's stated intentions of keeping the gold price in check. The attention unsettled Gould's fellow pool members. With short sellers gunning for them, they took their profits. "These fellows deserted me like rats from a ship," Gould said after.[6]

Gould was now alone and in deep. If the gold price moved against him, the losses would be ruinous. But if he unwound the trade and joined in the selling, he'd not only lose money, but he'd forfeit his chance for a gusher. Gould still had faith. To support the gold price, he bought more.

At this point in the story, Fisk was off elsewhere, away on assignment. While Gould was bulling gold, Fisk, who the papers called the Prince of Erie, was starring in a drama that featured New York governor John T. Hoffman, various units of the state militia, and J. P. Morgan, then a young banker who, at age thirty-two, was a year younger than Gould.

Gould had recently bought controlling interest in a small railroad, the Albany & Susquehanna, that had a route between Albany and Binghamton in New York. Fisk had gone to Albany to fetch the keys, but the railroad's executives declined to give them. Fisk retreated to Binghamton and sent a train manned by two hundred thugs to seize the railroad's stations along the way. The A&S put their own thugs on a train to Binghamton.

There was only one track. Trains from one direction let trains from the other pass by shunting to the side. This time, there was no shunting. The trains crashed head-on in a tunnel. Combatants leapt from the carriages and attacked with guns and metal pipes. The governor called in the militia to break it up. Fisk enjoyed the dust-up. He complimented his rival commander for his "manliness" and offered him a job. Morgan, in his first encounter with Gould, found another buyer for the railroad. Gould sold his stock at a profit.

Limping back to the Opera, Fisk discovered Gould at his desk tearing pieces of paper into confetti. This, he knew, meant Gould was on edge. "Every man has his peculiarities," Fisk observed. "When Gould snips off corners of newspapers and tears 'em up in bits, I know there's trouble."[7]

Amid the confetti, Gould gingerly brought up gold, which had edged lower while Fisk was away. "Don't you think gold has hit bottom?" Gould asked.[8] Fisk didn't know what to think. His mind had been on field operations. He asked how much Gould was in for. Gould said he was in deep—so deep that, with the price slipping, he was paying tens of thousands of dollars every night to keep the trade open. Gould then told Fisk the same things he told himself. Grant was on his side and Butterfield would warn if there was trouble. "If Butterfield gives any information, we will get it in time to get out," Gould said.[9]

By now, gold was the focus of financial markets. Horace Greeley condemned the "gold gamblers" driving up the price. The *Times* agreed. The sympathies of Democratic papers, however, aligned with the farmers. They urged the president to let the price run.

As action in gold intensified, Treasury Secretary Boutwell came to town for a speech at the Union League Club, a favorite Republican haunt. Boutwell assured listeners to have no doubt. While it might be years before the government could redeem greenbacks at par, the policy was firm. Recent events notwithstanding, it would continue to pressure the gold price so that, little by little, the gold price and the greenback price would converge. Hold on to those greenbacks, he seemed to be saying. The recent run-up in the price was a momentary spike that the market would sort out in time. The administration remained committed to driving gold down. The nation's honor was at stake.

FOURTEEN

THE MIX-UP

At this point the gold scheme took a turn. Gould was visiting Corbin every evening to make sure all was well. When Gould visited Corbin on the night of Boutwell's speech, Corbin told him that Boutwell had met with a crowd of bankers earlier in the day. Corbin knew this because he had snuck into the meeting. He listened as one banker after another jawboned about the evils of a strong gold price. When Corbin tried to talk to Boutwell, the treasury secretary brushed him off.

The snub alarmed Corbin. What was he to make of it? Boutwell knew that Corbin was the president's advisor and brother-in-law. Was Boutwell merely too busy to talk to him? Or had the treasury secretary somehow divined that Corbin had a financial stake in gold? And if Boutwell knew, did Grant know? This was a chilling thought. If Grant suspected that his brother-in-law had an interest in gold, he would surely release gold and smash the price. If he didn't and the newspapers found out, it would look like he was in league with Corbin. His presidency would be ruined.

Unsettled by Corbin's musings, Gould did something rash. He instructed Corbin to dash off a letter to Grant, repeat the arguments in favor of gold, and see what Grant said in reply. The reply was crucial. Gould hoped that Grant would communicate whether he still stood with the farmers. Gould ran to Erie headquarters to find Fisk.

"Who is the most confidential man you've got?" Gould asked his friend. Fisk volunteered a clerk named Bill Chapin. Grant was relaxing in the western Pennsylvania town of Washington. Gould told Chapin to get there as soon as possible and not to come back until he had a response from Grant. "See what he says," Gould told him. "Go from there to the first telegraph station and telegraph me what the reply is."[1]

Chapin left New York early the next morning. He crossed to Jersey City by boat, took a train to Pittsburgh, and, arriving after midnight, banged on the door of a stable owner who rented him a horse and buggy for an overnight ride through the mountains. After a few wrong turns, he found Grant playing croquet with his chief of staff, Horace Porter. As Grant maneuvered his ball through the wickets, he seemed the picture of repose. Chapin, dressed in a natty uniform and military boots, handed over the letter.

Grant took the letter and excused himself, saying his wife needed him but that he'd be back. Punchy from sleep deprivation, Chapin told Porter about the boat ride, the search for a horse, the midnight ride, and the wrong turns. Grant returned and gazed out the window. "Is all satisfactory," Chapin asked. Grant said it was. Did the president have a reply? "No," Grant said. "Nothing." Chapin left for the telegraph office. "Delivered," he wrote to Gould. "All right."[2]

Porter was disturbed by the exchange with the messenger. Why would Corbin go to the trouble and expense of sending a letter overnight that contained nothing urgent? He shared his thoughts with Grant. Edison had yet to invent the light bulb but it was as if one lit up inside the head of the president. Suddenly, it all made sense. The meeting Corbin arranged on Fisk's boat? The night at the Opera with Gould? Gould randomly popping up at Corbin's house whenever Grant was visiting? There was only one explanation. Corbin must be in cahoots with the gold crowd and had his own money on the line.

Sending the letter was Gould's first mistake. It alerted Grant to Corbin's interest. The second mistake was reading too much into the messenger's telegram. By using the words "All right," Chapin was saying nothing more than that Grant had received the letter, not that Grant remained on the side of a strong gold price.

That Monday, as the week that culminated in Black Friday began, Gould believed Grant was still with him. He bought more gold through an entity he registered as the National Gold Account, a name chosen to feed the narrative of government complicity. James Hodgskin, a banker, later recalled all sorts of rumors about how the gold clique included "pretty much everybody in authority in the United States, beginning with President Grant and ending with the door-keeper of Congress." Those who feared missing out bought gold. Those who discounted the rumors sold short. Volume climbed.

Gould bought more gold on Tuesday and, by Wednesday, the action in gold spilled over to the stock exchange where Gould, in a demonstration of second-level thinking, placed a side bet. He discovered through sources that Vanderbilt was on a train to Albany that morning for a secret board meeting of the New York Central. The board planned to approve a merger between Central and another Vanderbilt railroad, the Hudson. Although Vanderbilt controlled both railroads, they still operated as separate businesses. By merging them and eliminating duplication, Central would be more valuable. Gould bought some Central. Then he leaked news of the merger. As he expected, investors, knowing the Central would be worth more once it had the Hudson, bid up the shares. Gould sold at a profit.

That was fun. There was more to come. Vanderbilt was still on the train and out of reach when Gould sold Central short and made up a story. Through his brokers, he spread a rumor that Vanderbilt was dead. The train to Albany had derailed and the Commodore was a casualty. No one could immediately confirm the story. Skittish investors sold anyway. Central nosedived. Among the losers were friends of Vanderbilt who had borrowed money to buy the stock. Word soon came that there had been no derailment, no fatalities, and that Vanderbilt was very much alive. Central shares recovered. This all occurred in the space of a few minutes. Gould covered his short within the span and scored again. When Vanderbilt found out, "the sky over Albany was blue with the Commodore's curses," wrote Fisk's friend Robert Fuller.[3]

In the afternoon, a murderer's row of short sellers came out on gold. Foremost was Jay Cooke from Philadelphia. Cooke was the most powerful investment banker in the country. When banks and insurance companies refused to buy U.S. Treasury bonds during the war, he and his firm, Jay Cooke & Co., saved the effort—and gained Grant's everlasting gratitude—by hiring an army of salesmen, posting ads in newspapers, and selling bonds door-to-door. After the war, Cooke's brother and junior partner Henry, the first territorial governor of the District of Columbia, spent so much time at the Treasury Department that he practically worked there.

Cooke was tall, blue-eyed, and had a white beard that made him look older than his forty-seven years. Milking his Washington connections, he grew rich trading on inside information. He spent some of it on a lavish estate north of Philadelphia. Faux Roman ruins studded the grounds. At his vacation house on South Bass Island in Lake Erie, near his boyhood home of Sandusky, Ohio, he built a four-story watch tower and greeted visitors by firing a cannon.

Cooke shorted gold with confidence. His gold broker in New York, Harris Fahnestock, had told Cooke the week before that Boutwell was on their side and that he'd buy bonds with gold, thus releasing gold on the market, to keep the gold price in check. "I had a brief talk with Boutwell yesterday," Fahnestock wrote to Cooke on September 17. "He is committed unequivocally to bond purchasing."[4]

Another bear was James Brown of Brown Brothers in New York. Brown started his career in Liverpool and moved to New York when the Erie Canal opened. Over his four decades in New York, he became one of the most respected figures on Wall Street. Now seventy-eight, he was older than Vanderbilt and older than Drew. He had seen it all.

Brown refused to credit rumors that Grant sided with the farmers let alone the incredible notion that Grant had been bought. Experience told him Treasury Secretary Boutwell would intervene. Rather than wait, Brown proposed a risky plan to smash the price and, along the way, make a pile of money. He proposed to his fellow bears a test of wills. They should keep selling gold short and make the longs feel so exposed that, rather than risk ruin, they would bail out of the trade. "I myself suggested that a bold proceeding, such as giving them all the gold that they would take, would probably kill the bull,"[5] Brown said.

That afternoon, Brown, Cooke, and others aggressively shorted gold. Gould surprised them and carried the day by snapping up everything they sold. To put some upward pressure on the price, Gould also bought physical gold, funding the purchases with loans from a bank he owned with Tweed. Gold closed Wednesday at 141, up $4.

After the close, Gould went to Corbin's. He had every reason to feel terrific. He had profited on the New York Central trade, repelled a bear raid, and collected his winnings from shorts who settled their losses with him at the close of trading. Even bettter, the usual seasonal demand for gold was surfacing. As demand grew, the price would creep up and he'd be able to wrap up the trade and move on.

That evening, back at Corbin's, Gould found his lobbyist pacing the floor and looking like a taxi driver who had just run over somebody. Corbin hustled him upstairs to his library so his wife couldn't hear. Grant was on to them, Corbin said. He didn't know how. All he knew was that his wife, the president's sister, had received a letter from Julia Grant, the president's wife, earlier in the day. It revealed that Grant had guessed that Corbin had a financial interest in gold. "My husband is very much annoyed by your speculations," wrote Julia Grant. "You must close them as quick as you can!"[6]

The news was devastating for Gould. It made it all but certain that the president would dump government gold on the market and crush the price, lest he be seen as putting family interests before those of the people. Gould was sitting on millions of dollars of gold coins and contracts to buy more. Grant hadn't acted yet. That was a good sign. But an order from Washington could come at any time. If it came soon, Gould would be wiped out.

FIFTEEN

PUMP AND DUMP

Gold traded on the Gold Exchange, a small building on Broad
Street around the corner from the stock exchange. In the middle of the trading floor stood a golden statue of Cupid, a reference
not to erotic love but to cupidity, a word for greed. In case anyone
missed the reference, Cupid sprayed water into a pool of goldfish. A
clock-shaped dial above the floor showed the gold price. Otherwise,
the exchange was just a bare floor suitable for dancing. Traders took
positions on the floor and shouted offers to buy and sell. Another
dial was helpfully mounted outside the building for curbside gamblers. If the exchange had a provisional look, it was because its days
were numbered. Its purpose would vanish once the government returned to a fixed price for gold.

The curbside crowd showed up early Thursday morning. They
limbered up by trading gold among themselves as if laying bets on
that afternoon's baseball game between the Brooklyn Atlantics and
the Washington Nationals. As Broad Street filled, James Brown
gathered Jay Cooke's people and the other shorts. He knew nothing
about the domestic drama unfolding within the Grant family but
remained committed to take the price higher and find the clique's
breaking point. "Is this thing to be perpetuated?" he asked. "Are

we to stand and be flayed by this unscrupulous party?"[1] He volunteered to lead. Despite his advanced years, he'd join the scrum of the
exchange floor, try to break the price, and, if he succeeded, make a
killing.

Uptown, Gould went to check on Corbin. Corbin was up
$125,000 on the gold Gould had bought for him. Gould promised
to close the account and, in the meantime, advance him $100,000
to keep his mouth shut about the note from Julia Grant. "I am undone if that letter gets out," he said.[2] He dashed back to the Opera
to meet Fisk and grab a carriage with him downtown. They found
Broad Street mobbed with gawkers who came to catch a glimpse of
the famous combatants. By now, there was no mystery about who
belonged to the cliques. Gould and Fisk played for the bulls. Cooke
and Brown played for the bears. Fisk tipped his top hat and flashed
his diamond stickpin. Gould stroked his beard and tried to look
invisible. From Philadelphia, Cooke telegraphed with his brother in
Washington and with his broker, Fahnestock, in New York.

Gould needed to sell his gold as soon as possible. But he had to
do it in a way that didn't crash the price. To do so, he decided on a
technique as old as financial markets. He'd do a pump and dump.
Because nothing attracts buyers more than a rising price and the fear
of missing out, he assigned Fisk to buy just enough gold to make the
price go up. Gould would dump his gold on the other buyers that
Fisk lured in.

The plan sounded good but it wouldn't be easy to execute. For
one thing, Gould had to unload a lot of gold. Fisk would have to stir
up a storm of activity for Gould to sell all of it. If he wasn't careful,
he'd end up destroying himself to save Gould. Also, Gould wouldn't
be foisting his gold on amateurs but on Cooke, Brown, and others
who counted among the biggest names on Wall Street. These were
people who traded gold for a living. They knew the tricks as well

as all the traders on the floor. If word got back to them that Gould, the leader of the bull clique and the one who supposedly fixed the president, was a seller, the price would immediately crater.

Gould used his former partner Henry Smith to do the dumping. To cover Gould's tracks, Smith assigned a fleet of different brokers to execute the sales. He also planned to buy token amounts of gold to feed the idea that Gould was still a buyer. Fisk used a former partner of his own, William Belden, to carry out his trades. Belden, in turn, pawned off the work on the floor to a veteran named Albert Speyers. Speyers was in the words of the writer Stedman "an elderly man of small intelligence who was well calculated to do what he was told and ask no questions." A German immigrant with a face "crisscrossed with wrinkles," Speyers sustained himself by executing small orders for small buyers.[3]

Speyers was personally on the hook if his client didn't come through and pay for his trades. He insisted on meeting the man on whose behalf he would be buying. Belden took him to his office and pointed out Fisk. Here he was, the famous Prince of Erie, with the diamond stickpin glistening against his starched white shirt. Speyers knew Fisk only from pictures in magazines. He was awestruck. He had never worked for anyone so consequential. Bewitched by dreams of fat commissions, Speyers assumed his post on the trading floor, ready to buy at whatever price Fisk commanded while Gould, unbeknowst to him, would try to get out from under the country's largest hoard of gold not in government hands.

Gold opened to massive trading. Every tick in the price produced an explosion of transactions as other traders joined in, taking one side or the other in the war between the cliques. Caleb Norvell of the *Times* reached for metaphors. He described the "roar of battle and the screams of the victims." Floor traders, he said, "were undergoing torments worse than any Dante ever witnessed in Hell." The bears were the Dantes, gored by the unbridled buying of Fisk and other bulls. "The bear party at times seemed to be perfectly frantic while undergoing punishment at the hands of the defiant and exultant bulls."[4]

As the shorts underwent torments, they bombarded Boutwell with telegrams. "Bull clique are defying you to do your worst," said one. Another informed about "extreme anxiety among the banks" and warned of bank failures.[5] The telegrams did no good. The price crept up as the buyers stayed ahead of the sellers. Some of the bulls, even as they were buying gold, admitted the price made no sense. "We have no argument, only that we can put it up higher and intend to do so," said one.[6]

At about 11:30, Fisk felt the market needed a jolt and took to the floor himself. Traders fell silent as his huge bulk breezed past them. "Gold!" Fisk yelled. "Sell it short and invite me to your funeral."[7] He took bets that gold would hit 200. After whispering something to Speyers in full view of other traders, Speyers bought more at 143, then 144. Just as Fisk hoped, his enthusiasm inspired an army of copycats. The government's inaction served to endorse his bullishness. The longer Washington sat on its hands, the more credible became the idea of government complicity. Gold at 200 seemed possible. By noon, trading volume topped the already ridiculous level of the day before.

With mountains of gold changing hands at big prices, Smith, Gould's broker, sold as much of Gould's gold as he could. "Sell, sell, sell," came the command from Smith's office. "Do nothing but sell." In a head fake, Gould himself bought in small amounts. "I sold that day, and only bought enough to make the Street think I was a bull," Gould said afterward.[8]

In Brooklyn that afternoon, the Atlantics scored seven runs in the ninth to shell the Nationals 21 to 10. There was more excitement at the Gold Exchange. The copycats were falling for Fisk's trick, snatching up gold in the mistaken belief that Fisk had President Grant in his pocket. The pump and dump was working to perfection. By day's end, $320 million of gold changed hands, a new record. But Gould, because he had to be careful not to tip his hand, managed to sell only half his holdings. He needed at least another day to get out whole.

Brown went home to Brooklyn to lick his wounds. For the second day in a row, his furious buying failed to break the clique and he'd lost money. There seemed to be no limit to the price the bulls would pay. "The gold conspirators are holding high carnival," wrote the *Times*.[9]

SIXTEEN

BLACK FRIDAY

O n Friday morning, the *Times* ran a front page story rejecting the idea that Grant had been bought. "It is too monstrous for serious belief," it wrote.[1] The president would never stoop so low. The rumor, it argued, was nothing more than a story made up by Gould and Fisk to lift the price. Fisk later said he felt weak-kneed at seeing his name in the story. He worried it backed Grant into a corner. The administration would have to intervene now. Grant would look guilty if it didn't.

Gould grabbed a carriage, hurried downtown, and climbed two flights of stairs at the Sub-Treasury to find Sub-treasurer Butter-field. The Sub-Treasury, now called Federal Hall, was across from the Stock Exchange. Opened in 1842, it was the spitting image of the Parthenon and a tribute to the Greek spirit of democracy. If the administration planned to intervene in the gold market, it would have to notify Butterfield first. Butterfield wasn't in, but a clerk told Gould that no cables from Washington had come that morning.

Next, Gould raced back uptown to pick up Fisk at the Opera. Gould suspected the opening bell would be like a cannon shot in the Alps. With the *Times* egging on the government to act, he expected the shorts to sell with explosive force. If the avalanche broke the wrong way, Gould would get buried. It all depended on Fisk. Fisk had to keep the price aloft long enough for Gould to liquidate.

The mob was back on Broad Street. Before turning off Broadway, Gould, for tactical reasons, hopped from the carriage. Fisk, the theater impresario, had engineered a spectacle to dazzle the crowd. Replacing Gould at his side were Lucille and Patrie, two beauties from the Opera. Like his diamond stickpin, the dancers were props. Their presence advertised that Fisk was a winner. Their smiles broadcast a message. Buy gold and you, too, could be a winner.

Fisk wore a coat made of velvet and a cream-colored vest. He said goodbye to the ladies and connected again with Gould at Heath & Co., a brokerage with an office down from the Gold Exchange. Heath had a back room where Gould and Fisk could lie low. Fisk tossed off his hat and the corduroy coat. He paced the carpeted floor. The stickpin glistened. Gould sat in a chair and pretended to read the papers.

Gold opened at a price of 143. While Gould was selling, Fisk was buying. He ordered Speyers to bid 145. Others followed Speyers and bought at the same price. Gould's brokers sold them as much as they would take. After the shorts lost interest in selling at 145, Fisk revised his order. "Put it to 150 at once," he told Speyers.[2] "Take all you can get." Brown stepped up and sold him $500,000 worth of gold. Another spasm of copycat buying followed.

More telegrams fell on Washington. Jay Cooke urged Treasury Secretary Boutwell to act immediately, reminding him of "duty to keep things steady for the benefit of the honest interests of the country."[3] Sub-treasurer Butterfield sent Boutwell an update. "Gold is 150," he wrote, "much feeling, and accusations of government complicity."[4]

Western Union assigned telegraph operators to the exchange to send the fast-moving gold price to the world. One of the operators was a young man who three months earlier had won his first patent. The patent for an electronic vote recorder was one of more than a thousand he would win in his lifetime. Now from a desk inside the exchange, twenty-one-year-old Thomas Alva Edison watched the price indicator and sent electric jolts with his keypad every time it moved. Broad Street gasped as the price oscillated between 149 and 151. Edison struggled to keep up. The wires weren't built for such abuse. They crackled and went dead. On the floor, trading continued. Fortunes were made. Fortunes were lost. "The majority felt the ground breaking under them, and as they saw their margins gone, their fortunes broken and their hopes blasted, they stood bewildered," wrote the *Times*.[5]

To Gould's relief, Washington seemed to be sitting it out. To speed things along and give Gould more cover, Fisk told Speyers to raise the bid to 155. Brown stepped up and sold him $500,000 worth. But this time something odd happened. The copycats did nothing. Nobody followed his lead. No one else, no matter how greedy, would sell at 155. Doubts had surfaced. Could Fisk settle his trades? Did he have the money to close on his agreements? And what if the gold price fell back to earth? Would Fisk honor a commitment to pay 155 if Washington jumped in and the gold price crashed to 130?

Speyers himself had doubts. When no one joined Brown to sell at 155, he left his post, elbowed his way around Cupid, and fought his way through the crowd on the curb. His career would be over if Fisk welched. He needed to make sure Fisk remained committed. From his hideout at Heath & Co., Fisk told him to relax and to get back to work. "Go and bid gold up to 160," Fisk said. "Take all you can get at 160." Maybe no one would take the risk selling at 155 but, at 160, it could be worth the risk. A seller could make a bundle if the price cracked.

Back on the floor, Speyers made his offer. "160 for any part of five millions," he shouted. Brown watched the crowd. No one stepped up. Speyers raised his offer to 161, then 162. Okay, Brown thought. It's over. No one wanted to sell to Fisk. No matter the compelling price, it was too risky. Brown was certain the end was near. He only needed to sell a bit more to force a collapse. "Sold," Brown declared. "One million at 162."[6]

OVER AT THE Sub-Treasury junior bankers jammed the waiting room, anxious to hear if the government said anything about gold. Sub-treasurer Butterfield kept his door closed. At 11 a.m., at the same moment Brown sold $1 million worth of gold at 162, the door swung open. Butterfield stepped out to address the crowd. Butterfield said he had just received word from Treasury Secretary Boutwell. He read it aloud. "Sell four millions gold."

That was it. The pleas of the bankers had been heard. The government had stepped in. It didn't need to flood the market with gold to prick the bubble. It only needed to send a signal. Selling $4 million worth was the signal. The stampede from Butterfield's office began before he could pin the announcement to the bulletin board. His listeners tripped over each other as they crossed Broad Street and raced to the Gold Exchange to spread the word.

The story goes that floor traders got the news just as the bells of Trinity Cathedral began to toll the hour of eleven. Before the bells could finish, the gold price had crashed from 162 to 145. There is doubt about the story but no doubt that the price fell in a heartbeat. Bulls shouted offers to buy at the reduced price, believing they were snapping up bargains. Short sellers rushed to cover. Edison congratulated himself and a fellow telegraph operator for having nothing invested in gold. "I felt very happy because we were poor," Edison said. [7]

Speyers was terrified. If Fisk welched, he'd go down with him. He made an insane show of conviction. He could have bought all the gold he wanted at 145. Instead, he tried to turn back the clock and lift the price by offering 160. "He interposed his feeble weight to stem the tide," wrote the *Times*.[8] His eyes grew wild. He ran circles around the fountain. "160," he shouted. "160!" Other traders eyed him warily. They backed away. They didn't want to be near a crazy man. Speyers switched to his native German. "Mein Gott," he cried. "Mein Gott."[9] He ripped open his shirt and begged for someone to shoot him. "It took five men to hold him," Edison recalled.[10]

Brown grabbed Speyers and demanded he pay him at once. He wanted $1 million for the gold he sold him at 162 and $6 million for the rest. Speyers whined that he had only done as instructed. "Speyers," Brown said, "I want to know who your principals are. I want names."[11]

Speyers led him to Heath & Co. and talked his way in. "Gentlemen," Speyers said, "this is Mr. Brown. He has demanded a margin of me; you have not given me any, and, therefore, I refer him to you." Fisk turned his back and refused to meet Brown's gaze. Gould, ever civil, said he could do nothing at that moment. "If you do not make the margin tonight," Brown said, "I will have your heads."[12]

Those who had ridden Fisk's coattails lost heavily. Many were ruined. Fortunes accumulated over years were gone. A mob formed outside Heath. "Lynch, lynch," they shouted. Tammany sent police to maintain order. A militia unit in Brooklyn was told to stand ready. Unnerved, Gould ran through a back door and down an alley. He was a wildebeest pursued by lions. He made it to the back door of another of his brokers , Smith & Martin, and let himself in. Fisk turned the wrong way and almost ran into his attackers. Next came Fisk's broker Belden. "Which way have they gone?" Belden asked a bystander.

Alerted to the escape, the crowd moved to Smith & Martin and the police braced to defend the entrance. Fisk opened the front door of the broker's office, faced the mob, and begged for calm. An irate trader, moaning of losses, pushed through the police line and popped him in the nose. Fisk staggered back and mopped blood from his face.

SEVENTEEN

THE DAY AFTER

At the height of the Friday panic, Vanderbilt's men begged him to go downtown and show his face. The meltdown in gold had spilled over to stocks. Share prices, including that of his own New York Central, were crashing. Perhaps a visit by the towering, leonine Commodore, forehead gleaming in the sun, his manner imperious and confident as ever, would calm anxious investors. Vanderbilt waited until Saturday morning. A reporter for the *Sun* saw him and noted that he looked "calm, quiet and serene—the very picture of self-satisfaction."[1] And why not? It looked like the market had done for him what he had failed to do himself. It had flattened Gould and Fisk. Vanderbilt appeared as if "he had clinched a great victory of the bears over the wild bulls of the gold clique."

If he had peered inside the Gold Exchange, he would have seen a floor covered with muddy footprints, half-eaten sandwiches, and chewed tobacco. The gate around the Cupid fountain was destroyed. The goldfish were dead. On the street outside, broken bottles conjured images of a fraternity house after a party. "It smelt of the fray,"[2] wrote the *World*. Only a week before, Wall Street was happily in the throes of a bull market. "Now it was a valley of skulls," wrote Fowler. "It was Golgotha."[3]

As the losers tried to make sense of it, James Brown tried to collect his profits. After taking a carriage uptown, he pounded on the door of the Opera and got in. He hobbled down the hall, walking beneath the great ceiling murals and peering into offices, looking for Gould and Fisk. Guards stopped him before he got far. Brown demanded to see his creditors. The guards turned him away.

Gould had succeeded in selling almost all of his gold and he was solidly in the win column. But like James Brown, his wins were on paper. The Gold Exchange had the job to reconcile buy and sell orders and determine who owed what to whom. The work usually went quickly. But with the Street in tatters, there was an overwhelming volume of activity to sort out. Gould would have to wait for his payday along with everybody else.

An hour before midnight, a squad of black carriages pulled up at the Opera. Gould took one. Fisk another. Their lawyers rode in a third. The parade turned right on Broadway, drove through Union Square and over Chambers Street before stopping in front of the Gold Exchange. They wanted to find out where things stood on their trades. They found Henry Benedict, the president of the exchange, at his desk. He said $500 million worth of gold traded on Friday. This was an unimaginable sum. It meant all the gold in the country had turned over several times, passing between different buyers and sellers who were after quick gains. Despite the late hour, the room was full of clerks trying to make sense of the order receipts. Benedict complained that the receipts weren't worthy of the name. When a broker sold a gold contract, he was supposed to give a clerk a slip of paper with the amount of the trade along with names of the buyer and seller. But the trading had been so furious that many of the names were illegible, many of the numbers indecipherable, and many of the receipts torn to bits. Some orders had outright disappeared. Benedict, his voice rising in irritation, said he was doing all he could. He got back to work but not before blaming Gould for blowing up the market.

On Monday, Benedict gave up. He didn't have the manpower to trace the transactions. He pleaded with the Bank of New York to lend him some clerks. Bank officials threw up their hands. The job was too big for them. There would be ugly disputes between buyers and sellers. The bank wanted no part of it.

The Gold Exchange didn't open that day. The exchange elders pushed Benedict aside and created a group, the Committee of Twenty, to reconcile the trades and arbitrate disputes. The group included representatives from Brown Brothers, Jay Cooke & Co., and other short sellers. This was a disaster for Gould. Dispute resolution would be like elections where votes mattered less than who was counting. Considering the forces arrayed against him, he'd be lucky to get anything.

A couple of days later, with Gould no closer to getting his money, protesters returned to the Gold Exchange. A now familiar chant rose from the curb. "Hang them, hang them," cried the mob. Inside the building, the Committee of Twenty was settling down to business when a dignified-looking gentleman appeared in their midst. Sheriff's deputies were at his side. The man introduced himself as Augustus L. Brown. He had surprising news. He announced that a judge had just appointed him receiver of the Gold Exchange. He dismissed the committee. He was now in charge. By order of a court, he would take over the counting.

Augustus Brown, no relation to the banker James Brown, was a lawyer whose firm did work for Gould. Earlier that morning, Gould's lawyers had appeared before Judge Albert Cardozo, a Tammany judge whose son Benjamin would grow up to become a Supreme Court justice. They petitioned Cardozo to name Brown as receiver. Cardozo rubber-stamped the petition, testifying to the value of Gould's relationship with Tweed. Now, with one of Gould's own lawyers in charge of the money, Gould could count on getting his share.

Where did that leave Fisk? He had planned to limit his exposure by buying just enough gold to frighten the shorts into closing their positions by buying up the stuff at a loss. The terrified shorts would liberate Gould of his holdings. But the plan had gone awry. Others had indeed bought Gould's gold. But to keep the price high and the shorts on edge, Fisk had to buy more than token amounts. He had had to buy with abandon, grabbing large quantities at the highest prices of the day. When prices crashed, Fisk found himself millions in the red.

Fisk had to act fast. It might be too late, but at least he'd go down fighting. Acting on a plan that he and Gould prearranged, Fisk denied responsibility and pinned the trades on his broker, Belden, who agreed to take the fall, presumably in return for secret payments from Gould. On its face, the idea that Belden was the buyer seemed preposterous. Fisk was the one who appeared on the exchange floor and whispered orders to the floor trader Speyers. Even the newspapers put Fisk at the center of the activity. But there was no paper trail.

The cover-up would have been perfect except for one thing. Speyers, the grizzled German floor trader, had to play along. For the plot to succeed, Speyers needed to keep quiet.

Fisk invited him to the Opera. Speyers found Fisk at his unctuous best. Fisk asked about his health. He asked about his family. Expressing sympathy, Fisk said he felt sorry about the stress and asked what he might do to help. "All I want," Speyers said, "is that you should place me where I was when my credit was good, when my name was good and when I had a good business."[4]

A few days later, they met again. Belden was there, too, along with Fisk's lawyer Shearman. Shearman hinted at a cash payoff, suggesting he'd give Speyers $200,000 to join the plot. All Speyers had to do was declare that Belden, not Fisk, had given him his orders. Belden chimed in. "You know, Speyers," he said, "that you did it all for me."

Speyers thought for a moment. If he took the money, he'd never have to work again. But he refused to perjure himself. "Mr. Belden and Mr. Fisk, that is all nonsense to talk to me."[5]

EIGHTEEN

THE RECKONING

The mob chanting for executions embarrassed civilized New Yorkers. It wasn't that they disagreed. They understood why the mob wanted Gould and Fisk strung up. But frontier justice was for Dodge City, not a metropolis that took its social cues from London and Paris. In London and Paris, they didn't hang railroad executives in the public square. New York thought the gold clique deserved to swing, but also thought it deserved its day in court.

The papers were quick to judge. Surveying the wreckage, the *Times* likened Gould to Mephistopheles, the devil of German folklore. Greeley's *Tribune* called Gould and Fisk public enemies. The *Sun* said they were crooks and told prosecutors to leave no stone unturned. Insider trading was legal. Market manipulation was legal. But fraud and conspiracy were actionable, and punishable with jail.

Tweed was in their corner. He could probably stifle the district attorney. But what about the federal courts? Tammany's reach ended at the New York frontier. And federal judges, unlike New York judges, were appointed rather than elected. Beholden to no one, they might play it straight.

Unwilling to leave his defense to lawyers, Fisk launched a public relations campaign to shift attention toward Grant. Grant was the most popular man in the country. The hero of Appomattox was be-loved as a symbol of the best America had to offer—strength, brav-ery, devotion to country, modesty, and quiet resolve. The Siamese Twins, Corbin's name for Gould and Fisk, knew Grant was inno-cent. They would have tried to bribe him if they could, but Grant had never given them the chance to try. The public didn't know that. Maybe the Twins could raise enough doubt to blur perceptions and get everyone to forget about them.

A freelance journalist named George Crouch covered Erie for the *Herald*. Fisk invited him to his office. "I have the most astound-ing revelations to make," Fisk told him. "I can make Rome howl at somebody besides me." Fisk sat close to Crouch to make sure he was heard. "Everybody lays the blame on me," he said. "I am threatened with assassination. I'm caged up here like a tiger in a menagerie." But the mob had it wrong, he said. There were others more blame-worthy and more important than himself.

Fisk asked Crouch a question. Did Crouch really believe that he and Gould would attempt to buy millions worth of gold without assurances from the administration? Of course not. The assurances came from the highest levels, Fisk told him. "The president himself was interested with us in the corner," he said.[1]

He eyed Crouch. "This astonishes you, does it not?" Fisk told Crouch about Corbin's investments in gold. He told him about the conversation among Gould, Fisk, and Grant on the ship to Boston. He told him about the follow-up conversations between Gould and the president. He told him about the payments to Sub-treasurer But-terfield. Crouch, putting down his notepad, pushed back. There was a hole in the story. Fisk had provided no direct evidence of Grant himself making money on gold. Yes, Fisk had claimed that the pres-ident "was interested with us in the corner." But where was the proof? The *Herald* refused to publish the story.

Fisk turned to another paper, the *Sun*. The *Sun* was struggling financially. In return for a fee, the paper went with everything Fisk had told Crouch. Asked for comment, Corbin and Butterfield denied everything. The *Sun* followed up with sworn statements, canceled checks, and other bits of ephemera that proved the men were liars. The *Sun* called the evidence—all of which came from the files of Gould, Fisk, and Tweed— "conclusive and unanswerable."[2]

The articles put Grant in a tough spot. There was no evidence against him but there was plenty of smoke. The president gave a statement denying he had had any financial interest in gold. But the question lingered. If Corbin and Butterfield were lying, was the president lying, too?

Democrats in Congress demanded an investigation. Ohio congressman James Garfield, chairman of the House Committee on Banking and Finance and a Republican like Grant, called for hearings. When it came Gould's turn to speak, Garfield examined Gould himself.

In a soft voice, Gould talked about farmers. "We had an immense harvest and there was going to be a large surplus of breadstuffs, either to rot or to be exported," he said. To move the grain, the price had to be low enough to attract buyers in Liverpool. That—and, yes, his own financial interest—is why he lobbied Grant. "I thought to put [gold] up so as to start business and then quietly to sell mine off," he said.[3]

Garfield didn't care about breadstuffs. He wanted information to exonerate Grant and put Gould in jail. Gould admitted he had no evidence linking Grant to the scheme. As for his own actions, he had acted alone. He denied that he ordered Fisk to pump up the gold price so that he himself could sell out. He denied any knowledge about the broker Belden being a fall guy for Fisk.

"Were not orders given by you, or by Mr. Fisk for you, to Belden to buy large amounts of gold?" Garfield asked.

"Mr. Fisk never gave any orders for me," Gould said.[4]

Fisk came next. The *Times* called his testimony "theatrical and ludicrous in the extreme." When Garfield asked for a job description, Fisk drew a laugh. "My business is railroading, steamboating and I suppose, I may add, speculating," he said.[5]

The explosion on Black Friday arose from a misunderstanding, he said. When he strode into the Gold Exchange and bet the price was going to 200, he was just fooling around. It wasn't his fault that Belden and Speyers took him literally, bid up the price and attracted followers. "A fellow can't have a little innocent fun without everybody raising a halloo and going wild," he said.[6]

As for Belden and Speyers buying on his behalf, that was another misunderstanding. To prove it, he produced a letter he said was written by Belden. The letter authorized Fisk to execute trades for him. In other words, Belden wasn't the broker for Fisk. Fisk was the broker for Belden. "Dear Sir," it said. "I hereby authorize you to order the purchase and sale of gold on my account during this day to the extent you may deem advisable."[7]

Garfield was suspicious. "You know this to be a true copy?" he asked. Fisk assured him it was.

When Belden's turn came, he broke from the script. Unwilling to perjure himself, he said he bought gold on Fisk's orders. And what about the letter that Fisk had just produced? Belden said he couldn't recall. "These were days of such excitement that I cannot undertake to swear what I did or did not do," he said.[8] Speyers's testimony was more to the point. He identified Fisk as the principal.

Another tantalizing bit of evidence pointing to Gould's complicity came from a broker named Henry Enos. Enos was one of the traders that Smith, Gould's broker, hired to execute Gould's orders on the floor. Before the market opened on Black Friday, Gould instructed Enos to take the gold price higher and add to the buying momentum needed to sell the rest of his gold. "Enos, go put gold to $150," Gould had told him.[9] Fisk then told him the same thing. Gould and Fisk had claimed they had acted independently. Enos's testimony pointed to a conspiracy. Gould denied having anything to do with Enos. "I never knew this man Enos until the thing was over," Gould testified.[10]

The committee's report faulted Corbin for corruption and Sub-treasurer Butterfield for bad judgment. It exonerated Grant and put the blame entirely on Gould, Fisk, and Belden. It blasted Fisk for his "singular depravity" and called Belden "a man of straw." As for Gould, he was "the guilty plotter of all these criminal proceedings."[11]

The committee had no prosecutorial power and those who did never moved forward. Tweed persuaded the district attorney to stay away. Federal prosecutors brought no charges, presumably because the Grant administration wanted the matter to disappear.

There were, however, civil suits from broken investors trying to get back their money. They recovered little. The biggest winner was Gould's lawyer, Thomas Shearman. He defended Gould in more than a hundred cases. Following Gould's order to stall, Shearman dragged out the proceedings. It took a decade to clear the docket, "There isn't any secret," Gould once said. "I avoid bad luck by being patient. Whenever I'm obliged to get into a fight, I always wait and let the other fellow get tired first."[12]

What to make of Black Friday? With the perspective that comes from looking back over more than a hundred years, there is nothing inherently wrong with Gould having lobbied the government for a strong gold price. He was just one voice, albeit a loud one, in a legitimate public policy debate. Nor did he cross the line by trying to make a quick buck. This was nothing more than speculation, and speculation, despite its sometimes negative associations, fosters a ready market that buoys asset values and makes it easy for sellers to find an exit. Fisk's jawboning about gold going to 200 and government complicity, while morally repugnant, was just free speech as was Gould's manipulation of *The New York Times.*

But there is no question Gould behaved badly. Nowadays, he would go to jail for bribing a treasury official and for conspiring with the broker Belden to take the fall on Fisk's debts. Gould escaped prison because of yet another crime: his corruption, in collaboration with Tweed, of the New York judiciary.

Still, Gould is not alone in deserving blame. The gold trade went haywire because of deep-pocketed short sellers—men with strong ties to the Grant administration—who counterattacked. It was their selling, their effort to make money by destroying Gould, that forced Gould to elevate the gold price to the stratosphere. For these reasons, it's fair to lay an equal amount of blame on Jay Cooke, James Brown, and the other shorts. As Gould told Congress, "I did not want to buy so much gold, but all these fellows went in and sold short. I had to buy or else back down and show the white feather."[13]

❖ PART TWO ❖

NINETEEN

FISK'S REWARD

Gould's brazen attempt to manipulate the gold market woke up the British investors in Erie. Contrary to what stockbrokers told them, it turned out that not all the American railroads were winners and it actually mattered whether tracks terminated in New York City or Jersey City. It mattered whether a railroad had mountains of debt. It mattered if the railroad was run by a builder like Cornelius Vanderbilt or a "speculative director" bent on manipulating the stock price, robbing the corporate treasury, and awarding corporate contracts to himself and his friends.

In April 1870, British investors sued to oust the Erie board. A federal marshal served Gould and Fisk with a court summons. Fisk laughed. He invited the marshal to lunch. "If these Britishers prefer that their share of earnings shall be eaten up in lawsuits instead of being distributed in dividends, I can't help it," he said.[1]

Fisk could afford to laugh because his friend Tweed controlled the New York courts. But something disturbing was happening. The *Times*, under new management, had begun taking shots at Erie's guardian angel. It asked how Tweed, a public official, could afford a Greenwich estate, a Fifth Avenue mansion, a yacht, and a stable of horses. Tweed joked that he didn't care because his constituents couldn't read. But in the summer of 1871, Tweed, joined by Gould, nonetheless offered *Times* publisher George Jones the unfathomable sum of $5 million to call off the crusade. Jones turned them down. "The Times will continue to publish the facts," Jones said.[2]

The *Times* got a break when a disgruntled city accountant showed up at Jones's door with a clutch of ledgers. The documents proved that Tweed rented shacks and leased them to the city at ten times the market rate, received kickbacks from a plasterer the city paid an impossibly high sum, and took a cut when a vendor sold the city three tables and a few dozen chairs for the price of a house. Each day's newspaper brought new revelations. In October 1871 police arrested Tweed on $1 million bail. "I have my bail ready,"[3] Tweed told the sheriff. He produced a check signed by Gould.

The Erie Railroad, meanwhile, limped along. Its cars were full but interest on the debt was more than it could bear. Gould tried to raise $30 million on Wall Street but was having no luck. A stockbroker named William Duncan leveled with him. "Gould," Duncan said, "there is but one thing that can help Erie out of its troubles, give it credit and enable you to sell your bonds abroad and get money."

"What can be done?" Gould asked.

"Change the Board of Directors and put in some strong names,"[4] Duncan said.

Just like that, Gould dropped Tweed and his own brother Abram from the board. With regret, he also dropped his friend Fisk. In their places, he nominated an all-star team of New York financiers, all of whom despised Gould and wanted to put Erie on a respectable path. The names included John Jacob Astor, J. P. Morgan's father, Junius, and several Vanderbilt associates.

Fisk had other problems. His girlfriend Josie Mansfield told him she loved another. Ned Stokes was a tall, dashing figure who, at age thirty, was six years closer in age to Mansfield than Fisk. Stokes was broke. Out of desperation, he and Mansfield tried to blackmail Fisk and told him they would release his love letters to the press if Fisk didn't pay them off. The letters contained Fisk's most intimate and aching thoughts. Worse, they contained incriminating information about his business affairs.

Fisk went to the police. During the afternoon of January 6, 1872, Stokes was having lunch at Delmonico's when Judge Barnard, who was also at the restaurant, told Stokes he had been indicted. Stokes excused himself. Looking the picture of respectability and, according to the *Times*, "dressed with great elegance in clothing of light color," he walked into a Broadway gun shop, bought a four-round Colt revolver, and stuck it in his coat. Fisk was at the Grand Central Hotel at Broadway and Third Avenue when Stokes spotted him on a staircase. "Now I've got you," Stokes said. He aimed his pistol and fired. The shot hit Fisk in the stomach, knocking him off his feet. "Oh, no," Fisk cried. "Don't."[5] He struggled to get up. Stokes fired a second time, hitting him in the arm. Fisk collapsed on the stairs.

A messenger gave Gould the news. Fisk had been shot but was alive and at the hotel under a physician's care. Gould rushed over. Tweed was already there. They found bedsheets soaked in blood. A surgeon poked a finger into Fisk's gut. The bullet was too deep— and Fisk too large—for the surgeon to find it. Gould buried his head in his hands and fell into uncontrolled sobs. The Grand Opera canceled that night's concert, citing Fisk's critical condition. Fisk's wife, Lucy, took the night train from Boston. She arrived the next morning. Her husband, age thirty-six, was already dead.

The murder was front page news across the country. In New York, the *Times* gave it six columns. The *Herald* scooped its competitors with a reaction from Gould. Gould insisted Fisk had renounced debauchery. "Since the dissolution of whatever tie has existed between him and Mrs. Mansfield, he has been a changed man," Gould said. "He had ceased to practice many of the old habits and was in every sense becoming what all who loved him desired he should be."[6]

Throughout his life, Fisk loved the spotlight. He financed and led a militia unit that marched in parades. He spoke at Tweed's campaign rallies, promising to vote two or three times if that's what it took. Just four months before his death, he had sponsored a relief train after the Great Chicago Fire. New Yorkers mourned his death. They dismissed his financial treachery and thought about the jilted lover, the big-hearted Romeo gunned down by a madman. His funeral was one of the largest New York had ever seen. Thousands filed past his open coffin in the foyer of the Opera. Gould sat quietly beside the body, perhaps wondering who would mourn him when his turn came. He quietly slipped out before they closed the lid and covered it with an American flag. Severed from his partner in crime, Gould would never find another business associate with such complementary skills.

GOULD WAS WAITING for a meeting at the Brevoort House, near Washington Square Park, when Erie general counsel Frederick Lane found him. "There is a great conspiracy against you," Lane said. "You are being sold out by the Erie management."

Gould looked astonished. "What do you mean," he asked.

"A majority of board members have been purchased,"[7] he said.

Lane explained how James McHenry, a British railroad investor, was trying to take over Erie and was attacking on several fronts. McHenry hired George Crouch, the journalist who covered Erie, to bribe the board members. He had also hired Daniel Sickles, a famous Civil War general who had lost a leg at Gettysburg, to lobby Albany to overturn the law that insulated Gould from board removal.

The next day, at the Metropolitan Hotel, Horace Greeley entered the picture. A founder of the Republican Party and a brilliant journalist, he launched a generation of pioneers with the words "Go West Young Man." His editorials, said one admirer, had influence second only to the Bible. Greeley was a writer. He was also a businessman who was willing to forget his antipathy of Gould for a chance to make money. Angling for a seat on the Erie board, he introduced Gould to a young gentleman with manicured nails, patent leather shoes, and a silk hat. Greeley informed Gould his friend was Lord Gordon, a nobleman from the Scottish Highlands. Gordon told Gould he could buy enough Erie shares in London to give Gould majority control and protect him from board meddling. Stress might have been weighing on Gould because, against his better judgment, he gave Gordon $500,000 to buy shares. Gordon took the money and fled to Canada.

In all events, the Erie board scheduled a meeting to fire Gould. The Erie bylaws said that only Gould could call a meeting, but the rebellious board members, their wallets fattened by McHenry's payoffs, scheduled one anyway. They'd worry about the validity of the action later. Gould called Tommy Lynch, the gang leader, to keep the board members from entering the building. Gould was out of his element dealing with gang leaders. But with Fisk gone, Gould had become the widow whose husband had always taken out the trash and killed the spiders. He had to fend for himself. He deputized Lynch and eighty of his toughest friends as Erie security guards.

Gould showed up expecting to find Lynch holding the fort. He was surprised to see no one. He caught up with Lynch and his crew inside the building. They had their feet up on the French furniture and were spitting tobacco onto Erie's carpets. Gould also found a squad of New York police officers, who apparently came at the request of the board. He peeped into the boardroom. There they were, the traitors, chatting around the conference table.

Shearman, the lawyer, was waiting for Gould. He told Gould to stay out of the boardroom. His presence would give the meeting official sanction. To protect his legal position, he should go to his office, lock the door, and let the police remove him by force. Gould complied, locking himself in with Shearman. To bolster the defenses, he ripped a curtain sash off the wall and tied together the door handles. He shoved his desk across the room to block the entrance.

From behind the battlements, Gould heard shouts in the hallway followed by a lone voice outside the door. The visitor wanted in. Gould saw the doors shake. Next came banging and scraping. The hallway grew louder. Gould saw a letter opener slip through a crack in the door, sawing through the sash. Like a gopher chased into his hole by a snapping terrier, he dashed out a side exit. Toppling over furniture to slow the predator, he ran deeper inside the building and locked himself in another office.

Gould inched open the door to let in his lawyer. At that moment, a U.S. marshal dove for Gould and stuffed a letter into his pocket. "You have been served," he cried. The note informed Gould that the board had fired him. Shearman snatched the letter and declared it invalid because it wasn't a court order. "This isn't even a writ,"[8] Shearman scoffed. Gould slammed the door and barricaded himself inside with Shearman.

Early the next morning, they heard footsteps and an odd tapping sound that became more audible as it drew near. Someone was coming for them. Gould heard the tapping again, then a knock on the door. When the visitor identified himself, Gould knew the source of the strange noise. It was the wooden leg of General Sickles.

Fifteen years earlier, Sickles was in the news for shooting dead his wife's lover in Lafayette Square, across from the White House. A crime of passion, he told the court. The court agreed and set legal precedent by ruling him temporarily insane. Sickles had all his senses when he stood before Gould's door. He knew Gould still had some cards left. The law that gave Gould a five-year term on the board was still in force. Unless it changed, Gould was safe.

Sickles put his lips near the door and propped himself up on his cane. He offered Gould a deal. If Gould quit, the board would drop the legal challenges and repay $2 million that Gould had loaned Erie. Gould was unmoved. Running the Erie Railroad was the best job he had ever had. Even in the railroad's weakened condition, it offered opportunities for profit. It would take more than a promise and a loan repayment to get him to quit. Playing his last card, Sickles gave a stock forecast. "If you resign it will send the price of Erie up 15 points," he said. "You can make $1 million."[9]

Gould perked up. He had seen himself as a Vanderbilt, building a railroad empire. But he was sufficiently aware to know his reputation as Mephistopheles weighed on Erie's stock. Gould agreed that, once he vanished, Erie stock would rise and he would make a quick score.

Gould, the gopher, opened the door and stuck his head out, as if sniffing the air for danger. He took Sickles's offer. A reporter for the *Sun* watched as Gould staggered out into the hall. He described Gould as looking "ashen" and "scarce able to walk." Gould hobbled to the boardroom to find everyone assembled. He called a meeting to order. "Gentlemen," Gould said, "I herewith resign the office of President of the Erie Railroad Company."[10]

The board named John Dix as his successor. Dix was treasury

secretary under President Buchanan. A general in the war, he had arrested six members of the Maryland General Assembly and deprived Confederates of votes needed to secede. Gould took Dix to what had been his office. He apologized for the torn curtains and overturned furniture. "You won't find things in very good order," he said.[11]

Gould left the building and showed that, even when scarce able to walk and looking ashen, he could think. He already owned 66,000 shares of Erie. He bought additional shares at 30. Sickles forecast a 15-point rise to 45. He underestimated. Erie shot to 75. Gould didn't make $1 million on the sale. He made more than double that.

TWENTY

COWS IN THE MOONLIGHT

Gould was now thirty-six and had enough money to retire. He could easily provide for his children. He could even provide for their children. If he wanted to slow down, he could have returned to the Catskills and played country squire. Or he could devote himself to scholarship. But he needed the intellectual combat of business. From the moment he left Erie headquarters and stepped onto 23rd Street as an unemployed corporate president, he dreamed of new opportunities and greater riches.

Gould regarded his millions as a grubsteak, the starter money for making even more. "A little money and perseverance will make any man rich," he liked to say.[1] He had perseverance. And now he had money. He had the requisites for a spectacular fortune. The question was how to get it.

The sensible choice was railroads. He had already run two and knew how to use them to generate profit, whether by legal or questionable means. But railroads were expensive even for someone who had just scored a $2 million windfall. He had to find a good one at the right price. As he scouted for his chance, he filled his time by returning, as he had once told his father, to "the smoky world of stocks and bonds."

Being a private investor was different than being a "speculative
director," the insider who ran the stock price up or down to suit
his whims. As a speculative director, he had inside information. He
could see into the future. Without being on the inside, he'd be guessing. Andrew Carnegie was a year older than Gould. Before getting
into the steel business, he made a fortune as a railroad executive
trading on inside information. He thought only a fool invested without it. Daniel Drew agreed. To invest without insider knowledge,
Drew said, was like buying a cow in the moonlight. You only knew
what you bought after the sun came up. Gould would be buying
cows in the moonlight.

After watching Erie rocket to 75, Gould concluded it would
rocket no more. Maybe the new directors could raise some money,
improve its service, win more freight, and become everything that
Erie should have been all along. But Gould didn't think so. As far as
he was concerned, Erie's problems were the same as always: inade-
quate freight rates, high expenses, and excessive debt. He sold all his
Erie shares and then sold some more by going short.

He also went short another stock, Pacific Mail. Pacific Mail was a
steamship operator. It carried letters and freight from San Francisco
to New York over Panama. Based on analysis rather than inside information, Gould concluded the stock was overvalued, sold it short,
and tried to drive down the price.

Gould's broker, Henry Smith, his comrade in the gold pump
and dump, joined in both campaigns. Smith started as a banker in
Buffalo, moved to New York, and scored by hitching himself to
Drew before jumping over to Gould. He had strawberry blond hair,
a ginger beard, and sharp eyes that prompted one contemporary to
say he looked "Hebraic."

Despite Gould's prediction that Erie would flop without him,
Erie shot to a new high. Gould and Smith covered at a loss. Pacific

Mail went differently. Gould got advance word about some positive developments. He covered his short and went long. Smith, ignorant of Gould's activities, stayed short and watched helplessly as Pacific Mail rose from 30 to 103.

Gould had an office a few doors down from Smith. As brokers hounded Smith to cover his losses, Smith burst in on Gould. He demanded Gould make him whole. Gould refused. It wasn't his fault that Smith stayed too long in the trade. Smith screamed at Gould. "I'll get good and even with you," he said.[2]

Gould was not vengeful. But Smith had crossed a line by threatening him. When Gould got a chance to give Smith a kick, he took it. Two Vanderbilt cronies, Augustus Schell and Horace Clark, told Gould that they had bought some stock in the Chicago and North Western on behalf of themselves and Vanderbilt. Gould was intrigued. He knew Smith was short that stock, too, and did the math. With the Vanderbilt party owning as much Northwestern as they did, he could buy some shares, corner the market, and squeeze Smith like a maid wringing a mop.

Events intervened when a fire swept through Boston in November 1872. This came a little more than a year after the Chicago fire. Smith assumed the fire would wipe out Boston like it did Chicago and take the stock market down with it. He shorted another batch of Northwestern shares. Gould, meanwhile, bought more. To Smith's horror, the Boston fire torched a piece of downtown but left most of the city untouched. In the relief rally that followed, Northwestern jumped from 75 to 95.

The Victorians had rich vocabulary to describe financial calamity. "Shipwreck" meant a bad trade. "Absolute shipwreck" meant a worse trade. "Gone up" meant sudden, unexpected collapse. "Undone" was a devastating loss combined with humiliation. "Gone to the wall" meant financial death. It was interchangeable with "ruin," a word that meant the same then as now. It was the loss of everything—money, reputation, and the chance to get them back. Smith wasn't ruined. When trading in Northwestern opened the following morning, he was somewhere between shipwreck and absolute shipwreck.

Smith begged Gould for the stock needed to cover his short. "You must let me have Northwestern so I can get out of this fix," he said. Gould turned him down. Smith borrowed a page from Drew and threatened to turn over documents proving that Gould looted Erie. "You know what that means!" he said.

Gould knew all right. The ledgers could be his downfall. For a prosecutor, peering into them would be like slicing open a fish to see what it had for breakfast. They revealed everything: the details of the Opera swindle, the money siphoned to companies Gould owned on the side, the use of corporate funds to make investments for Gould's personal account. All told, Gould had helped himself to $9 million from the Erie treasury. He had to take Smith's threat seriously. Without Tammany judges to protect him, the evidence in Smith's hands could land him in jail. Still, Gould had cornered the market for Northwestern fair and square. It wasn't every day that he perfected a corner. When trading opened the next morning, he could charge Smith and other shorts whatever he wanted for his stock. Gould was at a crossroads. He could agree to Smith's demand and avoid the risk of prison. Or he could take his chances with the courts, score big on the corner, and make even more money. Smith demanded an answer. What did Gould want to do about the ledgers? "Very well," Gould said. "Turn them over. I have no objection."[3]

Smith ran from the office. He took the records to Peter Watson, the new president of Erie. Watson was a good man. He wanted to put Erie on the right course. He was delighted to see Smith. If Erie got back $9 million from Gould, it could put itself on the proper financial footing. Watson brought a theft charge against Gould and gave the records to a judge, who, convinced that foul play was involved, issued an arrest warrant for Gould.

The warrant gave Smith a small dose of satisfaction. But it did nothing to relieve his losses. Northwestern had closed the day at 90. When the market opened the next morning, the share price burst from the starting gate. By the time the sheriff found Gould on Broad Street and arrested him, Northwestern was approaching 200. It zoomed past 200 about the same time Gould's lawyer, the future secretary of state Elihu Root, paid Gould's $1 million bail. Gould was back in his office when, after trading hours, the stock hit 250. "I was induced," Gould later said, "to part with some at that price."[4]

Other investors who were short Northwestern were broken but not destroyed. They settled their trades and lived to fight another day. That wasn't the case with Smith. He had shorted sixty thousand shares at 75. His loss came to $10.5 million. Only a Vanderbilt had that sort of money. Smith was no longer in a shipwrecked category. He was ruined.

There remained the matter of Gould's felony charge. Erie dropped the charge after Gould awarded it a collection of stocks, bonds, and several properties that were not worth $9 million but at least worth something. "I do this for the sake of peace," Gould said.[5] True enough, but he also had another angle: insider trading. Gould bought shares in Erie before the settlement. Their price leapt on news of the deal.

Smith later saw Gould in the street and vented his rage. "I will live to see the day, sir, when you have to earn a living by going around this street with a hand organ and a monkey," he said.

"Maybe you will, Henry," Gould said, "maybe you will. And when I want a monkey, Henry, I'll send for you."[6]

* * *

A FEW DAYS after the Chicago and North Western corner, a financial newspaper, the *New York Commercial Advertiser*, published a letter from a reader eager to set the record straight.

> Sir: The recent "corner" in Northwestern has called forth much comment from the press. My name has been associated with that of Mr. Jay Gould and others in connection with this speculation and gross injustice has been done to me thereby. I leave, therefore, to say (once and for all) that I have not had, either directly or indirectly, the slightest connection with or interest in this matter.[7]

The letter, dated November 26, 1872, was signed "C. Vanderbilt." The Commodore hated Gould, and the idea that people would think he had partnered with Gould on a deal infuriated him. Not only had the Commodore lost some money to Gould, but Gould had accomplished something even more painful. He had embarrassed him. It was well known that Gould had outfoxed the Commodore by seizing Erie, by accelerating the Erie shareholder vote, and by successfully shorting New York Central with fake news.

There was also a little episode with the cows. Back when Gould ran Erie, Vanderbilt slashed New York Central's rates and offered to move cattle across New York State for the token amount of $1 a carload. Erie was pinched for cash. Vanderbilt was certain the move would bury the railroad and take Gould down with it. Instead, Gould and Fisk made a profit by buying cows in Chicago and shipping them to market at Vanderbilt's bargain rates. "When the old Commodore found out he was carrying the cattle of his enemies at great expense to himself, he nearly lost his reason," Gould's assistant Giovanni Morosini later recalled. "It was very blue in Vanderbiltdom."[8]

A reporter from the *Sun* caught up with Vanderbilt and queried his thoughts on Gould. "May I ask you," the reporter said, "if you have any especial reason for thinking ill of him?"

"I have had but one business transaction with him in my life. In July, 1868, I sold him some stock for which he paid me promptly," Vanderbilt said, referring to the sale of his Erie shares.

"Why then do you distrust him," the reporter asked.

"His face sir," said Vanderbilt, as if it was obvious, "no man could have such a countenance and still be honest."

The reporter wanted more. "But surely Mr. Vanderbilt, you must have some other reason besides that for your opinion."

"I tell you," Vanderbilt said. "God Almighty has stamped every man's character upon his face. I read Mr. Gould like an open book the first time I saw him."

The reporter paused, waiting for a zinger. "You have my authority for stating that I consider Mr. Jay Gould a damned villain," Vanderbilt said. "You can't put it too strongly."

Gould normally let insults pass. But Vanderbilt's words stung. When the reporter sought a reply, Gould hit back. Vanderbilt, he said, was seventy-eight and envious of the young. "He can no longer go around as he used to and attend to business, and he is feebly envious of those who can," he said. "There is a class of rising financiers whom the old hates. They are young, full of energy and possessed of modern knowledge and appliances to aid them in their business. The old Commodore is jealous of them."

Gould predicted that he, Rockefeller, Carnegie, and others of his generation would have even more brilliant careers than Vanderbilt. "These young businessmen are rising into financial power, which will exceed the old Commodore even in his palmiest days."[9]

TWENTY-ONE

UNION PACIFIC

Gould traded securities as often as he changed his socks. He bet on gold one day, a mining stock the next, and a bankrupt express company the day after. Along with the big bets, he made tiny ones hardly worth the effort, as if picking up a nickel spotted on the sidewalk. It was like he'd offend the gods by letting even a small profit slip by.

Flipping assets was fun, but his true passion wasn't trading. It was railroads. Railroads were changing the world. They fascinated him. When talking about railroads, he sounded like a kid with toy trains. "I have been interested in railroads ever since I was a boy," he told a reporter. "I now think a railroad train is one of the grandest sights in the world. I like to see the great driving-wheels fly around."[1]

He clung to a dream he developed at Erie, the dream of creating the nation's first seamless transcontinental line of railroad track. There was already the Union Pacific. Completed in 1869, it was called a transcontinental railroad because it connected east with west and had a monopoly over the Rockies, a mountain range previously considered forever impassable to railroads. But the Union Pacific was only a link in the chain. It didn't travel unbroken from sea to shining sea. It only covered the distance from Omaha to Ogden. To go sea to sea meant changing trains at least four times. Gould wanted to fix that by controlling all three thousand miles of the journey.

He returned to railroads late in 1872 by buying the New Jersey Southern. The New Jersey Southern had nothing to do with the transcontinental dream. All it did was transport fish. It took them from the Maryland shore up the East Coast. Gould named himself president and declared his intention to transform the fish hauler into a railroad "second to none of the great lines running into New York."[2] It was a tall order because the New Jersey Southern was a disjointed mess. When a train reached Delaware Bay, porters loaded the cargo onto a ferry. Another train received it on the other side to load onto another train. It was the same at rivers. Gould saw the potential. He could use the tracks as the foundation for a straight connection from Baltimore to New York. Needing money to finance his plan, he went to Wall Street. His timing was unlucky. Wall Street was about to suffer what could be fairly likened to an earthquake. The shock would have enormous consequences for Gould and devastating consequences for the country.

FIVE YEARS EARLIER, on a pleasant summer day in June 1868, the banker Jay Cooke was in Duluth, Minnesota, easing himself into a canoe. Wearing a top hat and overcoat, he listened as a member of a local Indian tribe described the highlights of St. Louis Bay. Cooke later became Gould's foe on Black Friday. For now, he was scouting an investment opportunity.

On a map, the western end of Lake Superior looks like the open jaw of a dog. Duluth sits at the hinge. Its winters are punishing. Visitors might suffer entire weeks when the temperature never tops zero. The wind whipping off the lake makes it feel even colder.

The way Cooke saw it, Duluth had an attribute that overcame the weather: location. It sits at the exact point where the Great Lakes waterway begins its journey to the sea. Other than by traversing Panama, the only way to escape the West in the 1870s was by a long and dangerous journey over land. The situation brightened in Duluth, where the traveler could board a boat and ride in comfort to Buffalo. Civilization began in Duluth.

Cooke got off the canoe and pronounced Duluth to be "the next Chicago." He returned to Philadelphia where he won investor backing to build the world's longest railroad, the Northern Pacific. He painted an exciting picture. All the timber from Washington, all the coal from the Dakotas, and all the wheat from the Red River Valley; all of it would fill its cars and move on its seventeen hundred miles of track. Trains starting at Puget Sound would be bursting with freight by the time they hit Duluth. The government awarded the railroad 44 million acres of land—an area the size of Missouri—to see the project through. There had never been a larger land grant. Vanderbilt seethed over the gift. "Building railroads from nowhere to nowhere at public expense is not a legitimate undertaking," he fumed.[3]

Cooke personally invested everything he had. He went all in because he believed in Duluth. The dream ran into trouble two years after breaking ground. In what must have been the most arresting statement to ever appear in an annual report, he flagged the cause of his ruin. "Our men and their escorts have been resisted and fought by the Indians," he wrote. "The company's engineers have in effect been driven by Indians out of the Yellowstone Valley."[4] Sitting Bull, the chief of the Lakota Sioux, had warned Cooke to stay away. When Cooke ignored him, Sitting Bull attacked. Cooke was a first-rate bond salesman. He was not a military strategist. Sitting Bull explained himself. "I hate all white people," he said.[5]

On September 17, 1873, Cooke hosted President Grant at his Philadelphia estate. The next day, his company failed and a panic began. Cooke was the country's most powerful and successful investment banker. If Cooke could fail, anyone could fail. And if Northern Pacific couldn't make it, what about the other western railroads? The failure crushed share prices. To break the fall, the stock exchange closed for ten days. When it reopened, shares changed hands at less than half their former prices. Grant did nothing. Asked to comment on Cooke's failure, Grant's aide General Orville Babcock said, "I can assure you the President, knowing little about financial matters, will express no opinion on the subject of this failure for he has none to express."[6]

It was no ordinary panic. A bubble had been pricked and, in the months and years ahead, land prices fell, crop prices fell, and unemployment hit a record high. In New York, one in every four jobs disappeared, storekeepers slashed prices, and rents dropped by a third. In Pittsburgh, steel mills laid off fifty thousand people. In San Francisco, ships stayed in port. In Providence, Rhode Island, A. & W. Sprague, a giant manufacturer that made everything from sewing machines to hay mowers, closed and sent ten thousand workers into poverty. The country had never experienced such a prolonged or agonizing period of weakness. Recessions typically last eleven months. The contraction that began in 1873 lasted five years. Called the Long Depression, it was the longest, most devastating period of economic weakness in the country's history and was unsurpassed until the Great Depression.

Railroads suffered like everything else. Within a few months of Cooke's failure, twenty-five railroads defaulted on their debts. Before it was over, half the railroads in the country entered receivership. The rest struggled to stay afloat. "I stay in my office not knowing what to do," moaned Collis Huntington, the president of the Central Pacific.[7]

Gould was heavily invested when the crash came. His assistant, Giovanni Morosini, later insisted that no one lost more money than Gould. But even after his losses, he still had resources. With bargains around every corner, he set his sights on the connecting fabric of the transcontinental rail chain. He wanted the Union Pacific.

At the moment, the railroad was recovering from a scandal. During the 1872 election, it came out that a construction company owned by the railroad's owner, the Crédit Mobilier, had bribed members of Congress in exchange for favors. The scandal made the words "Crédit Mobilier" synonymous with government corruption and dinged the Union Pacific's share price. The stock remained too expensive for Gould, but he put in an order in case it went lower. When Cooke failed, he got his price and bought enough shares to name himself president. "My orders caught it," Gould said.[8]

The Bostonians who created the Union Pacific still owned some stock. They didn't trust Gould. They knew Gould as the man who looted Erie, blew up the gold market, and had partnered with the debauched swindler from Vermont, Jim Fisk. Who could blame them for thinking that Gould had been suckled by a she-wolf? Or that he bought Union Pacific for speculative directing. They knew nothing about the Gould who bought the Rutland & Washington and immersed himself in the details by riding the rails and inter-rogating its engineers and traffic managers, or about the Gould who, along with his self-dealing at Erie, had won the railroad new business, improved its service, and frightened even Vanderbilt with his commercial ability. They didn't know the Gould who was the smartest guy in the room. They only knew the Gould who the news-papers said was a crook.

Gould invited the men to his home. He explained the situation and revealed his plans. The Union Pacific had gotten off to a slow start, he said. Despite its potential, it was losing money and was in no position to pay back the $46 million it had borrowed from the government to finance construction. Gould promised to turn it around. He said he knew how to make the Union Pacific pay and "make it a big thing." A quick buck wasn't on his mind. "I hold for the long pull," he said.[9] Oliver Ames, one of the Boston directors, allowed that Gould couldn't make it worse. "I feel he will not use his power adverse to the interests of the road," Ames said.[10]

Upon taking command, Gould deferred the question of the government debt and attacked an immediate problem by refinancing the debt held by private investors. Then he turned to taming competitors. Leadville and other Colorado mining towns were booming. The Kansas Pacific, a rival of the Union Pacific, connected St. Louis and Kansas City, and had a line into Denver. The Union Pacific also served the region. Gould persuaded the Kansas Pacific to fix prices at high enough rates for both to prosper.

The Pacific Mail, the trans-Panama steamship company, was a bigger problem. California shippers had two ways to move freight east. They could put it on the Union Pacific to cross the plains or load it on a Pacific Mail boat to Panama, where in those pre-canal days porters carried cargo over the isthmus, and then on to New York. Union Pacific was fast but expensive. The Pacific Mail was slow but cheap. Patient shippers opted for the Pacific Mail.

Russell Sage was president of the Pacific Mail. Creative, quick, and intelligent, he had survived a usury conviction and was known on Wall Street as "the Money King." Sage earned his stripes in upstate New York where he embarrassed veteran horse traders with a superhuman ability to buy good horses at low prices. Elected to Congress, he planned to shake down businesses by threatening offensive legislation but discovered his fellow lawmakers too focused on slavery to pursue supplemental income. He quit after two terms, moved to New York, and changed financial markets forever.

Before Sage came along, only bankers traded options, the securities that give investors the right to buy or sell at preset prices. Options offer long odds and big payoffs. Sage thought adventurous members of the public might be interested. He guessed right. From a downtown office with caged windows that looked like a betting parlor, Sage did a huge retail business in options.

Sage was a notorious cheapskate. Rockefeller, another penny-pincher, once calculated he could save Standard Oil $2,500 by using 39 drops of solder to make an oil barrel instead of 40. "Thrift is essential to well-ordered living," Rockefeller said.[11] Sage was just as cheap. He treated Delmonico's like a company cafeteria, but only because he could expense it. He wore used suits and once bragged to Gould about paying only a dollar for a hat. "Never pay more," he said. "Not worth it." Another time, he bragged about saving $3 by firing his office boy and hiring another who worked for less. "Well," Gould said. "Have you figured out how much you will lose on his blunders."[12]

At the Pacific Mail annual meeting in 1874, Sage told stockholders that their company was "destined to become great."[13] At the same time, he was whispering to Gould that the company was worthless. He invited Gould to short the stock with him and then buy it back at a low price.

The stock cratered when it became known that Sage, the company's own president, was a seller. Pacific Mail's other board members blasted Sage's conduct as "highly unbecoming" and fired him. Sage didn't care. He and Gould had bought enough shares to oust the moralizing board members and put Gould in charge. Gould created a price-fixing deal with Union Pacific similar to the one with the Kansas Pacific.

With the railroad's competitors neutralized, Gould attacked costs. He hired Chinese labor for less than he was paying Swedes.

He built a steel mill in Wyoming to supply track for less than outside suppliers. "Money is made by saving as well as earning," he told a subordinate.[14] He took trips out west, flying down the rails in a private train and dictating notes to an assistant. He courted ranchers and miners for business, and encouraged his executives to get out of the office and follow his lead. "Our men on the ground have intelligence we need," he wrote one executive.[15]

The Union Pacific was making astonishing progress. But Gould kept the good news secret and let the stock price drift as he prepared the ground for a short squeeze. "Tell our friends in Boston not to sell a share," he informed an associate. "I shall not sell a share of my stock at any price. I shall stand by it."[16] He promised they would be rewarded for their patience.

A small crowd gathered in Boston for the railroad's annual meeting. The press was on hand as the tall, craggy figure of Sidney Dillon, Erie's president, took the podium. Dillon was, like Gould and Sage, from a small farm town in New York. Twenty-four years older than Gould and a foot taller, he had been one of the Union Pacific's contractors during the construction phase and, on that great day in 1869 when the Golden Spike joined the Union Pacific with the Central Pacific in Utah, he was on hand. Dillon had pocketed some of the Crédit Mobilier profits and survived the scandal, and was a famous figure in the country's business scene. But on this day, he served as Gould's mouthpiece and reported on Gould's handiwork.

After greeting the crowd, he delivered stunning news. Revenue was up and costs were down. For the first time, the company was turning a profit. For the first time, it would pay a dividend. "There followed such a scene of frantic excitement as has seldom been witnessed on the New York Stock Exchange," wrote one reporter.[17] The Union Pacific dominated trading for several sessions. Over the next eight weeks, it shot from 40 to 77. The Bostonians no longer had doubts about Gould. He was as good as his word.

A MONTH LATER, Allen Thurman, a senator from Ohio, held a campaign rally. Thurman, a Democrat with populist leanings, was stumping south of Cleveland. His uncle was running for governor and Thurman wanted to give him a lift. Nearly a thousand mostly friendly people showed up. From a small podium draped with red, white, and blue ribbons, Thurman spoke on national affairs. His commentary on Reconstruction and currency reform failed to stir the crowd. "The Senate Chamber itself never listened more gravely and silently," wrote the *New York Times*. "The Allegheny highlands was never more chilling than his reception."[18]

Only toward the end of his speech did Thurman connect. Look at the collapse of the Northern Pacific and how it ignited bank failures, a stock market crash, and raging unemployment, he said. Look at Crédit Mobilier, the construction company that paid off dozens of congressmen and made sure the Bostonians behind the Union Pacific made money even if the railroad didn't. "Is there a man here who has not heard of the Northern Pacific Railroad Company and the Crédit Mobilier," he thundered.

The audience hooted in agreement. Thurman pressed on. He blasted Gould's insistence on paying Union Pacific shareholders— the Crédit Mobilier crooks—a dividend instead of paying back its debt to the government. "Is there any one of you," he asked, "who does not know that, by the frauds of these companies, the people of the United States are absolutely certain to lose not less than $46 million?" Taxpayers, not shareholders, should come first, he said. Something must be done. The hoots turned to boos, and Thurman finished his speech to raucous applause.

The outrage voiced in Ohio was widespread. In the 1874 mid-term elections, Democrats took the House for the first time since before the war. In the prairie states, a new political force emerged in the Grange, a populist organization that championed farmers and claimed 1.5 million members. The Grange demanded lower freight rates and fought to collectivize everything from grain elevators to insurance companies. Huntington, the boss of the Central Pacific, called the Grange a pack of communists. The Grange called Huntington, Gould, and other railroad bosses a pack of thieves.

Back in Washington, Thurman demanded that the Union Pacific make good to taxpayers. No matter that the law chartering the railroad gave it a long grace period before it had to repay anything. He put forward a bill ordering the railroad to pay immediately. The bill died in Congress. But Thurman didn't go anywhere. He found success a few years later, giving lawmakers a grenade that, in time, they would throw at Gould.

TWENTY-TWO

EDISON

The whistle blew and the race was on. There were two teams. The first was a group of Western Union telegraph operators. They typed frantically on their keypads. Tom Edison led the other squad. His men typed nothing. They just fed perforated punch cards into their leader's newest invention, a device that typed for them. The teams were competing to determine who could most quickly transmit the same message—an hour-long speech by Grant—from Washington to New York. If Edison's team won, he could look forward to selling his invention to Western Union at a big price.

Team Western Union took seventy minutes. Team Edison came in a minute quicker. Edison had won. But he didn't win by enough for Western Union. After paying for the punch cards, typing by hand was still cheaper. Western Union turned him down.

It had been five years since Edison fried the wires at the Gold Exchange. Unable to find work as an engineer because he lacked a college degree, he was living in Newark with his wife and newborn daughter, trying to support the family as a freelance inventor. He was twenty-seven years old. The light bulb, the phonograph, and the movie camera were years away. For now, he had to invent a way to pay his mortgage. He made some money assembling stock ticker machines for Western Union. It didn't bring in much. When the bank moved to foreclose on his house, Edison held it off by promising to pay at least $5 a week. "If you don't watch out that daughter of yours will be a pauper," said his lab assistant. "I'm in straits," Edison admitted.[1] He entered the contest confident he could sell his punch card machine. Now he was more worried than before about paying the bills.

Thomas Eckert was a top Western Union executive. He was angry at his employer for passing him over for the president's job—so angry that he was willing to betray it. One night, Eckert brought a bantam-sized visitor with a long beard to Edison's Newark workshop. To avoid recognition, the visitor turned up his collar and kept his head low. When he lowered his collar and revealed himself, Edison recognized the man as the pointy-eared Shylock from the Thomas Nast cartoons. It was Jay Gould.

Gould was keenly interested in the telegraph business. Telegraphy went hand in hand with railroading. Telegraph companies strung lines alongside railroad tracks. Railroads set up dispatch operations in their stations. Western Union dominated the business. It partnered with the New York Central, the Erie, the Pennsylvania, the Baltimore & Ohio, and nearly every other railroad. The Associated Press news service shared stories over its wires. Businesspeople like Gould and J. P. Morgan were steady customers, using secret codes to transmit their messages. One of the biggest companies on the stock exchange, Western Union was above all else a money machine. Gould coveted it. "I'd rather be president of Western Union than president of the United States," Gould told an associate.[2]

It would be a near impossible task for Gould to take it over. It was simply too big and powerful. But maybe he could shake it down. Core to his scheme was Edison's latest invention—not the perforated card reader but a machine that, by exploiting the time intervals between electrical pulses, could send four messages at once. It was the sort of thing that could revolutionize the industry. Edison called his device the quadruplex. He had already demonstrated the machine to Western Union. The company told Edison to work out the kinks and then get back to it. Western Union's dawdling left Edison free to shop it around.

Inside Edison's workshop, Gould asked Edison some questions and left without making an offer. He went to bed thinking about the quadruplex. The Union Pacific was one of the few railroads that had its own telegraph operation. Called the Atlantic & Pacific, it was a sorry affair compared to Western Union. But Gould concluded that if he and Atlantic & Pacific bought the quadruplex—and Edison got it to work—Western Union would come begging to buy him out.

The next day, Eckert invited Edison to New York at Gould's request. Eckert took the inventor uptown and snuck him into Gould's house through the back door. Servants directed them to Gould's basement office. Edison found Gould along with one of his own stock ticker machines. Gould told Edison he wanted to buy the quadruplex. "Make me an offer," Edison said.

"I will give you $30,000," Gould said.

"I will sell any interest I have for that amount," Edison said.[3] Gould wrote him a check. Edison agreed to come work for him and perfect the device.

Edison and Gould shared some traits. Both were rustics born into poverty. Both thought about little beside their obsessions— inventions for Edison, money for Gould. Both worked all the time. Both had spent their childhoods reading anything that came their way. They could compare notes on farming. Or rat traps. Like Gould's grandfather, who sent Gould to New York to sell his trap at the fair, Edison also had a trap. His rat trap not only caught the rodent but roasted it with an electrical current, which, as Edison described it, "would render up its soul and depart this earthly sphere."[4]

After Edison walked down to Gould's Fifth Avenue basement, he tried to lighten the mood with a joke. It wasn't recorded what he said. But it might have been the one he liked to tell about the Irish sailor. "How would an Irish sailor know where to find the rocks?" Edison would say. "With the bottom of his boat."[5] Gould offered his own attempt at levity. He said he had just sold a steamship for $30,000. That happened to be the exact amount he had just paid Edison. Gould said it was as if Edison swapped the quadruplex for a boat. Edison faked a chuckle.

Gould wanted the quadruplex for what it could do for telegraphy. He also considered the havoc it could cause the stock of Western Union. By being able to send four messages at once, Gould could tell a story about being able to undercut Western Union's rates and take away its business. Gould shorted Western Union and announced he now owned the technology that would change the industry. Western Union shareholders panicked. By the time they calmed down and realized Edison still had to make the thing work, Gould covered his short and earned several times what he paid Edison.

As an employee of Gould's, Edison came to appreciate what Fisk had called Gould's peculiarities. During one encounter, Gould rambled on about his plans for the Union Pacific. Edison was eager to get back to his workbench. But he tried to appear attentive as Gould unfurled maps and talked about rail lines. Gould spoke for three hours before exhausting himself. During that same visit, Edison noticed that Gould's stock ticker was gone. Gould explained that Western Union had infuriated him by raising the monthly fee. In a fit of quiet rage, he ordered the machine removed. "He railed over it," Edison said. "This struck me as abnormal."

Edison was the chief electrician for the Atlantic & Pacific. He lasted a month before he lost patience with the company's president, the imperious Thomas Eckert, who had quit Western Union to come work for Gould. Gould offered Edison thousands of Atlantic & Pacific shares to stay, but the inventor wasn't interested. Not only did he hate his boss, but he found Gould strange and unsettling. "Gould had a peculiar eye," Edison later wrote. "There was a strain of insanity somewhere."[6]

Edison was out but Gould still owned the quadruplex. He took the Atlantic & Pacific public and stunned Western Union by persuading the Baltimore & Ohio to break its contract and come to him. Pennsylvania, New York Central, and Erie followed. Western Union, the monopolist, suddenly looked vulnerable.

Vanderbilt was the Western Union's largest shareholder. The battle between Western Union and Atlantic & Pacific took a turn when, at age eighty-two, the Commodore died of old age. The papers mourned the loss. The *Times* recounted his triumphs on the front page. "A long and useful life ended," read the obituary headline.[7]

Vanderbilt had thirteen children. Not wanting to dilute the power of his $105 million fortune, he gave almost all the money to William, the oldest. At age fifty-five, William was fifteen years older than Gould. He was made of different stuff than his father. He didn't bash his way over Nicaraguan cataracts in a steamboat. Nor did he pick fights with heavyweight champions. A gentle giant, he liked nothing better than to play with his children and admire his horses. A friend joked how William would sleep with the horses if he could. Another said William "had a heart as tender as a woman's and as big as an ox."[8] His wife said he never uttered an unkind word.

Friends called him Billy. The Commodore called him "blockhead" and complained about his lack of initiative. "The substance of the Commodore's remarks was that William was deficient in brains," said William's brother-in-law.[9] While Gould had brought his son George into business as soon as he could, Vanderbilt thought Billy needed seasoning. He bought him some land on Staten Island and made him tend crops for twenty years before inviting him to join the board of the Harlem Railroad and naming him heir apparent.

About the only thing William had in common with his father was his appearance, particularly around the cheeks. The Gilded Age was a golden time for facial hair. No president before Grant had a beard or a mustache in their official portrait. Then came six in a row, one after another with chins and upper lips constituents would never see. It took William McKinley, who took office in 1897, to break the string. Gould had a lumberjack beard. Fisk had a waxed mustache with pointed tips. Telegraph pioneer Cyrus Field went Amish carpenter while Gould's partner Russell Sage preferred chin strap. Union Pacific president Sidney Dillon had fluffy white sideburns that made him look like a poodle. Walt Whitman could be mistaken for a bohemian Santa. Grant had it right. He kept his beard and mustache neat and close cut. Horace Greeley had it wrong. With no hair on his face, he let his neck hair run wild. It stuck out like a scarf.

The Vanderbilts had a signature look—muttonchops. The Commodore's chops nicely followed the contours of his cheekbones. They were evenly, precisely balanced. On the careless William Vanderbilt, one chop always looked bigger than the other.

William wasn't a blockhead. He just showed no interest in money. "He was not a bold venturer," Gould said. "He was satisfied with a small, or at least fair, return." [10] William's caution was something Gould thought he could exploit.

No sooner did the Commodore die than Gould, as if poking a dog to see if it would growl, shorted Western Union's stock and initiated a rate war. The young Vanderbilt showed mettle. He matched the low rates. If Gould wanted to fight, he'd fight. His nerve lasted only until the next board meeting. The rate war, the board complained, jeopardized the dividend. The fighting had to stop. To end the pain, Western Union bought Atlantic & Pacific for $5 million.

Sage was one of Gould's backers in Atlantic & Pacific. He had joined Gould in putting up $1 million to get the company started. It was one of their first deals together. In just a few months, Sage and his young partner Gould earned five times their investment, not to mention whatever they made by shorting Western Union. Sage was so impressed. He worked deals with Gould for the rest of Gould's life.

Edison could have scored, too. Gould had offered a cut of Atlantic & Pacific that the inventor refused. Nonetheless, Edison claimed to have no regrets about his experience with the financier. "I never had a grudge against him because he was so able in his line and, as long as my part was successful, the money with me was a secondary consideration," he said.[11]

While on the subject, Edison offered an assessment. "He certainly had one trait that all men must have who want to succeed," Edison said. "He collected every kind of information and statistics about his schemes and had all the data." He excused Gould's greed. "His conscience seemed to be atrophied, but that may be due to the fact that he was contending with men who never had any to be atrophied."[12]

The Atlantic & Pacific saga had a violent epilogue. When Gould was hammering the stock of Western Union with a price war, a speculator and Civil War major named A. A. Selover joined him in shorting it. Selover struck it rich in gold mining and was then adding to his fortune on Wall Street. When Gould switched from selling Western Union to buying, he didn't tell Selover. Selover stayed short and lost everything.

Selover was a muscular Californian. At six feet, two hundred pounds, he towered over Gould. One day, he spotted Gould on Broadway. "I'll teach you what it means to tell me lies," he bellowed. He swung at Gould much like the lawyer Joseph Marrin did four years earlier at Delmonico's. Gould dodged the blow. Selover swung again, landing several shots to Gould's chest. Gould reeled back. Selover sucker punched Gould from behind. The *Times* later criticized that punch as less than "gallant." Selover pushed Gould down a set of stairs that led to a basement barbershop. He followed him and landed more blows. "You are a damn liar," Selover said. "I am not," Gould cried.

Selover threw Gould against the shop wall with such force that a brandy bottle crashed from a shelf. A crowd formed. "Won't someone take this man away," Gould implored. "He will murder me." A bystander grabbed Gould's arm and tried to lead him away. Selover threw more punches, accompanied by more profanities. "Finally," the *Times* reported, "a colored boy, employed by the barber, ran up from the basement and shouted" in a way that startled Selover. Selover fled. Gould, weak and pale, took a seat in the barbershop to recover.

George Crouch, the journalist, happened to be walking by. He helped Gould out of the shop and into the street. Gould brushed himself off and continued down Broadway. The *Times*, noting that Selover served as a vestryman at a church, said his profane language did him discredit. "He is notoriously treacherous," said Selover, explaining his assault on Gould. "This is not the first time he has been punished for the same offense."[13] He was referring to how, a few days earlier, James Keene, another speculator and a friend of Selover's, had waved a pistol in Gould's face. Keene, too, had been caught on the wrong side of the Western Union trade. He vowed revenge. Two incidents in the same week were enough for Gould. From then on, he kept his husky aide, Giovanni Morosini, at his side as a bodyguard.

TWENTY-THREE

DIRTY TRICKS

One of the most criticized, convoluted, and ultimately lucrative campaigns of Gould's career—and the one that best evidenced his brilliance—began with a kidnapping. This was his takeover and sale of the Kansas Pacific Railroad. The four-year drama began in August 1876. Amherst Stone was a circuit court judge in Colorado. He was on a train from Golden to Boulder when the brakes screeched and the train lurched to a halt. Masked men with rifles leapt aboard and burst into his car. They wrestled Stone from his seat, jammed him into a carriage, and rode with him through the moonlit Colorado scrub to a ranch house in the middle of nowhere.

Stone was caught in the crossfire of a corporate takeover battle. The price-fixing deal between the Union Pacific and the Kansas Pacific had fizzled with cheating on both sides. Gould wanted to buy Kansas Pacific to stabilize freight rates, but its stock price was too high. To drive it down, he attacked the railroad in the mountains.

The mining boom was in full swing. Although the Kansas Pacific covered a thousand miles, most of its profits came from a single subsidiary, the Denver Pacific. The railroad covered the hundred miles from Denver to Cheyenne. It had no competitors. To break the monopoly and smash the stock price of the Kansas railroad, Gould bought a controlling stake in the Colorado Central, a small railroad that he could extend to Cheyenne. "We must so effectively clean them out of Colorado that they will sue for terms," Gould declared.[1]

William Loveland, a railroad entrepreneur, was founder of the Colorado Central and the largest shareholder until Gould swept in. Gould bought the stock in the open market and didn't pay the customary premium to take control. Feeling deprived, Loveland went to court and asked Judge Stone to void Gould's purchase and force him to pay more. He soon realized he had no chance in court; Gould had acted properly. Now desperate, Loveland switched to a less conventional and more daring plan.

The judicial term was about to expire. If Loveland could detain Judge Stone for just two days, keep him locked up and out of his courtroom for a mere forty-eight hours, the term would end and Gould would have to wait at least a year before getting the railroad. Gould, Loveland guessed, was in a hurry and would pay him something extra to close the deal right away. With time running out, he hired a band of silver miners to grab the judge.

Colorado governor John Routt learned of the abduction and sent a posse to the rescue. He also packed a replacement judge on a train to Boulder to clear the judicial docket. The governor took no chances. He gave the train a military escort and put a cannon on a flatcar. The new judge made it to Boulder, ruled in Gould's favor, and Gould got the railroad. The game was over. The kidnappers, who had made the judge comfortable with cigars and whiskey, set him free. None of the plotters talked. An investigation into the incident died for lack of evidence.

Just as Gould hoped, the Kansas Pacific, robbed of its Colorado profits, slid into bankruptcy. He could now buy the stock for a song.

But there was one more hurdle. The railroad had a crushing load of debt. Unless Gould could get easier terms from bondholders, the railroad might fall right back into bankruptcy. Germans owned the bonds. They hired a remarkable immigrant named Henry Villard to negotiate.

Villard was born Ferdinand Hilgard. He fled Germany after his father enrolled him in a military school. Escaping to New York, he took a French name so his parents couldn't find him. He studied law and, to pay the bills, became a Civil War reporter for the *New York Herald*. He married a daughter of abolitionist William Lloyd Garrison and was the *Chicago Tribune*'s Washington correspondent when Lincoln was shot. Later, he became a railroad entrepreneur himself.

A class of Kansas Pacific bondholders had already settled with Gould. Villard represented another class, the ones first in line to get paid back in a bankruptcy. Gould offered Villard a bribe to betray his clients. Villard turned it down. Gould cut freight rates some more between Denver and Cheyenne. Villard retaliated by going to Washington for legislative relief. Gould followed Villard to Congress with what Villard called "a barrel of money" to thwart him. Villard tried to sell the railroad to a Gould competitor. Gould blocked the sale. Back and forth it went.

Gould became a frequent visitor to Villard's office on Nassau Street. A relationship developed as they tried to settle. Villard and Gould were only a year apart in age. They talked about bond indentures. They also talked about Kaiser Wilhelm and Queen Victoria. Perhaps looking for clues about this fellow Mephistopheles to whom the *Times* compared him, Gould asked Villard about Goethe.

After two years of talks, Gould finally proposed terms Villard could accept. The bondholders would get their money and Gould would get his railroad. The negotiations exhausted Villard. He was packing for a European vacation when a telegram came. Gould, it said, had gone behind his back and reopened negotiations with other creditors. Villard exploded. He thought he and Gould had a deal. His vacation plans trashed, he went back to the battle.

TWENTY-FOUR

IN GOULD'S GRIP

In early 1879, Gould picked up a crop report. It predicted a weak harvest. He played it by shorting shares in the Chicago and North Western Railroad. The railroad was an old friend. It was the same one whose shares he cornered a few years earlier when he destroyed the broker Henry Smith.

The North Western hauled grain, potatoes, and sugar beets from the Upper Midwest to Chicago. Summer rains were heavier than predicted and Gould's forecast proved wrong. As yardmen stuffed the harvest onto the railroad's freight cars, the stock rose from 32 to 50. Gould was famous for squeezing the shorts. Now he was being squeezed. Rumors flew that he was finished. "Jay Gould's Difficulties," read a *Times* headline. "The Great Financier Getting Crushed."[1] The *Times* was openly gleeful. Gould, it wrote, was "one of the very few Americans whose misfortunes will generally be regarded as a public gain."

Anticipating Gould would have to dump shares at any price, traders shorted Union Pacific as aggressively as they had bulled Northwestern. The entire street seemed against him. Gould ultimately sold half of his Union Pacific shares but, to the disappointment of the *Times* and the shorts, Gould not only survived but added millions of cash to his war chest. He soon put it to profitable use.

WHEN GOULD'S FORTUNE was tied up with the Union Pacific, his interests and those of the railroad were aligned. Now that he had more cash and less Union Pacific, he could think broadly. The first indication of the new priorities came when Gould abruptly stopped dickering with Villard and settled with the Kansas Pacific bondholders at 100 cents on the dollar, the price Villard had been demanding all along. The second indication came when Gould bought stock in the Kansas Pacific, which the market assumed was on death's door. The third came when he resigned from the Union Pacific board. The reveal came when he offered to sell Kansas Pacific to the Union Pacific for nine times what he had just paid for it, demanding the outrageous amount of $100 a share. His demand came with a threat. If the Union Pacific didn't buy him out, he would use the Kansas Pacific to steal its customers and drive it out of business.

Sidney Dillon, the Union Pacific president, was appalled. This was blackmail. He considered Gould a friend and couldn't believe what he was hearing. He could understand why Gould wanted a good price. But a price of 100 implied the Union Pacific and Kansas Pacific were of equal value. That was ludicrous. The Union Pacific was several times larger. It had more track, hauled more freight, and generated more revenue. Then there was the not insignificant matter of its monopoly over the mountains.

After he calmed down, Dillon offered to pay 66, a price he considered more than fair. Gould wanted more. At a meeting of the Union Pacific board, Gould demanded nothing short of unconditional surrender. The board held firm. "Gentleman," Gould said, "you are making a mistake."[2]

Gould, as promised, did his best to destroy his friends. His first step was to buy a large partner of the Union Pacific, the Wabash. The Wabash carried freight between Toledo and Omaha. Then, to connect the Wabash with the Kansas Pacific and deprive the Union Pacific of its business, Gould went after a small railroad that ran a shuttle between Kansas City and St. Louis, the Missouri Pacific. C. K. Garrison owned the railroad. A onetime Mississippi steamboat captain and an ace euchre player, Garrison made a fortune in shipping and, after serving a term as mayor of San Francisco, went into railroads. Gould didn't like Garrison—they had clashed in the past about railroad matters—so he sent Sage to negotiate. Garrison read Gould's strategy perfectly. Without his little Missouri railroad, Gould's scheme for mid-continental mastery would crumble. Garrison asked for $2 million, a price well above market. Sage offered $1.5 million. Outraged at being taken for a fool, Garrison shot back. "The price," he said, "has advanced to $2.8 million."[3]

Gould went himself the next day. He agreed to Garrison's price. Forget it, Garrison told him. The price was now $3.8 million. Garrison added that if Gould didn't agree on the spot, he'd raise the price by a million a day until he did. Gould paid him. Gould later explained why he agreed. "You pay more for a ruby than for a diamond," he said, "and more for a diamond than a piece of glass."[4]

With his lasso tight around Union Pacific, Gould left for Europe with his son George under the guise of a summer vacation. Dutch investors owned bonds in the Denver Pacific, the Kansas Pacific subsidiary. Gould's competitive attacks in Colorado had crushed their price. Gould was in a hurry to buy because, once he sold Kansas Pacific to Union Pacific, the bonds would become the obligation of a merged and fortified Union Pacific and their price would soar. He arrived in Amsterdam early one morning, washed up, and had breakfast. He met the Dutch investors at ten and got them to part with the bonds at 74 cents on the dollar before noon. "I was afraid to go over," Gould later told a congressional panel, "because I had very little time and thought that they would probably take a couple days to smoke before finding out whether they would sell or not. But I was mistaken."[5]

By the time they returned to New York, the Street was awake to Gould's game and had hoisted the share price of Kansas Pacific to 97. That made the Kansas Pacific's stock market value nearly identical with that of the Union Pacific. Dillon hated surrendering to Gould. If he and the board agreed to Gould's terms, they'd be watering down the value of their own Union Pacific shares. Then there was the question of appearances. No matter how justified the merger in the face of Gould's attacks, other Union Pacific shareholders would say the board had conspired with Gould to cheat them. Oliver Ames, one of the Boston directors, said the thought of a merger sickened him. But the prospect of fighting Gould made him feel worse. Other board members, which included Gordon Dexter, a shipping merchant, and Oliver's son Fred, felt the same. "I saw Sidney Dillon and Dexter and Fred Ames, as gloomy and unhappy set of men as I ever saw," Oliver Ames later wrote. "Mr. Gould had them in his power."[6]

Gould and the Kansas Pacific were getting stronger every day. Knowing he was cornered, Dillon came to Gould on a January evening and negotiated with him until midnight. Instead of rejecting the 50/50 split, Dillon reminded Gould of their friendship and begged him not to demand even more. Gould agreed. And why not? He had made about $20 million on the deal, making it the most profitable investment of his career. Dexter, the board member, admitted he and his friends were no match for Gould. "A man of Mr. Gould's ability—with such a weapon as the Kansas Pacific, let alone the Missouri Pacific—could have built branches and cut rates and cut us all to pieces," he said.[7]

Gould congratulated the men on making the right choice. The Union Pacific had no chance. "I would have destroyed it," he said.[8]

TWENTY-FIVE

ACQUISITIONS

After the Kansas Pacific triumph, Gould embarked on a dizzying shopping spree. The pace and volume of activity was like nothing ever seen in corporate America. It was as if Delmonico's was offering railroads as entrees and Gould ordered everything on the menu.

Gould bought the Delaware, Lackawanna & Western; the Central of New Jersey; the Denver & Rio Grande; the International-Great Northern; the Missouri-Kansas-Texas; the New York & New England; the St. Louis, Iron Mountain & Southern; the Texas & Pacific; and the Utah Central. He didn't buy a hundred percent of any of them. With some he only took a small bite. But he bought enough of each to put himself in charge. In every instance, he became the sole decision maker.

The acquisitions gave Gould breathtaking scope. Only a year earlier, the biggest city he touched was Omaha. Now he was in Kansas City, St. Louis, and Memphis. He was in Dallas, Denver, and Detroit. He was in San Antonio. He was in Buffalo, Newark, Hartford, Cleveland, and Toledo. Some 115,000 miles of railroad track ran across the United States. Gould was the master of 16,000 miles by the end of 1881. That was one of every six miles, giving him 15 percent of the largest, most important industry in the country.

Competitors, bankers, and his own employees were baffled. Was he buying as a speculator, ready to sell shares on the first move in price? Was he buying to reduce competition? Was he buying to bring all those railroads together in a grand east–west, north–south transcontinental spiderweb? Or given the weak finances of many of the acquired roads, had he just lost his mind? The *Sun* quoted a stockbroker who characterized Gould's collection as "a heap of rubbishy Southwestern stocks." As long as a railroad was "rotten and southwestern," the broker said, it could find a buyer in Jay Gould.[1]

His reputation as a cutthroat helped him at the bargaining table. He was seen as the gangster who demanded a slice of a restaurant's receipts. The owner could either submit or suffer the consequences. Thomas Allen was a Missouri congressman and owner of the Iron Mountain. Allen didn't want to sell. Gould forced Allen to terms by buying his competitors and surrounding him. "I thought that by selling out I would be able to secure harmony," Allen said.[2]

No competitor was too big to attack. Gould bought the Lackawanna for the single purpose of pressuring the New York Central and intimidating William Vanderbilt. It worked. Vanderbilt shocked Wall Street by selling Gould a stake in Central, the jewel of his late father's empire. The public feared a combination between Vanderbilt and Gould, the two great powers of Wall Street and railroads. But Vanderbilt wasn't thinking about combinations. Like Allen of Iron Mountain, he wanted harmony. "It was a choice between continuing the competition for western connections or making its members my friends. I thought it wise to do the latter," he said.[3] Gould probably had something else on his mind. By getting his foot in the door of the New York Central, it put a seamless transcontinental system—a system that would deliver unmatched convenience and efficiency—within his grasp. If he somehow managed to get control of Vanderbilt's railroad, rather than just having a board seat, he would have an unbroken line as far as the Rockies.

Nowhere was foreboding about Gould's activities greater than in the halls of another powerful railroad, the Chicago, Burlington & Quincy. The Burlington started in Chicago and crossed nearly as much land as the Union Pacific. Its golden goose was a two-hundred-mile length of track heading east from the Missouri River across Iowa. Iowa was an agricultural paradise. In sunbaked and windy Nebraska, tumbleweeds rolled along the tracks of the Union Pacific. Not so in Iowa, where settlers planted corn in "black gold" topsoil fifteen inches deep. The *Railway Gazette* called the Iowa breadbasket "one of the most productive districts in the world." Burlington was the only railroad serving this heartland arcadia. It could charge shippers whatever it asked.

Three small railroads—the Quincy, the Peoria, and the Iowa—were building in the region when Jay Cooke failed and the economy froze. They were bankrupt when Gould embarked on his railroad shopping spree. Charles Perkins, the Burlington's vice president, worried that Gould would acquire the railroads and shatter Burlington's Iowa monopoly. He wanted to buy them before Gould did. His uncle, Burlington president John Murray Forbes, objected. Forbes said he didn't want to spend the money, particularly when he considered Gould in over his head. "The acquisition of so much railroad property should make Gould conservative," he said.

Perkins argued that the railroads were small, bankrupt, and wouldn't cost much. Besides, Gould was already buying everything under the sun. Why wouldn't he buy the Iowa railroads, too? "We all exaggerate Gould's desire to fight us," Forbes said. Frustrated, Forbes told friends he envied Gould's celerity and ability to act without consulting a board of directors. "Gould moves so rapidly," he said, "it is impossible to keep up with him."[4]

Just as Perkins feared, Gould bought the Quincy, followed by the Peoria, followed by the Iowa. With the pieces in place, Gould announced plans to lay track from Iowa to St. Louis and strip business away from the Burlington. The situation called for face-to-face negotiations between Forbes and Gould. But Forbes couldn't do it. "I know he don't like me, and I certainly don't like him," Forbes said. "I can do nothing with Gould."[5]

Forbes resigned his position in favor of Perkins. Perkins took to the ramparts. He threatened to spend a fortune to lay track across Nebraska all the way to Denver— a move that would spoil Union Pacific's Nebraska business. Gould's top priority was the Missouri Pacific, not the Union Pacific. But he still owned enough shares in the larger railroad to care about its fate. "Carrying out your menace of extending your line to Denver means war," Gould wrote to Perkins.[6] It actually meant peace. Perkins's threat worked. After Gould calculated that he was facing a determined and well-financed adversary, he backed off.

With his railroad purchases, Gould inaugurated the inevitable process of industry consolidation. There were too many competitors. Few could prosper. As William Vanderbilt observed about New York, it had five railroads but only enough business for two. The situation was more extreme in the center of the country. In Kansas alone, where anyone with a dollar could buy a charter from the state and start a railroad, there were forty of them. Competitors faced a choice. Either win the Darwinian battle of rationalization or get swallowed up. Gould was aware of how Rockefeller, from a small office in Cleveland, was using coercion to grab every oil refinery he could. Gould longed to lead a similar process in railroads. "Consolidation will prove both essential and inevitable," he wrote an associate. What was needed, he continued, was "unchallenged market domination."[7]

TWENTY-SIX

---◆◆◇◆---

WESTERN UNION

Now that Gould controlled a sizable chunk of the nation's railroad network, he had the muscle to launch another assault on Western Union. In the spring of 1879, he formed a new telegraph venture, American Union, to take on the telegraph giant for a second time. This time, he wouldn't do it with Edison and inventions but with something more prosaic—plain old commercial agreements. Gould canceled contracts between Western Union and his own railroads and awarded the rights to American Union.

Gould was ruthless, as always. Western Union operated a battery station in Omaha for the telegraph lines that ran along Union Pacific tracks. Gould's men cut the station's wires and hooked them to a station belonging to American Union. The same sort of thing happened across the country. At every Gould railroad, Western Union battery stations were left with nothing to power. Then he turned to persuading other railroads, notably the Baltimore & Ohio, to come to his side.

With the wind at his back, Gould took American Union public. The offering document echoed Gould's battle cry in the Erie War. It declared Western Union an evil monopoly and said that Gould created the new company to give the country an alternative. With attractive pricing and superior service, American Union promised to deliver customers a better deal. Western Union's share price was already sinking on prospects of a price war. The stock offering dealt it another blow.

Western Union's president, Norvin Green, was an Ohio physician who quit medicine for business. He had been in the telegraph industry for more than twenty years and, under his command, Western Union had become a powerhouse. As Green watched his customers flee, he begged William Vanderbilt to let him retaliate. Not only could Western Union contest the broken contracts in court, but it could offer the railroads better terms than American Union. If it came to it, it could even send men scrambling up telegraph poles to slash wires like Gould had done in Nebraska. Gould was spending a fortune to fight the rate war, Green said. Western Union had resources to outlast him. It only had to fight.

Vanderbilt ignored Green and instead took cues from the cautious bankers on his board of directors. Like in the earlier battle with Gould's first telegraph venture, the board prioritized the dividend. Better to buy out Gould a second time than forfeit profits in a price war.

Vanderbilt lived just blocks away from Gould on Fifth Avenue. He invited Gould over for peace talks. Gould arrived with Sage and Dillon, his two partners in American Union. Vanderbilt was stunned when he learned that Gould had already bought enough Western Union shares in the open market to make himself the company's largest shareholder. Vanderbilt and his allies still had more stock as a group, but Gould was gaining on them. The meeting broke up without a deal. "I have met the Great Mogul," Vanderbilt reported to Green.[1] But he and the mogul had not come to terms.

They convened again the following evening in a meeting that lasted half the night. Gould demanded that Western Union buy American Union at a price nearly four times the $4 million Gould and his friends had invested in the company. He also wanted a premium for some leftover shares he still owned in his earlier telegraph venture, Atlantic & Pacific. There was one more demand. This one hurt Vanderbilt the most. Gould insisted that Vanderbilt immediately resign as chairman of Western Union and cede the job to him. When Vanderbilt heard the demand, his face turned red and curses worthy of the Commodore spilled from his mouth. Vanderbilt was a head taller than Gould. As he berated his pint-sized antagonist, Sage and Dillon worried that Vanderbilt would take a swing at him. Gould was resolute. He vowed to buy even more shares in Western Union if Vanderbilt didn't step down. When Vanderbilt recovered his composure, he realized it was over for him. He bargained for a few crumbs including a cooperation agreement with Gould in a railroad matter.

Gould returned to the Vanderbilt mansion the next day to sign the papers. News of the deal sent shares in Western Union flying. Gould had paid about 80 for his Western Union shares. Confident that the price wars were over, investors bid the price up to 116. Gould's profit came to more than $2 million.

The Western Union building, located at the corner of Broadway and Dey Street, was among the most magnificent structures in the city and a symbol of New York's aspirations for greatness. Ten stories tall, it had an Otis elevator and mansard roof with a giant clock on the top that New Yorkers used to set their watches. A hundred telegraph operators sent messages from the eighth floor.

Like warlords seizing the imperial palace, Gould, Sage, and Dillon marched into their new offices. Gould had arranged a special elevator just for himself. He fired Norvin Green and brought back Thomas Eckert, the former Western Union superintendent who had introduced him to Edison. Gould stopped talking about Western Union as an evil monopolist.

* * *

WHEN WESTERN UNION'S stock price recovered, Gould wasn't the only one who cleaned up. While Gould and Vanderbilt were holding their secret talks, a storm struck New York and disabled Gould's private telegraph. The blackout forced Gould to contract with a messenger service to deliver his trading orders by hand. A cabal of crafty traders seized the moment. They grabbed one of the messengers and dressed one of their own to take his place to gather information on Gould's trades. For four days, they saw Gould's every order for Western Union shares. Guessing Gould was trying to take it over, they bought all the Western Union they could and paid the kidnapped messenger $500 to stay in a hotel and keep quiet.

In an earlier episode, another group of traders tried to provoke a panic by having a Gould look-alike fake an epileptic seizure in front of the stock exchange. That trick flopped. It looked like a gag. The one with the kidnapped messenger succeeded. The schemers bought Western Union at 80 and sold at 120, pocketing $500,000.

TWENTY-SEVEN

ELEVATED

Except for the Lackawanna, Gould's railroads were hundreds of miles from New York. He visited them when he could. To make the travel tolerable, he rode in a private railcar with four state-rooms, a butler's pantry, a kitchen, and a king-sized bed. The journeys sometimes took him away for months.

During his pursuit of Western Union, he took an interest in a railroad he could visit without boarding a Pullman, one that he could see right under his nose from the tenth floor of Western Union. It had steam locomotives and tracks like other railroads. It ran on the same standard gauge of four feet eight and a half inches. But the trains traveled at half the normal speed and chugged along trestles forty feet in the air. While other railroads carried freight, this one only carried passengers. They paid 5 cents a ride, gripped straps, and stood for the journey.

The trains belonged to the Manhattan Railway Company, the city's first commuter rail system and the precursor of the subway. Each day, the Els, as they were called, pumped tens of thousands of New Yorkers from their uptown homes to the burgeoning office towers and factories downtown. New Yorkers, especially those near the tracks, hated the noise, the stench, and the shadows it cast.

When the trains roared by, dishes rattled, soot blew through open windows, and conversation stopped.

For all its faults, the Els were a godsend. Horse-drawn omnibuses and streetcars had made the city close to unlivable. Crowded, uncomfortable, and slow, they jammed the streets and turned rush hour into a nightmare. There were other problems. The city's 150,000 horses each dropped about twenty-two pounds of manure and a quart of urine a day on the street. Those quaint stoops that lead into brownstones? They were needed to distance their front doors from horse dung. With the filth came flies, rats, and disease. "New York was stinking with the emanations of putrefying organic matter," said the street cleaning commissioner.[1] Something had to be done.

Tweed loved the idea of an elevated railroad. Here was another chance for large-scale graft. The idea stalled after he was run out of office only to spring back to life a few years later. By 1878, the New York Elevated was running from Grand Central Station to South Ferry. Another elevated railroad, the Metropolitan, served Second and Sixth Avenues. A third company, the Manhattan Railway, held a lease on both lines. In the summer of 1881, Gould joined with Russell Sage, Sidney Dillon, and Cyrus Field to buy the Manhattan Railway and take control of the system.

They had only owned it for two months when, one morning right after Christmas, Gould picked up his *New York Times* and found three columns on the front page about himself and the railroad. It was a massive piece of investigative journalism. Measured in column inches, the *Times* gave the story as much ink as the story that toppled Tweed a decade earlier. It was as if the *Times* believed that this was it for Gould: this was the silver bullet that would fell him and end his life of trickery.

Like with the Tweed story, the Gould exposé was dense. There were too many words, too many names, and too little context. Yet it was devastating. The essence was that Gould spooked the stockholders of Manhattan Railway into selling their shares to him at a knockdown price. In a classic example of the wolves slaying the sheep, Gould transferred $2 million from oblivious shareholders to himself and his friends by spreading lies about the railroad's financial condition. "Public Trusts Betrayed," blasted the *Times* headline. "The Stock Jobbing Scandal of the Elevated Roads. How the Gould Clique Gained Their Present Control."[2]

According to the paper, Gould had accomplices. They included the New York State attorney general, a friendly state court judge, and the editor of a rival newspaper, the *New York World*. Gould had acquired the *World* with his takeover of the Texas & Pacific, which happened to own it. As part of his scheme, the *Times* said, Gould used the newspaper as a weapon of terror. The St. Louis newspaper magnate Joseph Pulitzer later bought the *World* and turned it into one of the finest, most progressive newspapers in the country. For now, the *World* was an also-ran. The fifth-largest paper in the city, it catered to a working-class audience and lost money. George Templeton Strong, a priggish chronicler of Gilded Age New York, called its editor, William Hurlbert, a "fetid bug," accusing him of loose morals and complete absence of journalistic integrity. "He is among the very few human creatures whom I loathe," Strong wrote.

Gould, said the *Times*, gave the *World* something to write about by siccing the state attorney general and a friendly judge on the railroad. The Manhattan Railway and the two railroads it leased had been feuding in court over how to split the profits. Attorney General Hamilton Ward launched an attack reportedly cooked up by Gould. Ward blamed the feud for delays, crowded carriages, and accidents, and concluded that the railroad was too important to leave in the hands of petty, warring shareholders. He sued to revoke its corporate charter. Judge Theodoric Westbrook, also said to be on Gould's payroll, let the case proceed. Ward followed up by throwing the system into receivership. Westbrook, not to be outdone, appointed two Gould associates as the receivers.

The *World* danced to Gould's tune. It hammered readers with stories about the railroad's precarious finances. For anyone with money invested in the Manhattan Railway, the articles were terrifying. May 10: The Manhattan is a "gigantic swindle." May 21: "The Attorney General is waiting and working up his case." May 28: "The stock has nothing behind it but a general potentiality of rickety iron bridges." July 9: "It is hopelessly insolvent." July 19: "It has nothing but debts." August 4: "A number of weak spots have been discovered." October 2: "It is an even bet that the assets of the Manhattan will be sold at auction within ninety days."

The stock price was 55 before the *World* began the campaign. As its shareholders lost faith, selling begat selling. The share price tumbled. "Batches of it were let loose on the market by timid shareholders," said the *Times*.[3] The share price lost nearly three quarters of its value, crashing all the way to 16. Gould was there with a fishing net. He scooped up the shares.

The *Times* was struck by how the *World* abruptly turned bullish as soon as Gould finished scooping. Just two weeks after declaring Manhattan bound for bankruptcy, it proclaimed the railroad a great thing. The *World*'s financial columnist became the railroad's biggest tout. "As I said long ago, the elevated franchise is a thing too big to give away," he wrote. "I never believed that the Manhattan would not be rescued by men who have the means and brains to change it most."

The stock almost tripled by Thanksgiving. Shares that Gould bought for less than $1 million jumped in value to $2.6 million.

From a quick reading of the *Times*'s attack, a reader could conclude that the newspaper proved its case. But it had no smoking gun. Unlike with its Tweed articles, it had neither receipts, nor accounting statements, nor canceled checks. By its own admission, all it had were "inferences." Its most damning fact was that Judge Westbrook sometimes used office space at Western Union. A jury couldn't convict on that. Unable to get to the bottom of the story on its own, the *Times* demanded an investigation. It urged those with subpoena power to pick up the case. "Gould and his accomplices have won millions of dollars," it wrote. "But what are the gains of the public officials who lent themselves or sold themselves to the service of the stock operators?"

The city's other newspapers yawned. They saw the affair as a spat between the *Times* and the *World*. Better to stay out. The only person who seemed to care was a twenty-three-year-old law school dropout then serving in the State Assembly. His name was Theodore Roosevelt. Scion of a rich New York family, Roosevelt considered Gould "a bloated monopolist" who needed to be deflated. With the New York City district attorney refusing to act, Roosevelt produced his own evidence against Judge Westbrook and proposed that the legislature itself launch a probe. But the legislature, "under mysterious influences" according to the *Times*, refused to back him.

The Manhattan Railway saga revealed something about Gould that his opponents may have forgotten. He was above all a pragmatist. If Gould had been a crazy dreamer like Jay Cooke, the money he invested in Elevated would have instead gone to buy railroads or track that advanced a transcontinental vision. But Gould only dreamed when it didn't conflict with the prime directive, which was to deploy capital where it could earn the most. The Manhattan Railway was an opportunistic purchase, not a strategic one. He still wanted to create a coast-to-coast railroad, consolidate the industry, and put a stop to the rate wars. But not at the expense of making money. In only a few months, Gould was firmly in the black on Elevated. Years of dividends followed. It was one of the best investments he ever made.

TWENTY-EIGHT

WARES AT A BAZAAR

In the early 1880s, the mood on Wall Street was giddy. The economy had shaken off the Long Depression and stock prices were soaring. The Gould stocks, the Street's term for his holdings, rose along with the rest. Gould used a spectacular rise in Wabash to fuel his purchase of Kansas Pacific and Missouri Pacific. The Kansas Pacific bonanza fueled his takeovers of Western Union and Manhattan Railway. The more profits he earned, the more collateral he could offer the banks. The more collateral, the more he could borrow and the more he could acquire. With nothing but prosperity on the horizon, lenders advanced him money on easy terms.

As the money poured in, Gould became, for the first time, extravagant. He and his family had lived at 578 Fifth Avenue for a decade. In keeping with his heightened affluence, he traded up for a bigger house across the street. The three-story mansion at 579 Fifth had a mansard roof, a grand, tasteful portico, and, on the front steps, two lampposts left over from its prior owner, a former New York mayor. Gould moved his flower garden to the roof. Ellie's tastes were sophisticated. She kept the interior elegant, refined, and comfortable.

Home was central to Gould. Other luminaries led busy lives outside the office. Carnegie went to concerts and hosted salons.

Rockefeller played nine holes of golf every morning. Gould was a homebody whose routine left no time for diversion. He rose at 7:30, ate breakfast at 8, and, with a secretary, wrote letters until 9:30. He had lunch at noon with Sage and Dillon at the Astor House or, after it opened in 1888, the spectacular Café Savarin. On other days, he and his friends met in the Western Union executive dining room. Gould ate light. He liked snails until he had a bad one, got sick, and never ate another. He drank lots of coffee. He stayed downtown until 4:30 when he came home for dinner with the family. After dinner, he headed to the Fifth Avenue Hotel to talk markets with stockbrokers who traded there after-hours. Then he read in his library until it was time for bed at 11. He spent Sunday in the office as if it were a regular day. When he was at home and needed air, he pruned the flowers.

"I have the disadvantage of not being sociable," he told a reporter. "Wall Street men are fond of company and sport. A man makes $100,000 there and immediately buys a yacht, begins to drive fast horses, and becomes a sport generally. My tastes lie in a different direction. When business hours are over, I go home and spend the remainder of the day with my wife, my children and books of my library. Every man has natural inclinations of his own. Mine are domestic. They are not calculated to make me particularly popular on Wall Street, and I cannot help that."[1]

His home office was a cavern mostly occupied by a large table covered in unkempt piles of documents, letters, and memos. A fireplace burned on one end. Bookshelves lined the sides. A large map of the U.S. hung above a long sofa. There was a clock above the fireplace. On the day a *Tribune* reporter visited, the hands were stuck at five minutes to nine. Gould was too preoccupied to wind it.[2]

He added to his real estate portfolio by buying a summer residence up the Hudson in Tarrytown, New York. Called Lyndhurst, the house was a Gothic hulk of pink and gray granite adorned with spires, turrets, and other medieval flourishes that gave it a ghoulish chill. The point was later brought home when Lyndhurst served as a movie set for the 1960s vampire soap opera *Dark Shadows*. Gould filled the house with books, including the classics and at least one volume on phrenology. He covered the walls with paintings by Corot, Courbet, and other French realists.

The grounds included the country's biggest greenhouse. It burned down shortly after Gould bought it. He rebuilt it and channeled his inner Frankenstein by cultivating new breeds of orchids. To walk through the greenhouse was like strolling in the tropics. On cold winter days, Gould ambled along the humid pathways amid the ferns and exotic trees.

His neighbors rode the train to work. Preferring a more comfortable commute, Gould bought a steamship built not for the slow-moving waters of the Hudson but for stormy ocean crossings. Named *Atalanta* after the speedy Greek huntress, it measured 205 feet. The Larchmont Yacht Club on the other side of Westchester County took him as a member. The New York Yacht Club turned him down, wanting nothing to do with the mastermind behind the gold caper. Gould also started his own club, the American Yacht Club, in Rye. To get there and wherever else he might want to go, he kept a fleet of expensive carriages complete with landaus, broughams, and, for summer, cabriolets.

The toys brought Gould scrutiny. *The Dallas Morning News* did some digging and discovered Gould had seventy servants and a French chef. Indignant, it said the chef's annual income came to several times that of a messenger boy. Imagine the outrage if it had done the math on Gould himself, whose dividends on his stocks alone amounted to $4 million a year.

Gould was now in his forties and settled into middle age. A loving husband and father, he had six children, all healthy. George, the oldest and heir apparent, was sixteen. Gould was already bringing him to business meetings. The youngest, Frank, was two. Ellie enjoyed being a mother. A homebody, she was active in the church and became close friends with Russell Sage's wife, Olivia. Lady Astor, the queen of New York society, disdained railroad men and never called. Ellie didn't mind missing Astor's balls. But she had two daughters to think about. At some point she and Jay would have to introduce them into society.

Gould's niece Alice Northrop was a frequent guest at Lyndhurst, where she rode horses and took boat rides on the river. She became best friends with Gould's daughter Helen. They saw shows together in the city. One day, Northrop walked into Gould's study and found him staring at a telegram, looking pale and agitated. "Garfield," Gould muttered, "has been shot." The president was at a Washington train station at the start of a summer vacation when a lunatic ambushed him and fired two bullets into his back. Garfield had been in office less than four months. More than a decade had passed since Garfield, then a young Ohio congressman, had grilled Gould about the Gold Corner. Gould bore Garfield no ill will. When Garfield died from infection three months later, Gould took it hard.

The Garfield shooting terrified the country, raised fears of a recession, and demolished the optimistic tone on Wall Street. In the flash of an assassin's gun, the rally was over. Stocks began to swoon. Western Union and Missouri Pacific fell in line with the market, losing about 10 percent of their value in the ensuing weeks. Wabash fell by half. After one particularly brutal day for stocks in February 1882, Gould joined with William Vanderbilt and Cyrus Field to calm the market with bullish predictions. Stocks moved higher. But the recovery was short-lived. Investors were soon selling again. Gould's banks became nervous.

To ease concern, Gould engineered a spectacle worthy of Fisk. He invited Sage, Cyrus Field, and Vanderbilt protégé Frank Work to his office, and told his aide Morosini to fetch the bags in the back room. On Gould's orders, Morosini opened the bags and dumped stock certificates across Gould's desk. Millions of dollars' worth of Union Pacific shares, millions' worth of Missouri Pacific, millions' worth of Western Union spilled across the mahogany surface. The shares represented a material chunk of the American economy.

Go ahead, Gould said. Check the backs for signatures. They're clean. Signatures meant the shares were pledged as collateral. These certificates were unsigned. All told, the value of the bundles came to $40 million, or $1 billion in contemporary terms. And that was just the stocks, Gould had another $20 million of bonds if they cared to see them. The bonds alone covered his debts. It was a staggering display of wealth. Gould didn't mind if people thought he was a thief. But he cared deeply about how the world evaluated his net worth because it affected his negotiating leverage and ability to borrow. Even worse, if creditors and investors thought he was busted, there would be an avalanche of selling. Gould had debts taken on during his railroad shopping spree but was still tens of millions to the good. Still, in a severe panic, there was a chance, however slight, of insolvency.

Gould asked his friends to tell the newspapers what they witnessed. Sage advised against it. Publicity would only raise more questions and invite scorn. Gould insisted. When the papers reported the incident the next day, they ridiculed Gould's stunt just as Sage predicted. The articles cast Gould as a desperate merchant displaying his wares on a bazaar carpet. Who shows their goods other than those trying to sell? Gould must be in trouble, they concluded. Wall Street took a different view, however. Gould's financial health was better than it imagined. Investors figured that if Gould owned that much stock, they should own more themselves. On the same day the papers reported the story, stocks resumed their upward march.

A LOT HAD happened to Charles Francis Adams since he wrote "A Chapter of Erie." He served ten years on the Massachusetts Railroad Commission, dominated its proceedings, and realized his ambition of obtaining national influence. His vision proved correct. A data-driven technocrat, armed with communication skills, could make a difference. Other states followed his insistence on standardized financial reporting for railroads—a change that made it easier for investors to separate the wheat from the chaff. His advocacy of George Westinghouse's air brake, a brake that could be put on every car of the train, made the devices the industry standard and saved lives. Railroad men read Adams's reports. Lawmakers sought his counsel. Newspapers reprinted his speeches.

Adams, as always, was hard on himself. He listed in his diary as many failures as successes. He was ferocious with others. The directors of the Board of Trade, he wrote, were "blockheads." He described civil servants as unimaginative "asses," a failing he attributed to their pedestrian backgrounds. A "thick witted lunkhead," was how he characterized one executive with the Pennsylvania Railroad.[3]

Adams and his wife, Mary, had five children and lived in a big house in Quincy. His inheritance gave him $5,000 a year. His job as a commissioner paid $4,000 a year. By comparison, a skilled craftsman like a furniture maker or a blacksmith would be doing well to earn $400 a year. Money also came from his wife's side. She was an Ogden, a well-to-do New York family. Adams met her in Newport, which had shed its whaling heritage to become a playground for the rich.

Adams was rich himself. But some of his Harvard friends were even richer. As he sailed on their yachts and ate oysters on their terraces, he dreamed of attaining fantastic wealth. "I have all I want," he wrote. "But I want a great deal." Doing nothing more than serving on a state panel no longer measured up. "I could do more for my own success by getting rich than by slaving my life away in mere political action," he wrote. "Can I ever get rid of this beastly commissionership?"[4]

His friends brought him investment ideas. Concern about conflict of interest barely crossed his mind. To him, being an investor and being a regulator were not opposed. As long as he avoided investing in the Massachusetts railroads, he considered himself safe from reproach. He bought shares in Westinghouse and profited off the air brakes he promoted. He invested in the Marquette, Houghton & Ontonagon, a railroad in Michigan. He served on its board and, before it collapsed, he lost sleep "thinking, thinking, thinking" about how to save it. He scored on Calumet & Hecla, a Michigan mining company, but lost on another one, Champion Iron. He "took a gamble" on Robinson Consolidated, a copper mine in Nevada, and lost his entire investment. He bought shares in Union Pacific and, for a year, sat on the board as a government-appointed director. No sooner did he and Gould exchange an awkward greeting at a board meeting, than he began to form a more nuanced view of his literary antihero. Adams had once tried to destroy Gould in a bid to boost his own career. Now they were, for better or for worse, allies.

Adams had friends who owned the Kansas City stockyards. They invited him to invest. Adams visited, decided the president of the stockyards was a "bad fellow," and convinced his friends to fire the man and install him in his place. Adams ran the yards from Boston and found a Harvard man, Charles Morse, to work in Kansas City as the operations manager. Kansas was among the country's fastest growing states in the 1870s. As it grew, so did the stockyards. Under Morse's skillful management, the stockyards produced a gusher for Adams. He made a hundred times his initial investment. Adams made equally fantastic returns on Kansas City real estate, buying downtown land for as little as $150 an acre on the Kansas side.

Through it all, Adams retained his sense of outrage. He continued to denounce the Wall Street crowd as "monsters," "buccaneers," and "gamblers." True, he personally engaged in what he called "financiering," but financiering, he insisted, was different than speculating. He was morally pure because he wasn't a trader but an investor. Investors were builders. They were employers and agents of progress. Traders were quick-buck artists. Adams considered himself more Cornelius Vanderbilt than Daniel Drew. And now, thanks to Kansas City, he was rich beyond his dreams. He wasn't the most accomplished of the august line of Adams. He needed to be president of the United States for that. But no Adams had ever had as much money.

In December 1882, he read in the *Boston Advertiser* a letter from someone calling himself the Investigator. The Investigator asked readers how to value railroad stocks and weigh fast-money "Wall Street values" against "intrinsic value," the true value of a security based on its expected, long-term cash generation.

Adams replied in the next day's *Advertiser* with a recommendation to buy Union Pacific. The stock had sold for 120 early in the year. Now in the grip of a bear raid on accusations that Gould cooked the books, it fetched less than 100. Adams wrote how he had recently spent two weeks out west performing due diligence. He had inspected the railroad, interviewed managers, and pored over the financial statements. He was bullish.

Adams wasn't blind to the challenges. He conceded there would eventually be competing railroads over the Rockies. But he assured that the Union Pacific, as the first mover, would remain dominant. The competitors would be "what Third or Sixth Avenues are to Broadway,"[5] he wrote. He and some of his Boston friends had been buying heavily. He invited *Advertiser* readers to come along with them and dilute the power of Gould. Investors should act soon, he urged. The shares "have been drifting to Boston in considerable quantities," he reported. "The object of my present writing is, in so far as I can, to cause it to drift here faster."

The Investigator followed up with another letter, this time accusing Adams of naïveté. "Intrinsic worth is not always the base of stock values," he wrote. "The discoveries made by Mr. Adams in the methods of Wall Street for making and unmaking stock value may be new to him, but they are very old to those who have been diligent students within its classic shades—and paid dearly for their tuition." Gould wasn't the Investigator. But he would have agreed with everything he said.

TWENTY-NINE

———◆◆———

TERROR

It was another day of terror on Wall Street. Grant & Ward was a brokerage firm backed by the former president as a favor to his son. On May 6, 1884, it collapsed amid fraud. "We are all paupers now," moaned the blindsided President Grant. "We are ruined."[1]

Fear sent New Yorkers racing downtown. Carriages jammed the streets. Men in top hats packed the sidewalks. The economy was healthy and business conditions strong. But confidence, the bedrock of financial markets, had turned to dust. Confronted with proof that assets could crash to zero, everyone wanted out. Lines of anxious depositors formed outside banks.

This was a scandal made for cartoonist Thomas Nast. He could sketch the fast-talking mastermind Ferdinand Ward, leaping over an agonizing Grant with a bag of loot. Or he could show Ward, with a knife, stabbing Grant as Lady Liberty watched through tears. Nast didn't make a sketch because he didn't like self-portraits. He had personally invested all he had in Grant & Ward. He lost everything and joined the lecture circuit to pay the bills.

The failure of Grant & Ward toppled several banks and obliterated stock prices. Gould wasn't involved. But because he had been buying stocks on margin, rumors of his demise resurfaced. Investors pounded the Gould stocks, anticipating Gould would be selling them to raise cash. Missouri Pacific went from 78 to 67. Union Pacific from 45 to 39. Western Union from 54 to 49.

Asked if Gould was liquidating, Gould's broker, Washington Connor, replied with one word: "nonsense." Morosini, Gould's assistant, feigned surprise. "Pooh, pooh," he said. As fear reached its height, a *Times* reporter found Gould walking up Broadway. Despite "rumors of his own impending ruin," Gould seemed unruffled. "He was apparently as calm as though there was no panic."[2]

Investors jammed the stairs outside Russell Sage's office and spilled onto the street. Sage had sold them put options, investments that would rise in value if the market turned south. Elated by the panic, they shoved receipts into the hands of Sage's tellers and demanded their winnings. Stalling for time, Sage planted dummies in the line to slow its progress. When the clock struck the customary closing time of 1:30, clerks jumped from behind their windows and pushed the throng from the office. One enraged investor rammed the office door with his shoulder. "If Sage doesn't open the door, I'll burst in," he cried. Another shouted, "If the old man has gone up, why doesn't he come out like a man and say so." Gould, with Morosini to protect him, came into the room and flashed his cane at the crowd. As if speaking to children up past their bedtime, he took out his watch and ordered the mob to go home. "It's 2 o'clock," he said. "You can't put in any more today anyhow."

Later that afternoon, Gould invited a *Tribune* reporter to his office. The reporter found Gould at the ticker machine, pulling the tape through his fingers. "This disturbance today is a senseless thing," he said. "The general calling of loans has been wholly unnecessary and foolish." Stocks were cheap, he said. "I think the worst is over. People will regain their senses by morning."[3] He offered a stock tip: Western Union.

Gould visited Sage at home that weekend. The man known as the Money King was in bed, overcome by stress. "He is a gentle old man and the turmoil around his office has completely unnerved him," Gould told reporters camped outside.

Sage's problem was liquidity. He had the cash to pay his debts. He just needed time to get his hands on it. Gould's issue ran deeper. Two years earlier, when Gould dumped share certificates on his desk as if displaying wares at a bazaar, he was flush. Now, with stocks having taken a bigger hit than in the last downturn, he was on edge.

Charles Woerishoffer was a German immigrant and skilled gambler who, as a young man, busted more than one faro bank. He was the leading bear on Wall Street, fabled as much for his nerve as his good humor. "He could have marched upon a cannon's mouth with a smile on his lips," said an associate. One victim was his countryman Henry Villard, the onetime agent for Kansas Pacific bondholders. Villard had become a railroad baron himself, having taken control of the Northern Pacific by buying the stock on margin. A year before, Woerishoffer led a bloody bear raid on the company. Northern Pacific hit the toboggan slide and Villard was wiped out. Edison, a friend of Villard's, described his friend as being "in a stupor" and sought to cheer him up by telling him about his latest invention, an electric light bulb. Villard tried to be philosophical. "What a revolution in the wheel of fortune," he said.[4] He sold his Madison Avenue mansion and returned to Germany.

Now Gould was in Woerishoffer's sights. Believing Gould too indebted to defend his positions, he shorted the Gould stocks and smashed their prices. Woerishoffer had read the situation correctly. Gould was indeed overextended, so overextended that the rumors of his demise might become reality. As the value of Gould's collateral declined with each downward tick in stock prices, banks issued margin calls. They demanded Gould sell stocks at whatever price he could. Gould couldn't stall by closing a teller window like Sage. He had to pay. "He had to throw stocks overboard like men unloading a ship at sea," wrote the *Herald*. His selling drove prices down further. He'd be bankrupt if prices didn't turn.

GOULD AND ADVERSITY were well acquainted. As a young man, he had to shoot his way back into the tanning business. Then he clawed out of the rubble of the gold fiasco only to find himself shoved aside at Erie. This was worse. It was worse because during the same week that Grant & Ward collapsed and shook Wall Street, a U.S. senator tried to make political hay by putting Gould in jail. As stocks were crashing, Senator George Edmunds of Vermont put forward a bill ordering the attorney general to press criminal charges against Gould and other directors of the Union Pacific for ignoring the Thurman Act, the law requiring the Union Pacific to immediately repay its government debt. The Thurman Act was the law of the land. The Supreme Court had upheld it. But Gould was thumbing his nose at it. He still paid dividends to shareholders instead of paying the Treasury.

Battling not one but two of the scariest crises of his career, Gould met with the other Union Pacific directors in search of savior, for someone to send to Washington and beg. Gould, of course, couldn't do it. The populists considered him the pilferer in chief. Union Pacific president Sidney Dillon, tainted by Crédit Mobilier, was no better. Fortunately, there was one among them who still had credibility, Charles Francis Adams. Now one of the railroad's largest investors, he was linked in the public mind with reform. His successful military career added to his stature. And who better to lobby Congress than a member of America's royal family? Gould had not forgotten "A Chapter of Erie" and the part where Adams accused him of "unspeakable effrontery." But he agreed with the choice. Adams was just the man to rescue the Union Pacific and keep lawmakers off Gould's heels.

Adams took the train to Washington and found Edmunds in combat mode. Edmunds showed Adams a report that he kept in his desk under lock and key. It chronicled in great detail the railroad's disregard for taxpayers. Edmunds threatened to release the report if the Union Pacific didn't come around. Adams appeared before his Senate committee and groveled. He said if the government enforced the Thurman Act, the railroad would go under and small investors would be wiped out. He reminded them of the toll on employees, thousands of whose jobs a bankruptcy could jeopardize. Then Adams said something that must have shocked even himself. Even worse, he continued, Jay Gould would be wiped out. Gould might deserve ruin, Adams said. Taxpayers should by no means cry for him. But if Gould failed, the failure of Grant & Ward would look trivial. The failure of Gould would be like the failure of Jay Cooke, a catalyst for another Long Depression. Gould—a man Adams himself had condemned as a monster—needed to be saved for the good of the republic. Edmunds persisted. The republic, he believed, could survive even if Gould did not. There were also principles involved. It would be unconscionable to let Gould squirm out from under the law.

It was up to Senate majority leader George Frisbie Hoar to bring the Edmunds bill to a vote. Hoar represented Adams's home state of Massachusetts. He agreed to table the Edmunds bill on two conditions. The first: Union Pacific had to participate in a deep investigation of its affairs. Once Congress had all the facts, it would consider what to do about the Thurman Act. The second demand was extraordinary, especially in a time when laissez-faire was supreme: Gould, Dillon, and the entire board had to resign and Adams himself had to take over from Dillon as president.

For Gould, there was no point in arguing. Regretting that he had to put his transcontinental ambitions on hold but having no choice, he gave his consent. He had been the guiding force behind the Union Pacific for more than ten years. He had pressured it into the costly merger with the Kansas Pacific. But he had also increased its revenue, doubled its miles, and raised its banner in several new states. Gould did this while beating back competitors, preserving the railroad's monopoly over the Rockies, and, if one overlooked the interest charges the company should have been paying the government, turning a profit. Now he was out.

Gould's Union Pacific problem was solved, at least for now. But his fight against Wall Street remained unresolved. He still had the banks chasing him for cash. Facing insolvency and the fearless Woerishoffer trying to push him off the ledge, he cabled William Vanderbilt. He urged Vanderbilt to support the market with some buy orders. Confidence was the problem, Gould believed. An expression of faith from the country's richest man could turn the mood and lift stock prices. Vanderbilt, despite his antipathy to Gould, had answered such calls in the past. He refused this time, essentially telling Gould to get lost. It was as if he would rather forgo profits than let Gould wiggle out of another jam. "I guess I won't buy anything for the present," Vanderbilt wrote back.[5]

What happened next comes from an account in the *Herald* written years after the fact. The story might not be true in every detail but the substance of it makes sense. According to the *Herald*, Gould responded with a show of force. He sailed aboard the *Atalanta* to Long Branch, a summer retreat on the Jersey Shore where Woerishoffer was in residence. Woerishoffer had a paper profit of $1 million on his Western Union short sale. He could either close the position and realize the profit or keep pounding the stock, force Gould to sell even more and make even more money for himself. Gould sent an emissary ashore with an ultimatum. The messenger said Gould was willing to sell Woerishoffer all the Western Union stock he needed to cover his position for $2.5 million—a price that would net the short seller more profit than if he bought on the open market. But if Woerishoffer refused, Gould would file for bankruptcy. Gould's man pulled a bankruptcy petition from his pocket, already drawn up and signed. Woerishoffer took the deal. He didn't want to cause a panic and damage his other investments.

Woerishoffer considered the money he paid Gould a brandy shot for a dying man. It wouldn't save him, only make his death less painful. Gould was still dangerously overexposed; his collateral terrifyingly thin. Feeding this narrative, the *Herald* reminded readers of Villard's failure a year earlier. It saw Gould "hastening towards the same termination—a grand collapse."[6]

DURING THE SIEGE of Petersburg during the Civil War, Union forces burrowed under rebel fortifications and packed the end of the tunnel with dynamite. Grant planned to break the siege by blowing the rebels sky-high. A colonel lit the fuse. Kaboom! The explosion blasted a Confederate regiment to bits and left a hole two houses deep.

With his back to the wall, Gould plotted a similar trick for the short sellers. In another colossal show of nerve, he took all his money—everything he had—and, instead of paying back creditors, he stuffed a tunnel with explosives by going all in on a single stock, Missouri Pacific, the backbone of his rail network. It was a high-risk, Hail Mary move. He already owned a majority of its shares and short interest was high. By buying more, he might be able to corner it, pocket a profit, and pay the banks. But if he ran out of money before perfecting the corner, he'd be left with nothing to repay what was essentially a severely overdrawn checking account. The banks would foreclose. He'd be finished.

Undaunted, he commanded his brokers to buy all the Missouri Pacific they could. Their buying pushed the price from 64 to 100 and pinned it there. In the siege of Petersburg, some rebels died in the blast but enough survived to, in the words of one Confederate general, "turkey shoot" Union soldiers who emerged from the tunnel. Gould fared better. Woerishoffer had already covered his shorts. But other short sellers hadn't been as careful. Gould obliterated them. He sold at a fantastic profit and repaid his creditors. He was saved.

The close call changed Gould. He didn't want to end up broke and disgraced like Daniel Drew. Nor did he want to be like Jay Cooke, surviving on the gifts of friends. Nor did he want to find himself "in a stupor" like Henry Villard, nor ruined like President Grant, nor, like Trollope's character Augustus Melmotte, who killed himself by drinking poison. Gould declared an end to his life as a trader. No more speculation. No more going into debt to maximize his profits. From then on, he'd be nothing but a railroad man. "I am out of the Street and nothing whatever could induce me to go back into it," he told the *Tribune*.[7] Few believed him.

THIRTY

THE STRIKE

I n the spring of 1886, Gould was on the *Atalanta* touring the Caribbean. He loved his yacht, loved being on the water, and, most of all, loved being out of reach. Stocks might crash. Companies might fail. But as long as he was aboard *Atalanta*, dozing in a deck chair, book on his lap, he could forget his troubles. All was calm on the water. The danger was onshore.

By the time Gould reached Havana, he had been at sea two months. He tied up at the port, not far from the old Baroque cathedral that claimed to house the bones of Christopher Columbus. He was twelve hundred miles from home, gazing upon white-sand beaches and palm trees. He probably felt a world away from the bustling corner of Broad and Wall Streets.

A telegram jolted him back to reality. It was from H. M. Hoxie, the general manager who ran his western railroads. Gould looked at the note and learned about what came to be called the Great Southwest Railroad Strike. Frustrated by management's refusal to negotiate with their union, workers at Gould railroads in St. Louis, Fort Worth, and other cities were torching depots, tearing up tracks, and draining the boilers of steam engines. While Gould was floating in azure waters and listening to the happy squawks of seagulls, freight waited in the yards. The strike was in its third week by the time Gould got word.

As a news story, the strike was bigger than Gould and the workers because it stoked fears about the radical left. Irish Republicans had recently bombed London Bridge, Parliament, and the Liverpool police barracks. In Germany, Marxists were calling for revolution and stirring protests in the cities. Back at home, New York railcar operators, Pennsylvania coal miners, and Baltimore factory workers walked out demanding better treatment. That single year alone brought 1,400 strikes. European radicals played to the frustration over working conditions and the resentment over wealth disparity. A German immigrant named Johann Most won a following for his book *Science of Revolutionary Warfare.* It told how to make bombs, poisons, and chemical weapons. A Chicago gun dealer reported a brisk business with militant socialists. "Socialist bodies in this city have all the arms, powder and ball for a stubborn and bloody battle," he said.[1]

VIOLENCE WAS THE last thing Terence Powderly wanted. Powderly led the Knights of Labor, the nation's largest union. A high-minded organization that took its cues from the New Testament, the Knights fought to give workers a better shake by creating a cooperative commonwealth with worker ownership of factories, mines, and railroads. The Knights believed in temperance. Because it was the right thing to do, they believed in nonviolence. Because it would free up time for self-improvement, they believed in the eight-hour day. Membership induction ceremonies were held in secret, cloaked in ritual, and echoed religious conversions.

Powderly was the opposite of a brawny union boss. He wore glasses and read as much as Gould. A labor newspaper said he looked like a poet. Before taking the job with the Knights, he was mayor of Scranton, Pennsylvania. He earned $1,500 a year as mayor. He earned $400 a year with the Knights. He took the pay cut because he believed in the cause.

A year before, Gould employees across the Southwest had struck over a pay dispute. Before the strike, a freight handler or switchman made $1.50 a day. That's wasn't much but it was enough. Rent at a boardinghouse cost 50 cents a day. The rest covered food, whiskey, and tobacco with some left to send home. There was nothing left to send home after Gould cut their pay.

The Knights hadn't called the 1885 strike. But Powderly took it upon himself to bargain with Gould in New York. With the public overwhelmingly against him, Gould agreed to restore wages and, more significantly, to bargain with the Knights to settle future grievances. The fight left Powderly bedridden, but the victory made him a hero. "No such victory has ever been secured in this or any other country," wrote the *St. Louis Chronicle*.[2] The *Richmond Labor Herald* took a shot at Gould. "What a contrast!" it wrote. "Brother Powderly, as noble, liberal hearted, fine-looking man as this country can boast of, standing face to face with that little insignificant-looking specimen whose gold is his god."[3]

Membership in the Knights swelled from 100,000 to 700,000. The group became the largest labor organization in the country and the only one with a national membership. With representation like that, the Knights looked invincible. Martin Irons, a St. Louis railroad mechanic and well-spoken Scottish immigrant, had joined the Knights in the wave that followed the 1885 settlement with Gould. He quickly became one of the organization's leaders. He shared Powderly's vision of a cooperative commonwealth. The difference was timing. Irons was in a hurry. The Knights, he believed, were strong enough to confront the capitalists, show them who was boss, and accelerate the march of socialism. He wanted nothing less than for workers and employers to be full partners. "I wanted something substantial," he later told Congress.[4]

Looking for an excuse to strike, Irons found his opportunity after Gould's Texas & Pacific fired a Knight in Marshall, Texas, for attending a union meeting. Irons called on all workers throughout the Gould system to walk out and picket the railroads. Workers in five states heeded the call. "Traffic throttled," read a headline in the *St. Louis Post-Dispatch*. "The Gould System at the mercy of the Knights of Labor."[5]

Powderly didn't know the strike was coming. When he found out the next day, he was horrified. If he knew one thing about strikes is they could spin out of control. He had not forgotten the horrors of the Great Railroad Strike of 1877. After eastern railroads cut wages, workers downed their tools, smashed trains, blew up bridges, and paralyzed rail traffic for months. Egged on by rail bosses, troops moved in. "Give them a rifle diet for a few days and see how they like that kind of bread," said Tom Scott of the Pennsylvania Railroad.[6] The National Guard, aided by federal troops and vigilantes, restored order by shooting dead scores of strikers.

Powderly worried about a repeat. There was no telling what could happen after workers walked out. He faulted Gould as much as Irons. It seemed to him that Gould had engineered trouble to worm his way out of the 1885 agreement. "The railway companies precipitated the fight themselves," he said.[7]

Hoxie, Gould's man in St. Louis, couldn't settle the strike without consulting the boss. But the boss was out of touch in the Caribbean— intentionally out of touch, Powderly believed. The strike gathered power like a storm over St. Kitts. When Gould finally returned, he invited Powderly to Fifth Avenue to talk it through. Powderly was staying at the Astor Hotel downtown. He paid the nickel fare and rode uptown on Gould's elevated railway. He was surprised when Gould said he would stick to their original deal. As far as he was concerned, he had never strayed from it. Sure, there was specific instances where his railroads breached the terms. But the same could be said of the workers. Gould promised that if Powderly called off the strikes, he would tell Hoxie to arbitrate. He drafted a statement for Hoxie and showed it to Powderly. "We see no objection to arbitrating any difference between the employees and the company, past or future," it said. For his part, Powderly wired Martin Irons, the Knights' leader in St. Louis. "President J. Gould has consented to our proposition for arbitration," he wrote. "Order the men to resume at once."[8] Powderly praised the merits of one-on-one negotiations. "It's a pleasant ending," he told the newspapers. "The result we attain is almost always sure to come when the heads of institutions come together."[9]

The country awoke the next morning to celebratory headlines. "The Great Strike Ended," announced the *Times*. The *Sun* ran a flattering profile of Powderly. "The Knights recognized," it wrote.[10] Strikers returned to their jobs, thrilled that Powderly had for the second time bested the Wizard of Wall Street.

But there was a glitch. When the men came to work, guards turned them away. Contrary to what they were told, there was no deal. Powderly hurried to Gould's office at Western Union to straighten things out. Gould apologized for the misunderstanding. He said that he had not agreed—nor had he ever agreed—to let the Knights negotiate on behalf of all the workers. When he talked about arbitration, he only meant his willingness to arbitrate grievances with individual workers, not with the Knights as a whole.

Powderly felt conned. At their earlier meeting, Gould had been clear about accepting collective bargaining. But now Powderly realized that Gould wanted to make him look like a fool by announcing the strike was over. Having no choice but to stand his ground, Powderly wrote a note to his men in the field. "Gould the money monarch is dancing over the grave of our order," it said. "Let no man grow weary until, like Goliath, our giant is dead at our feet." It was a call to arms. "Gould must be overthrown," read a newspaper ad placed by Knights in Texas. "Workmen of the world. Marshal yourselves for the battlefield."[11]

Gould, too, was finished talking. State governors, under pressure from business, had taken his side, stepping up efforts to get the trains moving. Gould told the press he should have taken on the Knights sooner.

EAST ST. LOUIS isn't in Missouri but in Illinois, on a swampy patch of land on the east bank of the Mississippi. In the 1880s, it had a population of five thousand except, the story went, on election day when it swelled to rig the outcome. "It bore the reputation for being the wickedest community in the country," the *Times* wrote. "When a Missourian is too bad for his own state, he goes to East St. Louis." A dozen railroads converged on the city. They came for one reason: the bridge over the Mississippi that opened the door to the West. A showdown was coming between the strikers and the management, predicted the *Times*, and it would occur on the bridge. "The bridge," it wrote, "will ultimately be the battleground on which the fight will be determined."[12] It quoted an unnamed member of the Knights' executive board. "This will be a fight to the death," he said. "Stay in St. Louis if you are anxious to see a fight."[13]

Gould was a hardcore capitalist. He believed unions held back the ambitious, that organized labor protected loafers, and the market should determine wages. He believed the eight-hour day, an idea then on the political agenda, was foolish. "Your best men do not care how many hours they work," he said. "They are looking to get higher up."[14]

Expanding on the theme, he later told a congressional committee that the best workers didn't complain about pay. They put in extra hours, saved their money, and went into business for themselves. As for immigrants who complained about pay, they should go home. "They get better pay here than in any other country, and that is why they come here," he said. Government should stay out of the labor market, he said. "People who think they can regulate all mankind," he said, "cause much trouble to both employers and employees."[15] For what it's worth, there is no evidence that he said "I can hire half the working class to kill the other half," a quote attributed to Gould that is found online and even in recent books on labor history.[16]

The confrontation in East St. Louis came not on the bridge but in the nearby railyards. Hundreds of strikers and sympathizers convened at City Hall and spilled out onto the street to take positions on the tracks. No trains got in or out. About a dozen guards stood by, protecting property of the Louisville & Nashville, a railroad not owned by Gould but one whose workers had walked out in sympathy. The mob taunted the guards. They called them names. Some threw rocks. A protester pulled a gun. "Kill the cowboy!" cried a guard.[17] He fired into the crowd. Others joined him. The air filled with gunpowder smoke and the cries of victims. Seven protesters fell dead.

Pursued by the mob, the guards ran across the bridge and surrendered to St. Louis police. Illinois governor Richard Oglesby sent in troops and declared martial law. The railroad yards became a tent city. With soldiers to protect them, trains pulled out unmolested. Powderly telegraphed Gould. "By your action in refusing the peaceful negotiations," he wrote, "you and you alone must be held responsible for the death of these innocent people."[18]

Public support for the strike, already thin, collapsed after East St. Louis. The strike wasn't about something tangible like a wage cut. It was about the vague matter of recognition. Was that really worth striking over? As for this fellow Martin Irons, the union leader who called the strike, the papers said he was a drunk and a wife beater. Texas governor John Ireland called for trains to be put back in service "even if it takes every man in the state who can bear arms."[19] Realizing the cause was lost, the Knights called off the strike.

A few months later, Gould read in the papers that Powderly was in New York and invited him over. Gould introduced him to his daughters and inquired about his health. "I didn't ask you here to quarrel but to say that it is my ambition to build up a railroad system such as the world never saw before," Gould said. "You know I can't take it with me when I die and I don't want to. I want to leave it as a heritage to the American people."[20] Powderly was suspicious. Gould, he believed, wanted to soften him up in for future battles. But he had no doubt about Gould's ambition and his dream for railroad domination.

GOULD HAD NO love of organized labor, but he had a soft spot for certain employees. He doted on Silas Clark, who had been his superintendent at Union Pacific. He had repeatedly urged Clark to delegate and spare himself the wear and tear of operating minutiae. "In regard to your health let me advise you to do no work or think of business after 4 p.m. and get someone to read to you to sleep nights," he wrote to Clark. "I do that and get a good night's sleep in that way."[21]

Gould also looked after promising young associates. Not all appreciated his embrace. Edward Bok worked for Gould as a stenographer when he was eighteen. Bok later became a Pulitzer

Prize–winning writer, the editor of *Ladies' Home Journal*, and the person credited for the term "living room." For now, he was writing letters for Gould, a job that made him privy to each of his boss's transactions on the stock exchange. One day he asked Gould if he could piggyback on his trades. When Gould said nothing, he took it as permission. Bok bought shares through a broker he knew from church. The broker noticed the young man was a remarkably successful investor. The stocks he bought always went up. He followed Bok's trades, buying shares for himself and his clients on margin.

During the battle between American Union and Western Union, Gould pounded Western Union by publicly denying plans to end the price war. All the while, Gould was buying Western Union's stock, confident he would ultimately merge the two companies. Bok bought Western Union for himself. So did the broker and the broker's clients. As Western Union kept falling on Gould's denials, Bok's followers received margin calls. The broker agonized over what to do. Should he sell the stock and save his business or should he risk everything for a big score?

After church one Sunday, he took Bok aside, told him he was deep in Western Union and asked for reassurance. Bok squirmed. He refused to reveal the source of his intelligence. After some nervous back-and-forth, he told his friend to hang tight. Three days later, Gould announced the merger. Western Union soared. Bok felt more relief than joy.

Gould later asked Bok to take notes at a Saturday afternoon meeting. At noon, Gould told him he could get something to eat and come back in an hour. While Gould and the others ate a splendid meal, Bok spent his train fare on three apples. Back at the meeting, Bok took notes until late in the evening. His transcript reached forty pages. Gould asked him to write up the notes and deliver them to his house by eight the next morning. Bok walked home to Brooklyn and spent all night working. He left his home at sunrise for Gould's house on Fifth Avenue. When Bok delivered the notes, transcribed in flawless handwriting, Gould took them without a thank-you. In his memoirs, which Bok wrote in the third person, he voiced outrage. "Edward felt that this exceeded the limits of fair treatment," he wrote.

Not long after, Bok told Gould Wall Street wasn't for him. He'd be happier in another industry. "And what business is that," Gould asked.

"The publishing of books," Bok said.

"You are making a great mistake," Gould said. "Books are a luxury."

Gould told him there was no money in books because readers could get them for free at libraries. "A promising boy such as you are, with his life before him, should choose the right sort of business, not the wrong one," Gould said, offering him a raise. Bok left Gould for a job with the publisher Henry Holt.

Years later, Bok was boating on the Hudson with some friends and sailed past Lyndhurst. Gould's orchids were famous. When his friends said they wanted to see the greenhouse, Bok sent a note ashore. Gould was home. He invited them to dock and led the group on a tour. Afterward, Gould asked to talk to Bok alone. "Come and sit down with me," he said.

"Well," Gould began. "I see in the papers that you seem to be making your way in the publishing business. I have always felt you had it in you to make a successful man. But not in that business. You were born for the Street." Gould said he envisioned a financial career for Bok and that it wasn't too late to come back. Bok declined. "He felt that his path lay far apart from that of Jay Gould—and the farther the better!"[22]

THIRTY-ONE

A Gould Wedding

Gould was at Lyndhurst one September afternoon in 1886 when he ordered the household staff to meet in the parlor. Reverend Choate, the pastor at the Presbyterian church in Irvington, stood at Gould's side. Although it was a Tuesday, Choate wore his clerical collar and the black robe used to celebrate the mass. Ellie and the children joined them. As the servants gathered in the glow of the stained glass windows, they saw Ellie sobbing.

The papers had been reporting gossip that George Gould, Gould's firstborn, had secretly become engaged. New Yorkers were shocked that the rumored bride wasn't a Murray Hill debutante or the daughter of a Gould executive, but someone who, in Victorian New York, was only one step above a prostitute on the social scale. She was an actress. This was a scandal the family could ill afford. The Goulds had two unmarried daughters. Ellie feared George's marriage to an actress would further tarnish the family's reputation and destroy the chances of the girls making good matches.

Gould made an announcement. "George is to be married," he said.[1] The wedding would occur that very moment. No guests, no music, no celebration. Just a light lunch after the service. The staff could watch the ceremony. Then it was back to work.

Edith Kingdon, twenty-two, was beautiful and talented. A Canadian from a modest background, she toured with a Boston theater company before her installation at New York's Daly Theatre where she turned in a winning performance as Mrs. Margery Gwynn in *Love on Crutches.*

Ellie was distraught, but Gould was understanding. He had come from nothing and appreciated that Kingdon had made her way in a tough profession. "She went on the stage to earn her own living and that, I think, was very much to her credit. I honor her for it," he said.[2]

Under the gaze of the mystified staff, the couple exchanged vows and Gould signaled his approval by kissing Kingdon on the head. She retired from the stage and, a year later, gave birth to Jay Gould's first grandchild, Kingdon, and a year after that, a second grandson, Jay Gould II. Ellie loved the grandchildren but never recovered from the shock of her son having married an actress. She was long dead when Jay Gould II won the Olympic gold medal for court tennis at the 1908 London games, defeating England's Eustace Miles in the finals on the strength of a withering backhand.

GOULD SUFFERED FROM facial neuralgia, a chronic neurologic condition that made his cheeks and forehead feel as if they were pricked by needles. He was also afflicted by a persistent cough. His personal physician, Dr. John Munn, ordered a vacation. Gould reluctantly agreed to spend a few days yachting aboard the *Atalanta* with his family. They cruised down the coast, past Philadelphia, into Chesapeake Bay, and up the Potomac before tying up on the Virginia side at Mount Vernon. "I'm not dead yet," Gould told reporters.[3]

Colonel Harrison Dodge, the superintendent of Mount Vernon,

gave the Goulds a tour. Jay was struck by the sweeping lawn and the balanced proportions of the architecture. Gould felt a personal connection. His ancestors had left England in 1647, ten years before Washington's family had made its own voyage to America. Gould's great-grandfather Abraham had been a lieutenant colonel in Washington's Continental Army. He fought in the Revolutionary War and died in the Battle of Ridgefield. The prior owner of Lyndhurst had put a life-size bust of Washington inside the foyer of the mansion. Gould kept it when he moved in, a reminder of his family's storied past.

As Gould walked the grounds, his attention turned to a serene parcel of land in the distance. Dodge told him the owners planned a tavern for the site. Washington himself had been one of the country's largest whiskey makers and might not have objected. But Gould was incensed. There would be no tavern at Mount Vernon as long as he could help it. Washington was the father of the country. His memory shouldn't be insulted with drunkenness. On the spot, Gould said he would buy the property and donate it to the Mount Vernon Ladies' Association, the group that preserved—and still preserves—Mount Vernon.

At the time of the gift, Rockefeller and Carnegie were urging rich people to give away their money, encouraging their fellow titans not to take it with them. Gould saw no rush to commit. Unlike Rockefeller and Carnegie, who were already semiretired in their fifties, Gould was still absorbed by business. He wasn't a miser. When yellow fever hit Memphis in 1878, killing more than a third of the city's 47,000 residents, Gould wired $5,000 to a Memphis aid association and kept giving as the city struggled to recover. "Keep at your noble work until I tell you to stop," he wrote to the organization's leadership. "I will foot the bill."[4]

Like his gift to Memphis, Gould's gift to Mount Vernon was

made on a whim and done without publicity. If Fisk had made the donation, he would have hired a band, put on his colonel's outfit, and hosted a reception. Carnegie would have attached a plaque with his name. Gould took a different approach. He told Dodge to keep his gift secret. Gould's record is replete with one-off gifts like the ones to Memphis and Mount Vernon. He never got credit because he didn't want credit. To deter solicitors and cranks, he wanted the public to think he gave away nothing. He'd let others get the glory. "Mr. Gould has many properties," said one of his stockbrokers, "but a brass band is not one of them."[5] The *New York Tribune* saw it the same way. "He never bought a eulogy," it wrote after his death.[6]

THIRTY-TWO

IN THE DOCK

A gang of masked men hopped from their horses and boarded a Missouri Pacific train north of Austin. They fired shots in the air, piercing the car roofs. Passengers screamed. Working their way front to back, the robbers cleaned the riders out of their cash and jewels.

The gang leader looked like a cowboy in his chaps, Stetson, and mask. When he got to the train's mailroom, he thought for a moment and, in a flash of patriotism, decided to leave the postal clerk and his safe alone. He explained that he wasn't after "Uncle Sam's money, only Jay Gould's."[1]

The Pacific Railway Commission had the same intent. The commission was the investigative panel the Senate created following the prior year's debate over the Thurman Act. The Union Pacific owed the government $46 million. Officially, Congress empaneled the commission to determine how to get back the money. Unofficially, the commission met to crucify Gould. It subpoenaed dozens of witnesses in search of evidence to put him away.

The committee met in a conference room at 10 Wall Street across from the stock exchange. After the first few days of testimony, the committee had little to show for itself. When Russell Sage testified, he shuffled in his chair and looked guilty, but said nothing useful. Union Pacific president Sidney Dillon was "sphinx-like," evading questions. The next day was more interesting. The first witness, the banker John Pondir, accused Gould of bribing a senator.

Gould walked into the hearing room looking relaxed. He had survived the short-seller attack after the Grant & Ward collapse and was again on firm financial ground. True to his word, he had sworn off speculation and had whittled down his debts to the point where he could survive the worst market panic. Gould wore a dark gray coat and a business suit. His hair and beard were neat and trim after a visit to the barber. Pondir was still being questioned when Gould took a seat to wait his turn.

Pondir finished and looked surprised when he turned to see the man he had just accused of bribery. "Good morning Mr. Gould," Pondir said awkwardly, shaking Gould's hand. "I didn't say all I know, but left something for you."[2]

Gould took Pondir's place at the witness table, put on gold-rimmed glasses, and studied some notes before rising to take the oath. The chairman of the commission was former Pennsylvania governor Robert Pattison. He had already decided Gould belonged in jail. He sat beside Gould at the head of a long table, staring at Gould and trying to read him.

E. Ellery Anderson, a New York corporate lawyer, led the questioning. He dove into a dissection of one of Gould's masterpieces, his merger of equals between the Kansas Pacific and the Union Pacific.

"Did you make any transactions in the stock market with a view towards the consolidation?" Anderson asked.

"Not a share," Gould said.

"Did you hear of any objection on the part of the government to the consolidation?" Anderson said.

"No sir," replied Gould.

Anderson wanted Gould to admit that the merger harmed the Union Pacific and, hence, taxpayers. "How did it affect the government?" Anderson asked.

"It put a stronger company behind the debt than ever before," Gould said.[3]

Gould's facial neuralgia was acute during the hearings. Despite the discomfort, Gould gave a cool performance, easily swatting away questions about dates and numbers. He gave vague answers or outright denials when accused of anything damning.

Gould endured three days of questions. In contrast to Sage and Dillon, Gould proved himself an unflappable and even entertaining witness. He sprinkled his comments with investment advice, reminding that growth offered more upside than dividends. "We should consider the future more," he said. "That's the way I've made my money." He drew laughs with a story about a small railroad he had bought in Colorado. When he inspected it, he saw trains busily rolling in and out of the switchyard. He later learned the bustle was all for show. "I thought it was doing a big business," he said. "Afterward, I learned they had kept the freight back a week to impress me." He talked about a Union Pacific conductor who survived an Indian scalping. When Gould met the man, the conductor lifted his cap to reveal a deep scar that stretched the length of his head. Gould's point? The brave men of the Union Pacific advanced the cause of Manifest Destiny and American greatness. The western railroads had their faults, but they delivered taxpayers infinite benefit. "The government has received in advantage more than it paid for the road," Gould said.[4]

On the final day of testimony, Anderson asked Gould point-blank if he broke the law by paying dividends in defiance of the Thurman Act. "Did the Union Pacific ever violate the provision of the law that no dividend should be paid out except out of net earnings?"

"We were exceedingly careful not to do so," Gould said.

Gould's testimony was a triumph. He impressed observers as forthcoming and credible. His anecdotes and easy demeanor made him sympathetic. Never before had so many words spilled from Gould's mouth in public. Even the *Times* put aside its hatred. "He was a charming witness," wrote its reporter.

The commission issued two reports. The majority report acknowledged the terrific weight of the government debt on the Union Pacific and favored easier payment terms. Chairman Pattison, however, wanted blood. In his dissent, he recommended revoking Union Pacific's charter and handling its assets to a new company, actions that would wipe out the shareholders. He thought that by bankrupting Union Pacific, he'd destroy Gould. What Pattison didn't know is that Gould had sold most of his stock after he resigned as president. Charles Adams and his Boston friends would suffer the loss, not Gould. Grover Cleveland, now in the White House, returned the commission reports without comment. He'd let Congress sort it out.

THIRTY-THREE

BAD NEWS

The *Umbria* sailed at noon. The Duke of Alba was on board. So was an Austrian count, a handful of barons, an aide to Queen Victoria, and a former Michigan governor. The ship could handle a few hundred passengers. Several times that gathered on the pier to say goodbye. Three Western Union board members—Sage, Dillon, and J. P. Morgan—came for a last-minute conclave with the ship's most famous passenger, Jay Gould.

A gaggle of reporters zeroed in on the financier. "What will you do without me?" Gould asked.[1] A reporter asked if he was taking along his physician, Dr. Munn. No, Gould said, no need.

The last time Gould crossed the Atlantic was in 1879, eight years earlier. On that trip, he left Ellie behind and took his son George, who was now twenty-three. This time, George stayed behind, with Sage and Dillon looking over his shoulder, to oversee the family's affairs. The papers said Ellie looked in "splendid health." The truth was she was exhausted. Sensing this might be her only chance to see Europe, she dragged herself up the gangplank along with four of her children, her sister, and her brother.

The Goulds had booked a six-room suite near the bow. It included the captain's quarters. The captain had agreed to stay elsewhere. Ellie was inspecting the rooms while Gould, dressed in a suit with a loose fit, lingered on the pier. The reporters asked when he was coming back. Gould said he didn't know. Maybe in three months. Maybe in four. It depended on circumstances. Looking up from his notepad, one of the reporters commented on the fine weather. October was coming to a close and New York was experiencing some of the clearest days of the season. Gould said he couldn't ask for more. "I hear that the Atlantic last week was as calm as a mill pond," Gould said. "I might just as well have gone in the yacht."[2]

Gould was lucky to escape New York. A group of Kansas Pacific bondholders had accused him of fraud. Their lawyer urged District Attorney Randolph Martine to indict Gould and keep him at home. The day before the trip, Martine informed Gould's lawyers he lacked evidence. Gould could go as he pleased.

The boat deposited the Goulds in Liverpool. From there, they took the train to London and stayed a week, visiting Big Ben and the Tower of London. Gould only knew London from Dickens and Trollope. He was captivated. Here was Clerkenwell, where Fagin lurked in *Oliver Twist*. Here was Grosvenor Square, where Trollope's character Melmotte hosted his fabulous ball for the Chinese emperor. Gould's favorite attraction was underground. The Circle Line had opened three years earlier. Steam locomotives were roaring through tunnels under the streets, carrying passengers in carriages lit with gas lamps. Gould was struck by the fares. While the Elevated only charged a nickel, the Circle Line charged the equivalent of 31 cents. That was for a short ride. It charged more for long rides. Gould was envious.

As he rode, he glanced at his pocket watch. The trains were slower than the Elevated. The worst thing was the air. Smoke from the coal-powered locomotives watered his eyes and made it hard to breathe. "I felt on some occasions as if my breath would be choked out of me," he said.[3] He believed New Yorkers would never go for an underground system, not with the Elevated working so smoothly.

When he reached France, it was the taxes that surprised him. The French taxed everything from eggs to potatoes to beef. He complained to a French reporter and said his visit to France made him love America all the more. In Italy, he griped about lazy telegraph operators who only sent messages when it suited them.

The *Atalanta* and its crew traveled to Europe on their own. In Marseilles, Gould met up with them, and visited Nice and San Remo where, he noted, the Emperor Frederick of Germany had recently stayed. He took in Leghorn and Florence in Tuscany. From Rome, he went to Sicily, then Greece. In Alexandria he received a telegram from George. Gould had instructed George not to cable him with stock prices. George disobeyed the order when the price of Burlington fell and looked attractive. Gould took no action. He wanted a lower price. After Malta, Gould stayed on the south coast of the Mediterranean and visited Tunisia and Algeria before passing through Gibraltar for the trip home. Tired but relaxed, he landed in St. Augustine, Florida, then a favorite destination of the New York elite. He had been gone five months.

"Well," he told a *Tribune* reporter, "I am home again and, as you can see, in pretty good health." The trip worked wonders, he said. He was ten pounds heavier. The facial neuralgia had vanished. "Yes sir," Gould said, "the enemy which has tormented me for so long has left me, somewhere deep in the Atlantic."

Back in New York, with the weight of business back on his mind, he slept poorly and ate little. He fell ill. This time, it was more than facial neuralgia or a head cold. This time, when he coughed into his handkerchief, he found flecks of blood. Dr. Munn told him hard nodules were forming in his lungs. They were eroding his blood vessels and would make it more difficult to breathe. He diagnosed tuberculosis. Gould was fifty-two years old. Had he been as healthy as Vanderbilt, Carnegie, or Rockefeller, he'd have at least three decades of life ahead of him. Instead, he had, at best, only a few years.

Gould discussed his illness with no one—not his wife, not his children, not his business associates. No one could know. If word got out, competitors would attack his properties on the stock market and in the field. They'd test his strength and seek to peel off his allies. They'd drag their feet in negotiations, hoping that time would deliver a less determined opponent.

Gould worried his symptoms would betray him. As much as he tried to keep low, he was one of the most scrutinized people in the country. The New York press kept a steady watch. Desperate for quotes good enough to earn a freelance fee, reporters camped outside his door on Fifth Avenue and just beyond the gates of Lyndhurst. The safe thing for Gould would be to hide because his appearance alone raised questions. The color had drained from his face and the weight loss made him look cadaverous. But being a shut-in would raise questions, too. Gould and Munn concocted a story. When asked about Gould's health, they'd say he suffered from indigestion. Nonetheless, a rumor circled that Gould had cancer.

GOULD HAD ALWAYS been thick-skinned. When Charles Adams attacked him in "A Chapter of Erie," Gould kept quiet. When the *Times* called him Mephistopheles, he said nothing. When Nast drew him as Shylock, he let it go. Apart from the time he poked fun at Vanderbilt and called him an old man, he avoided personal insults. He didn't see the point of engaging. Better to stay quiet, check his emotions, and wait for whatever it was to blow over. His friends marveled at his restraint. Self-control was a strong suit. He rarely if ever lost his temper. "Do you read the newspapers much Mr.

Gould," a reporter once asked him. "Oh yes," Gould said. "And see all the cartoons of you?" "Yes," Gould said. "Some of them are very funny and I enjoy them immensely."[4]

But as his health faded, he became cranky. In March 1887, *Herald* editor James Gordon Bennett accused George Gould of the legal but morally outrageous act of short selling Missouri Pacific. Enraged at the attack on his son, Gould shot back in the *Tribune* and accused Bennett of sour grapes because of his refusal to put Bennett on the Western Union board. Bennett responded by calling Gould a "ghoul in human form."[5] Gould dredged up publicity about Bennett's love affairs and called him a notorious "libertine" whose life had been "one of shame . . . a succession of debauches and scandals."[6] Determined not to give Gould the last word, Bennett declared Gould a "ruffian to wreck railways, subsidize newspapers, buy legislators, own judges, degrade American credit, acknowledge no law in dealing with his fellow men but the law of the highwayman."[7] Joseph Pulitzer, the new owner of the *World*, sided with his newspaper compatriot and urged prosecutors to indict Gould for swindling taxpayers while running Union Pacific. A grand jury met and elected to do nothing.

As Gould grew more ill, he tried to keep appearances by embarking on yet another western tour. The journalist Henry Davenport Northrop caught up with Gould in Colorado. Northrop had interviewed Gould several times in New York and was on friendly terms with him. They were standing near snowcapped Pikes Peak when Gould kicked at the rocks at his feet. He was thinking about ways to profit. "There are many chances to make money in this western country," he said. "That rock may contain valuable mineral. A little money and hard work will make any man independent, particularly in the West."[8] Gould looked toward Cheyenne Canyon, one of the most picturesque spots in the mountains, and lamented that he was too weak to hike it. Noting Gould's fascination with orchids, Northrop observed that Gould's love of nature went beyond the attraction of mineral wealth. "It is strange that this appreciation of pure and poetical things should exist in the soul of a man of such financial grimness," Northrop wrote. "But it was doubtless in Mr. Gould's nature before his life took on its acquired thirst for gold."[9]

In Memphis, Gould attended a public reception where city elders thanked him for his aid during the yellow fever epidemic and discussed plans for a Jay Gould University. In Chattanooga, he took a train up Lookout Mountain. In Winfield, Kansas, he answered questions about his health. "I feel first rate and have been taking three meals a day right along," he said. "I am feeling better than when I left New York."

Back in New York, he took his family to Saratoga where they rented two cottages at the U.S. Hotel. Gould dozed on the porch, had dinner in the public dining room, watched a circus parade, and took walks with his bodyguard Morosini. Dr. Munn gave him massages to help him sleep. The idyll was broken when Ellie suffered a stroke. She returned to Lyndhurst while Gould, thinking it might be his last chance, took his children to Roxbury to show them his boyhood home.

THIRTY-FOUR

---·◆·---

MORGAN

The Union Pacific wasn't the only railroad in financial trouble. Overbuilding had fueled murderous competition. One after another, railroads were going bankrupt. If left on its own, the market would sort it out. The healthiest railroads would combine and become stronger. The weak ones would liquidate, toss workers into the streets, leave shippers stranded, trash stock prices, and, because of the damage caused to banks and investors, throw the economy into recession. There had to be a better way. But the railroad men were too suspicious of each other to stop their throat cutting and the government, which in 1887 attempted a cure by passing the toothless Interstate Commerce Act, was incapable of bold action.

Charles Adams found inspiration in Germany. Under Prussian leadership, Otto von Bismarck had forged a world power from a collection of small kingdoms that had been feuding for a thousand years. If Germany could consolidate, so could America's railroads. "What's needed," Adams declared, "was a railroad Bismarck."[1]

It was a role Gould imagined for himself. He wanted to be the one to consolidate the industry, bring order to freight rates, create the seamless coast-to-coast connection, and reap the profits. But he was too sick to meet the challenge. With the industry in crisis, J. P. Morgan summoned the country's leading railroad and banking executives to his home. He'd try his hand at being Bismarck. Morgan was a year younger than Gould. Imperious and condescending, with an acne-scarred nose that looked like a raspberry and made him more intimidating, he had yet to embark on his buying spree of antiquities or commit his most famous act, that of stopping the Panic of 1907. But three years earlier, he had earned a reputation as a conciliator when, on a meeting aboard his yacht the *Corsair*, he forced the New York Central and the Pennsylvania to fix prices and stay out of each other's territories. If he could bring peace to New York and Pennsylvania with the Corsair Agreement, he could perhaps forge a truce everywhere else.

Gould stepped through Morgan's massive oak door at 219 Madison at 36th Street followed by Adams for the Union Pacific, George Roberts of the Pennsylvania, and Chauncey Depew of the New York Central and other Vanderbilt railroads. The men took up seats around a large table in Morgan's dining room. Gould shuffled in looking, in the words of Adams, "dreadfully sick and worn."[2] Adams didn't know it but Gould's wife, Ellie, had just suffered a second stroke. Gould had spent a sleepless night at her bedside, holding her hand and trying to will her back to health.

Gould struggled to concentrate as Morgan launched the meeting with a fiery attack on the railroad men. They were to blame, he declared, because they were the ones who overbuilt. They were the ones who cut rates and tried to save themselves by destroying others. "This is not elsewhere customary in civilized communities," he roared.[3]

George Roberts of the Pennsylvania fumed. "On behalf of the railroad people of this country, I object to this very strong language, which indicates that we, the railroad people, are a set of anarchists."[4]

The bankers were the anarchists, he said. Hungry for fees, they financed "blackmail roads," railroads created only for the purpose of selling to the established roads they threatened.

Adams took a philosophical view. He spoke up to blame human nature, citing "covetousness, want of good faith and low moral tone." Sounding like the preacher Henry Ward Beecher across the river in Brooklyn, he said greed was at the core. If the assembled were less greedy, they might make less money but they and society would be better off. "That is the whole thing in a nutshell," he said.[5]

Gould found the strength to speak. Exhausted, depressed, and terminally ill, he offered a solution. He suggested the creation of a super cartel involving all the railroads, endowed with the power to set rates and enforce compliance. Morgan dismissed the idea and moved on to his own scheme. He said if the railroads promised to stop fighting each other with discounts and new track, the bankers would promise not to finance redundant railroad lines. "I wish that distinctly understood," Morgan said.[6] The meeting adjourned without an agreement. They'd try again the next day.

Adams walked uptown with Gould. As they talked, looking like two old friends rather than enemies brought together by a cause, Adams floated a heretical idea. How about letting the Interstate Commerce Commission, the newly formed government agency, adjudicate disputes and enforce discipline? It was a neutral third party. By involving the commission, the railroads would eliminate public suspicion about collusion. It would be like Gould's super cartel but, instead of railroads enforcing order, the government would do it.

Gould perked up. "He picked up on the idea instantly," Adams said.[7] Gould agreed to put forward the idea himself the next day. He'd suggest letting the commissioners into industry meetings and having them "cooperate in the scheme." There was no other way. Neither bankers nor railroads would behave unless ordered by a higher authority. The Interstate Commerce Commission was, like it or not, a reality. Industry could use the muscle of the government to achieve objectives otherwise impossible.

Adams returned to his hotel excited for the dawn. With Gould on his side, he felt he could win over the crowd. He had found his railroad Bismarck. It was the federal government. It would impose rules formulated by technocrats informed by industry and labor. It was the framework that Adams, the apostle of regulation, had championed his entire life. He felt gratified that Gould agreed with him.

Back at Morgan's, Adams was eager for Gould to present the plan. But when he looked around for Gould, he couldn't find him. He wondered what happened. Gould eventually trudged in, looking more tired than the day before.

Adams encouraged Gould to speak. Heads turned. Morgan gave Gould time to compose himself. Gould could barely get the words out. His voice was feeble and his comments, Adams said later, were vague and did not "take hold." Where was the Gould of old, the vigorous pirate of lore?

Adams tried to make the case on his own. "I spoke the truth that was in me," he wrote.[8] Morgan and others were unmoved. They wanted nothing to do with bureaucrats meddling in their affairs. They instead agreed to create a self-regulating organization to maintain rates, adjudicate territorial disputes, and level fines on malefactors. They would take it upon themselves to enforce the rules. Morgan took the credit but the idea wasn't anything more than a watered-down version of Gould's original plan for a super cartel.

Gould was disappointed. He believed the enforcement mechanism needed more teeth. Morgan, however, thought he had another Corsair Agreement. Reporters had been waiting outside all day. Morgan threw open his front door and, with Gould on his heels, walked outside to make a statement. "It is the most important agreement made by the railroads in a long time," he said. "Think of it. All the competitive traffic of the roads west of Chicago and St. Louis placed in the control of about thirty men!"[9]

Peace lasted all of a month. Railroads were soon back to cutting rates. By the time the signatories met again in Chicago, the deal was effectively dead. "Is it worthwhile for us to be represented," Gould asked his lieutenant Silas Clark, "or should we just send flowers to the corpse?"[10]

THIRTY-FIVE

CHANGE AT THE TOP

About a month after Gould's meetings with Morgan, Ellie, her body ravaged by two strokes, suffered a paralytic attack and fell into a coma. Gould sat by her side, staring at her small, exhausted face. He hoped for a miracle. They had been together twenty-six years. She had given him six healthy children. The Goulds were rich and lived in comfort. But it wasn't always easy for her. She had to endure the snubs of the old-money New York elite, the people that used to be her tribe. She had to stand by as rivals, victims, and reformers dragged her husband's name through the gutter. Early in their marriage, with Gould up in Vermont resurrecting a railroad, she hardly saw him. Later, after they were financially secure, she sat home alone while Gould did his western tours. His fidelity was never in question. Enemies would have enjoyed exposing an affair. But there was not even a whisper about that. Gould tried to compensate for his time away by keeping regular hours when home. He always made it back to Fifth Avenue for dinner with the family. On nights when Gould, overwhelmed by the stress, wanted to eat in silence, it fell on Ellie to keep the children quiet. Others in her circumstances farmed out child rearing to nurses. She didn't. She raised them herself.

She was surrounded by family when she died the day after losing consciousness. She was fifty. From then on nothing mattered
to Gould except preserving his empire and preparing the children,
George in particular, to carry on without him. Done with speculation, he threw his energy into fortifying what he already owned.
He fired memos to Silas Clark about coal volumes, rail routes, and
departure times. He studied depot workflows and suggested ways
to relieve bottlenecks.

His immediate concern was Western Union. John Wanamaker, a
Philadelphia department store magnate, became postmaster general
in 1889 by vowing to shake things up. Upon taking office, he banned
the sale of lottery tickets through the mail because, he argued, lotter-
ies encouraged gambling. He banned the shipment of books through
the mail because some might be obscene. He fired thirty thousand
postal workers so he and political allies could award jobs to others.

Wanamaker also took aim at Western Union. He believed the
company had too much power and, for the interests of the country,
should be nationalized. He didn't say it, but he might have been
thinking about the 1884 election when Gould was accused of delay-
ing the transmission of vote totals over the Western Union wires.
Gould, the story went, wanted to give his candidate, James Blaine,
time for find more votes. As the delays dragged on, mobs marched
in front of the Western Union building calling for Gould's head.
Gould denied wrongdoing and unofficially declared an end to the
presidential contest by contacting Grover Cleveland and congratu-
lating him on his win.

Cleveland didn't move against Western Union. But now Wanamaker, appointed by President Benjamin Harrison, thought it
was time to corral the company. To prevent that, Gould called in
a favor. As it happened, Gould had donated $100,000—about $2
million in current money—to the Harrison campaign of 1888. Har-

rison told Wanamaker to back off. "The effect of your work," the president told Wanamaker, according to the *Times*, "is to deprive my administration of valuable friends—friends who deserve better treatment and are not to be slighted. To attack them is political insanity." The Western Union nationalization drive stopped dead. The *Times* threw in an opinion. "Mr. Gould never gives money for fun," it wrote.[1]

Gould offered no comment. But he was more open than most about what he expected of politicians. "It was the custom when men received nominations to come to me for contributions," he said when he was with Erie. "I made them and considered them good-paying investments for the company."[2]

The Plaza Hotel opened in New York on October 1, 1890, advertising itself as "absolutely fireproof." That same morning in Boston, Charles Adams awoke "in a regular panic." It was his reputation that was going up in flames. The Union Pacific had released ugly numbers the day before. The railroad had reported a loss, confirming fears about its viability. While most stocks were flat on the day, Union Pacific took another tick down, bringing its decline since the start of year to 20 percent. It was down more than half since Adams had recommended it on pages of the *Boston Advertiser.*

Rumors flew that Gould wanted to take back the railroad. Adams didn't believe it. The Union Pacific was a bigger company than when Gould bought it the first time. A takeover would be a "task of enormous proportions even for Gould," Adams wrote in his diary. Besides, Adams and his Boston friends owned a large block of the stock. Even if Gould got on the board, he wouldn't be able to oust him. "Rumors that Gould is making a drive at me," he wrote. "Let him drive!"[3]

Yet there was no denying that Union Pacific was in trouble. Adams used to call the Union Pacific the "Broadway of the West." Now with losses mounting, he called it a "skeleton in my closet," a "prison house," and "a valley of exasperation."[4] He only stayed because he feared humiliation.

Unable to sit still and leave his fate to outsiders, he jumped on a train to Omaha. He had long thought the real problem with the Union Pacific wasn't competition, overbuilding, low freight rates, or government debt. It was managerial incompetence. Try as he might, he had not been able to find a chief operating officer who met his standards. He had long ago fired Gould's man Silas Clark, declaring him a "monkey head" and a "henchman of Gould."[5] He found his own choices to be no better. One lacked "nerve and backbone," another was "a promoted brakeman with a brakeman's limitations," and a third was a "bewildered barnyard hen, which goes flapping and fluttering about in abject terror."[6] The only executives he liked were the young Harvard graduates he hired for the junior ranks. Unlike the monkey head, the promoted brakeman, and the flapping bird, he thought they could grasp the big picture.

After inspecting the books in Omaha, he concluded management wasn't solely to blame. In fact, no amount of management tinkering could save his railroad. Falling revenue and the government debt were too much to overcome. He left the city knowing his time as a railroad man was over. "As we pulled out of Omaha and I crossed the Missouri, I looked back on the city—its smoke rising against the glowing Western sky—and in my bones I felt it was the last time. I was nearing the end."[7]

BACK ON FIFTH Avenue, there was a scene at the Gould house. Gould informed his family that the rumors were true. He wanted to take another run at the Union Pacific. With the erosion in the company's stock, he could make a fortune if it recovered. Plus, he could use the railroad to make trouble for competitors of Missouri Pacific. He could, for instance, bar other railroads from access to the Union Pacific's bridge over the Missouri River. While the takeover would mean a lot of work, the task was manageable because, as Gould told his family, Sidney Dillon would assume the presidency and look after operations.

Alice Northrop, Gould's niece, begged Gould to let it go. Didn't he have all the money he needed? And what about his health? She didn't know about his disease, but anyone who looked at Gould could see he was unwell. The strain of running yet another railroad could kill him. But Northrop didn't understand her uncle. Illness hadn't changed his character. He always wanted more. A few days after Northrop's appeal, she and Gould were chatting when a butler came with a telegram. Gould read it carefully. There is no record of what it said, but it related to the railroad. "About the Union Pacific," he said to his niece, "I have decided to go ahead."[8]

After that, curious stories about the Union Pacific began appearing in the press. Some highlighted Union Pacific's falling revenue and its wretched financial condition. Others attacked Adams. "A general feeling prevails in railroad circles that Union Pacific is managed by Harvard graduates who have big heads and small experience," wrote the *New York Herald*.[9]

Recognizing the attack as a smear campaign likely organized by Gould, Adams accused unnamed short sellers of spreading lies to drive down the stock price. The Union Pacific, he said, had $2 million of cash in the bank. Yes, it had a lot of debt but it didn't have an interest payment due until the following year. "The whole pack, headed by Gould, are now at work to bring me down," he wrote to a friend.[10]

Luck favored Gould. In the middle of his bear campaign, the government released a report saying the Union Pacific, while still profitable, earned less than a dollar for every ten it owed the government. With debt like that, it wouldn't take much to topple the railroad into bankruptcy. On a typical day on the stock exchange, a couple thousand shares of Union Pacific traded hands. When the government released its report, forty thousand shares changed hands and its value slipped another 10 percent. It would have lost more except for the presence of a big buyer. Adams correctly surmised the buyer was Gould. "The Jaybird had me," he wrote.[11]

Just as he was accumulating shares, Gould caught another break. Argentina defaulted on its debts and brought down Baring Brothers, a giant London bank famous for having financed the Louisiana Purchase. The collapse panicked the market and, because Baring Brothers was the Union Pacific's primary lender, it was a double blow to the railroad. The share price fell further and Gould bought more shares.

Adams was ready to surrender but not to Gould. Looking for an alternative, he came to New York and met with Vanderbilt's man Marvin Hughitt at the Union League Club. Hughitt was sympathetic and agreed to take the matter to the family. While the Vanderbilts deliberated, Adams bought an engraving of a Meissonier portrait of a defeated Napoleon on his return from Russia, "it being suggestive of my recent experience."[12] The next day, Adams waited at another club, the Knickerbocker, to hear from Hughitt. Hughitt came late in the afternoon along with Fred Ames, the largest of the Boston shareholders. Hughitt said he was sorry. The Vanderbilts had no interest in making investments west of Chicago. They would not be buying the Union Pacific.

Adams went to see Gould the next day in his office. He found Gould to be "quiet, small, furtive and inscrutable." In what was the single most humiliating moment of his life and among the most gratifying for Gould, Adams told Gould he was done. If Gould wanted to give the Union Pacific another try, he was welcome to it. They set a date for the handover. Gould showed Adams to the door. "As we formally shook hands, the little man seemed to look smaller, meaner, more haggard and livid in the face and more shriveled up and ashamed of himself than usual," Adams wrote. "His clothes seemed too big for him, and his eyes did not seek mine, but were fixed on the upper buttonhole of my waistcoat. I felt as if in my hour of defeat, I was overawing him—and, as if he felt so, too."[13]

Adams felt the loss as a loss for his people—the well-bred, exquisitely educated nativists who played by the rules. "Today I ceased to be president of the Union Pacific and so ended my life of railroad work," he wrote. "Gould, Sage and the pirate band were scrambling on deck. As far as the management of railroads is concerned, I am the most discredited man in America, and my class is discredited through me, and that hurts."[14]

The triumph exhilarated Gould. He declared that he'd combine the Union Pacific with his other railroads to create the seamless transcontinental system that had long been his dream. When the press asked why, at his age, he'd want to do something so challenging, he said he couldn't help it. The vision of an end-to-end rail link between the East Coast and California was too beautiful to let go. Although he had once left the Union Pacific out of necessity, he never stopped loving it. "There is nothing strange or mysterious about it. I knew it very well when it was a child, and I have merely returned to my first love," he said. "I think we will have good times in the future."[15]

THIRTY-SIX

WOODLAWN

Gould's dreams for the Union Pacific were better suited for a young man than one who knew his time was up. In his enfeebled state it took all his strength to get out of bed. Sidney Dillon, reinstalled as president, was no help. Dillon was twenty-four years older than Gould. Now almost eighty, he was in poor health himself. The railroad drifted in the absence of leadership. Rumors of bankruptcy stirred anew. On the first anniversary of Gould's return, Union Pacific stock sold for two points less than the low price at which he bought it.

Gould had other headaches. The Rock Island, a Missouri Pacific competitor, had launched a price war. As the two fought for customers in Illinois, the Missouri Pacific suffered losses. Gould had owned the Missouri Pacific for a decade without ever once missing a dividend payment. At a board meeting, Russell Sage, Gould's frequent partner, urged paying the dividend by borrowing the money. Not wanting to put the railroad at risk, an outraged George Gould glared at Sage. "Suppose you put your hand down in your own pocket and paid it," he said.

"My own pockets? My own pockets?" Sage said in astonishment. "That's different."[1]

Gould watched in pain as his son and best friend shouted at each other. Falling short of breath, he gasped a few comments in support of George. Suddenly, he started shaking, unable to control himself. He collapsed unconscious into a chair.

Gould recovered but word of the episode slipped out. Adams, in Boston, heard about it the same day. The *Times* put the story on the front page. "Gould's Days Numbered," read the headline.[2] It recounted the dividend fight with a nearly verbatim transcript. Shares in Missouri Pacific fell on heavy volume.

Gould returned to the office the next day to show he was still breathing. The Missouri Pacific issued a statement declaring Gould's health was "about as usual." Sage described Gould's condition as "nervous prostration." Gould made a show of strength by attending the Westchester County Fair. He rode up on a buckboard, an open wagon that farmers used. He held the reins and guided the horse as if he was back in Roxbury. The *Times* reported that "he looked pale and thin."[3]

THE INVITATIONS WENT to Elihu Root, J. P. Morgan, Navy Secretary William Whitney, and Postmaster General John Wanamaker. One went to Cyrus Field. Another went to Russell Sage, who had just survived an assassination attempt; a madman blew himself up in Sage's office with the Money King standing only a few feet away. President Harrison got an invitation as did Julia Grant, the widow of President Grant.

Join us for a Christmas party, it said. Only the Vanderbilts and the Astors—the snobs who had been cruel to the Goulds—were excluded. As long as Gould made the decisions, they would never step foot into 579 Fifth Avenue.

Gould hated parties and he especially hated dress balls. Even in the best of times, he would rather answer a margin call than stand in a receiving line. But this party was different. Sick or not, he felt obliged to introduce his oldest daughter, Helen, to society before the tuberculosis killed him.

Helen was twenty-three. She was Gould's favorite. Reclusive like her father, she considered the Fifth Avenue crowd shallow. On the days Gould coughed into his handkerchief, she ministered to him. On nights he couldn't sleep, she read to him from Dickens, Scott, and Twain. They played bezique together and went to the opera. She filled her days with church and charity work.

Her status as a rich scion brought out cranks. Suitors wrote letters asking for her hand. "I have gone into the matrimonial market and your name is in my catalogue," wrote Joseph P. Megler, one of the cranks. He had also written to an eligible Vanderbilt. "Be kind enough to write me of your approval." [4] Others demanded money and made threats. Gould insisted on precautions. On carriage rides, he ordered her to stay on Broadway because Broadway was safer than side streets.

Gould wanted the Christmas ball to be perfect. When the day arrived, ferns, palms, holly, and mistletoe arrived from the Lyndhurst greenhouse. Munczi Lajos came with his Gypsy orchestra. Delmonico's came with food. President Harrison was a no-show. Almost everyone else came. Gould stood in line and greeted every guest. Afterward, he was satisfied that he had done his duty. Helen could expect invitations in return. Gould hoped one would lead to marriage.

Gould had another physical breakdown—this time at a Union Pacific board meeting. Despite his feeble condition, he took another western trip in the spring. He traveled aboard a customized Pullman as far as El Paso. The dry air did him good but the desert heat was overwhelming. He rode up the mountains to Pueblo.

Gould spent the summer out west and returned to New York in September. On October 26, he attended his son Edwin's wedding. The date had been moved up at his request. Gould feared he might not live to see it otherwise. He presented the bride with a diamond necklace. One night just after Thanksgiving, he went to Madison Square Garden to a horse show and came home spitting blood. "It was worth going to but I believe I have taken a cold," he told his niece Alice.[5] Dr. Munn told the family it wouldn't be long.

Gould's room was on the second floor next to his study and overlooked the conservatory. It was the same room where Ellie died three years before. Gould was in bed for a week, in and out of consciousness, before the press found out and posted reporters outside his door. The death watch was on. At 2 a.m. on December 2, 1892, he regained consciousness long enough to ask Dr. Munn to gather the staff so he could say goodbye. Gould died at 9:15 that morning.

His death wasn't a surprise. It had been clear to everyone he was just hanging on. The only mystery was the cause. Apart from Dr. Munn, only Sage, Dillon, and George knew the truth. The rest of the world only later learned it was tuberculosis.

Reporters filed their stories and, soon, newsboys were on the streets calling out his death. Black crepe was draped on the doorbell of the house. Black and white ribbons were hung on the cars of the Manhattan Railway. Downtown, a flag over the Western Union Building was lowered to half-staff. Gould's body was put in a rosewood casket, suspended on a bed of ice, like an oyster.

The invitation-only funeral was at the house. Hundreds of gawkers mingled outside. A trade in counterfeit tickets developed. Security shooed out intruders. George and Edith Gould sent a four-foot display of roses, hyacinths, and ferns. It stood near the casket on a pedestal with the word "Father" written with violets. An arrangement from a grandchild said "Grandpa." Helen Gould laid a bouquet of orchids on the center of the casket.

Gould's friends—Sage, Morosini, Dr. Munn, and the Seligmans—were there. So were Gould's rivals, including Huntington and Villard. Morgan came up from Madison Avenue. William Rockefeller, the cofounder of Standard Oil and the brother of John D. Rockefeller, also came to pay his respects. A string quartet played "Nearer, My God, to Thee."

After the funeral, the family boarded carriages and rode to Woodlawn Cemetery in the Bronx for the burial. The family watched as gravediggers spooned hot lead onto the edges of the coffin to seal the sides. In 1878, robbers had unearthed the remains of department store impresario A. T. Stewart from his plot at St. Mark's church and demanded ransom for the bones. Stewart's widow paid $20,000 for them. The thieves left the bones in a burlap sack on a country road upstate. The lead seal would let Gould's bones rest in peace.

Gould chose to be buried in what is now the most interesting cemetery in America. Bonaventure in Savannah, with its live oaks and Spanish moss, is spectacular for its ghostly, antebellum beauty. Arlington, with its miles of identical headstones spaced at equal intervals, is a humbling tribute to sacrifice that celebrates collective effort. Woodlawn celebrates individual achievement. There are headstones. But what hits visitors as they make their way through the winding roads, is the abundance of mausoleums and obelisks. In the nineteenth century, headstones were for ordinary people. The Jupiters buried at Woodlawn required marble crypts shaped like pagodas or, for those who sought status in verticality, pillars that looked imported from the Nile.

No mausoleum at Woodlawn is bigger than Gould's. With Doric columns, a sturdy pediment, and proportions that follow the Pythagorean ratios, it looks like the Parthenon. Other mausoleums, ones the size of garden sheds, sit close to one another. Gould's mausoleum, which occupies the highest ground in the cemetery, sits alone. It is surrounded by a lawn and encircled by a road that cuts it off from others. A giant weeping beech provides shade.

Some of Gould's friends are nearby, as if ready to consult if needed. Gould's longtime sidekick Sidney Dillon is there. So is August Belmont, Joseph Pulitzer, and another Gould contemporary, Herman Melville. Cornelius Vanderbilt is buried on Staten Island but a collection of his heirs is at Woodlawn.

Plots at Woodlawn are not only marked with names, but sometimes nicknames and even helpful explanations of how family members are related. Some grave sites feature portraits of the deceased in bas-relief. Others have photographs of the deceased inside the tombs. There are no pictures in the Gould crypt. Nor are there names. Like in life, Jay Gould wanted to keep people guessing.

While friends and gawkers went uptown for Gould's funeral, investors massed on Wall Street to see how his death would hit the market. A similar scene unfolded on Throgmorton Street near the London Stock Exchange. Who knew? Maybe bargains would emerge as the estate dumped stocks to pay debts. No such luck. Gould had put his affairs in order, paying back the banks, and, in case there was trouble, transferring millions' worth of assets into a trust protected from creditors. Rather than nosedive, the Gould stocks—Missouri Pacific, Western Union, Manhattan Railway, and Union Pacific—rose modestly. Unlike Vanderbilt, who gave almost all his money to a single heir, Gould split the pie. His will assigned George $15 million and gave him sole responsibility for the business. The other five children received $10 million apiece. Gould also gave them some simple advice: live off the interest and don't touch the principle.

THIRTY-SEVEN

AN APPRAISAL

There's a stretch of road by Woodlawn Cemetery where truckers pull over to sleep. You can hear the engines while standing under Gould's beach tree. The trucks carry freight that in the old days moved by rail. Nearby, commuters wait for the Harlem line trains just like in Gould's time. Much has changed in the century and a half since Gould heard their whistles. But there are still traces of how it used to be. With Jay Gould, the traces are all that's left.

We build monuments to those who do the impossible or save people from death. We build monuments to explorers, artists, scientists, and inventors. We build them for generals and fallen soldiers. We do not build monuments for businesspeople. It doesn't matter how many jobs they created. It doesn't matter how they changed the world. They have money. If they want statues, if they want people to stand before their frozen features and consider their magnificence, they can build the damn things themselves.

Zadock Pratt, Gould's early backer, commissioned a likeness of himself above a village in upstate New York. Vanderbilt paid for a statue at Grand Central. Jay Gould did not commission a likeness above Manhattan nor a statue outside the stock exchange. Nor did he build a concert hall in Midtown. Or a skyscraper. His monument was a career like no other. No one before or after locked up the money supply to bring down every stock on the exchange and profit from the decline. No one else ever held the country's gold market hostage. No one else used the tricks of Wall Street to grab control of the nation's most important communications business and to dominate many of the country's most essential transportation lines. Nobody other than Jay Gould, a poor country boy who fought ill health all his life, used the same mix of brains, guile, and brute force to build one of the country's great fortunes.

Gould did more than pile up wealth. In his prime, he was among the country's largest employers. While he put money in the pockets of lawmakers and judges, he also paid hundreds of thousands of engineers, switchmen, brakemen, mechanics, ticket takers, porters, conductors, coal miners, iron workers, cooks, telegraph operators, accountants, lawyers, secretaries, and clerks. He was not the most generous employer. He was quick to replace cheap labor with even cheaper labor. But his checks cleared, and he put food on the tables for families that might otherwise have gone hungry.

More broadly, he accelerated growth and helped steer the country on a course to become a world power. It was one thing for Horace Greeley to urge young men to go west. It was another to get them there. Gould was the master of sixteen thousand miles of railroad track, four thousand miles that he built himself. No other rail baron built more. The Ohio farmhand who dreamed of a plot of his own in Kansas. The New Jersey store clerk eager to open a shop with his name above the door. They boarded Gould's trains to start new lives. Sure, others would have sold them tickets if not for Gould. But that's like saying someone else would have refined crude oil if not for Rockefeller or rolled steel if not for Carnegie. That fact is it was Gould who did it. It's a rule of economics that productivity gains advance living standards. In the nineteenth century, railroads drove the advance. Motivated by profits, Gould accelerated productivity as much any contemporary and, in doing so, improved the lives of most Americans.

As much as Gould's career showed the creative power of laissez-faire economics, it also shone a light on its shortcomings and made a mockery of Emerson's faith in free markets. Before Gould came along, villainous traders cast no shadow beyond the small community of investors. To be a Wall Street moneyman was to play cards at a poker table. The only winners and losers were the gamblers who played along. It made no difference to the general public if Jacob Little, the most successful trader before the Civil War, manipulated the shares of Morris Canal & Banking Company or bought Norwich & Worcester Railroad on inside information. These companies, although large for their time, had little influence on the country's economic life. If Little told a lie about a company's prospects, even the victims might agree that, in the abstract, it was a small price to pay for economic liberty. If Little created a bear pool to destroy some bulls, no one seriously suggested restricting commercial development, let alone campaigned for a vast regulatory bureaucracy for the sake of investor protection.

The situation was different by the time Gould showed up. Companies were larger, more wealth was invested in the market, and the economy was more integrated. That meant more money—and power—for those who could work the system. Bare-knuckled capitalism now had far-reaching consequences. It was one thing if a gangster shot and killed another gangster. It was another if bystanders got mowed down. Gould's capture of Western Union made him a toll collector on communications. His takeover of Manhattan Railway robbed small investors who naively believed the scaremongering of Gould's *New York World*. Taxpayers financed the dividends that Gould pulled from Union Pacific. Farmers suffered the monopoly rates he demanded on short hauls. Families across the Southwest did without so that Gould could make more money. His gold adventure nearly brought down a presidency.

This was new. Before the Civil War, Adam Smith's invisible hand gently guided the economy by the arm. After the war, as Gould's exploits demonstrated, the invisible hand could apply a choke hold. Mark Twain argued the exploits had lasting consequences. By disregarding social norms in pursuit of lucre, Gould inspired others to follow. "The gospel left behind by Jay Gould is doing giant work," he wrote. "Its message is get money. Get it quickly. Get it in abundance. Get it in prodigious amounts. Get it dishonestly if you can, honestly if you must."[1]

Gould's nemesis Charles Francis Adams saw the risks early on. After studying the Erie War, he argued that people like Gould, if left unchecked, held a gun to democracy. He warned of "Caesarism," a condition where a handful of businesspeople amassed more power than the state and grabbed the nation's wealth for themselves. Despite the Erie episode and Gould's subsequent transgressions, Washington waited until 1887, toward the end of Gould's career and nearly twenty years after the Erie battle, to enact the Interstate Commerce Act and get into the regulation business. Three years later came the Sherman Antitrust Act. The laws were meant to combat price fixing and monopolies. Both were ignored. It would be another decade before Teddy Roosevelt came along and put the laws to good effect. And it wasn't until the Great Depression, with the Securities Act, that the government went after securities fraud, insider trading, and market manipulation.

In our own time, Massachusetts senator Elizabeth Warren has cast a doubtful eye on Big Tech and likened Amazon, Apple, Facebook, and Google to the railroads of the nineteenth century. The technology giants are more than companies, she says. They are networks that, like the railroads, are too essential to be left alone. During her run for president, she referenced the Gilded Age and sounded like Charles Francis Adams warning of "Caesarism" and threats to the republic. "Today's big tech companies have too much power—too much power over our economy, our society, and our democracy," she said.[2] *New York Times* columnist Paul Krugman also reaches back to Gould's day to make a point. He compares the wealth disparity of our present era to the times when Gould cruised Long Island Sound aboard the *Atalanta*. "Needless to say," Krugman writes, "the armies of servants are back, too. So are the yachts."[3]

As I write this, the stock market is hitting record highs. A pack of small investors has cornered shares in video game retailer GameStop. Auditors are under attack for missing a $2 billion fraud at the software company Wirecard. Texas is dealing with power outages created by the deregulation of the state's energy markets. In response, lawmakers are rewriting the rules to make sure such events "never happen again." There will be more scandals in the years ahead followed by more rules to protect investors, protect consumers, and flatten the economic cycle. There will be more agencies, bureaus, and commissions to root out malfeasance. But short of a full attack on for-profit enterprise, the unscrupulous will still bribe politicians, welch on debts, and find ingenious ways to commit fraud. They will betray loyalties, squeeze labor, ignore moralizers, and rationalize their actions. They will still die, fortunes intact, without having seen the inside of a jail cell.

As Gould's experiences show, less government intervention could be part of a solution because there is no bigger punisher than the market. Would the financial crisis of 2008 have happened if mortgage traders, like latter-day Jay Goulds, faced annihilation for misplaced bets? Would the subsequent recovery, among the weakest in history, have been more robust if the government had let the market find its level like it did after the gold fiasco? Would the public have more faith in the system if contemporary Jay Cookes died penniless rather than walking away when their banks collapsed? These are not crazy ideas. Even Elizabeth Warren, about as progressive a politician as they come, acknowledges the value of risk and reward as a tool to advance public welfare. "I love markets," she says.

What can Gould teach investors? The great 1920s stock trader Jesse Livermore said it makes as much sense to study Gould's methods as it does for a West Point cadet to study archery. Rules and technology have changed. The old tricks no longer apply. But while the financial ecosystem is different, human nature is the same and Gould still offers useful lessons. Beware tips and rumors. Trust contracts and not handshakes. Dig behind the headlines. Believe in oneself and ignore the crowd. Hire good lawyers because they are worth the money. Be patient. Remember the human element because it can be as important as the numbers. In negotiations, the right approach might be sycophancy or bullying or something in between. The list goes on.

Livermore admired Gould. As we've seen, many of Gould's contemporaries held a dimmer view. One called him "a despicable worm." Henry Adams called him a spider. Another called him the "the skunk of Wall Street." James Keene, the trader who pulled a gun on Gould, called him "the worst man on earth since the beginning of the Christian era." There were cracks about his height. Gould was "the little wizard" variously described as slight, elfin, and impish. Critics couldn't find enough ways to say pirate. Gould was a freebooter, a corsair, and a buccaneer.

The insults continued after his death. In the middle of the Great Depression, the writer Gustavus Myers called Gould "a pitiless human carnivore," and Robber Baron author Matthew Josephson trotted Gould into service as an argument against capitalism. For these two socialist writers, Gould was a rapacious, loathsome, and felonious union buster, the embodiment of why America needed a Lenin to overthrow the system.

Historians of more recent vintage offer some balance. They argue Gould should be judged in light of his times and against his peers. Insider trading and market manipulation were legal so Gould can hardly be faulted for that. Bribing the New York legislature was morally reprehensible but, given the corruption of the age, a cost of doing business. In a 1986 biography, University of Rhode Island professor Maury Klein suggested Gould be judged in his entirety rather than on his business activity alone. Gould's record as an upstanding family man should be figured into the equation. Wharton professor Julius Grodinsky, who in 1957 completed the first serious analysis of Gould, took pains to credit Gould's contributions. Gould's aggressive track building lowered freight rates. His success as a railroad investor attracted speculative capital into a vital industry when other sources fled the field. But after examining every transaction of Gould's career, poring over every scrap of correspondence, considering every accusation of victims, and compiling spreadsheets to measure Gould's investments, Grodinsky couldn't pull the trigger on a definitive judgment about his subject. His conclusion was unsatisfying. "He had his virtues and he had his faults," he wrote.[4]

Poets might come closer to the truth. In *Babbitt*, written in 1922, Sinclair Lewis dissected American values and reproached the moneygrubbing businessmen of a fictional midwestern town. He could just as easily have been talking about Jay Gould when he describes the "clean, kind, industrious family men who use every known brand of trickery and cruelty to ensure the prosperity of their cubs." Gould was all these things. Lewis's judgment hits it on the head. "The worst thing about these fellows is that they're so good and, in their work at least, so intelligent. You can't hate them properly."[5]

That's the thing about Gould. He lied. He cheated. He stole. But he was so good at what he did, so intelligent in the execution, and such a "clean, kind, and industrious" family man that, try as you might, you can't hate him properly.

EPILOGUE

The Gould children ignored their father's advice about only spending the interest. They proved as adept at spending the family fortune as Gould was at making it. They weren't as frivolous as Mrs. Stuyvesant Fish, the Gramercy Park socialite who once held a champagne-soaked dinner party for a monkey. But some came close.

After George Gould received his inheritance, he spent $500,000 on a diamond tiara for his wife, Edith, that was previously owned by the emperor of China. He built one of the largest private homes in the country. Called Georgian Court, it occupied 152 acres in Lakewood, New Jersey, and came with sunken gardens, statues of Greek gods, and a golf course. Inside were forty rooms, inspired by Versailles, with murals, tapestries, mirrors, and gold leaf. There was an enclosed recreation center with a swimming pool, a bowling alley, and a riding ring. *Harper's Bazaar* gushed that there was no better estate in the country.

When George wasn't playing polo or hunting foxes, he tried to prove himself by accomplishing his father's dream of creating a true transcontinental railroad that stretched from New York to the Pacific. He underestimated the forces aligned against him. When he floated plans to extend the Union Pacific to California, he backed down after Edward Harriman, the owner of the Central Pacific, threatened to destroy him.

George was overextended and ill prepared when in 1907 yet another panic seized Wall Street. The Missouri Pacific filed for bankruptcy and, under pressure to raise cash, he and his siblings sold so many shares of Manhattan Railway and Western Union that they lost control of both. George also sold Georgian Court. The Sisters of Mercy, a Catholic charity, bought it in 1908 and turned it into a liberal arts college, Georgian Court University.

Another of Gould's sons, Frank, became a playboy in the south of France and married an actress. Howard, a third son, also married an actress. When she sued for divorce, he claimed she was having an affair with William Cody, better known as the Buffalo Bill of Wild West Show fame. The court awarded her $36,000 a year, then the largest divorce settlement in American history.

Anna married a penniless French count who spent their money on a Paris mansion, countryside villas, and a yacht so big it was confused with a warship. After his womanizing proved unbearable, she divorced him and upgraded by marrying his cousin, a duke.

The two other Gould children led respectable lives. Helen, the elder daughter, devoted herself to charity. In 1913, when she was forty-four, she married an executive with the Missouri Pacific. Edwin, the second oldest of the sons, made a sensible marriage and became a railroad executive himself. He created successful companies, sat on several boards, and gave away most of his money. Edwin might have been a better choice to run the empire than George.

In 1874, three years after Gould posted his bail, Tweed was convicted and sentenced on more than two hundred charges of embezzlement. He died five years later in the Ludlow Street Jail. As for

Tweed's judges, the New York Assembly impeached Judge Barnard and removed him from office. Judge Cardozo avoided a similar fate by resigning his post.

Sidney Dillon and Cyrus Field both died in 1892, the same year as Gould. Dillon died rich. In Nebraska, the city of Sidney took his first name. In Montana, the city of Dillon took his last name. Field died broke and humiliated. He lost everything after his unsuccessful attempt to corner Manhattan Railway. Some accused Gould for luring him into the trade so he could steal his stock. Field admitted he had only himself to blame.

Russell Sage was a tightwad until the end. He died in 1906 at the age of eighty-nine, without ever having given away a dime. His wife spent the rest of her life finding good homes for the cash. The Russell Sage Foundation remains active, funding research in the social sciences.

Henry Villard, after losing the Northern Pacific, regained control and recovered his fortune. He endowed the University of Oregon and, with Edison, created what became the General Electric Co. For a time, he owned the *New York Post* and *The Nation*.

After leaving the Union Pacific, Charles Francis Adams wrote about history, served as chairman of the Massachusetts Park Commission, became a follower of Henry George and an advocate of a flat tax. He called the Union Pacific episode the worst experience of his life.

ACKNOWLEDGMENTS AND SOURCING

I was able to access research materials at the New York Public Library, the New-York Historical Society, the Massachusetts Historical Society, the Morgan Library, and Gould's summer home, Lyndhurst, before the pandemic hit. I was unable to make it to the Library of Congress, which holds many of Gould's papers. As a result, I relied more heavily on secondary sources than I cared to. The most useful secondary sources were Maury Klein's *The Life and Legend of Jay Gould* and Edward Renehan's *Dark Genius of Wall Street*, which nicely covers Gould's early years.

Fortunately, much of what Gould said, such as in his testimony before various congressional committees, can be found online. The Howard Gotlieb Archival Research Center at Boston University library provided me photocopies of Gould's correspondence with Zadock Pratt. Finding old articles from *The New York Times* was easy enough thanks to the paper's miraculous TimesMachine feature. My ace research assistant Natasha Gross brilliantly chased down articles from other publications. I want to thank Scott Overall and the rest of the staff of the University Club Library in New York for finding articles from old magazines and borrowing books from other libraries, which worked great until interlibrary lending shut down in the crisis.

My reading circle of John Bensche, Doug Lavin, Bob Clymer, and my brother Art made this book better by identifying parts I should scrap and where I needed more context. My editor, Priscilla Painton at Simon & Schuster, encouraged me to think more broadly and kept the narrative on course. My family deserves thanks for putting up with me while I was juggling this, dog walks, and a day job.

NOTES

Introduction

1 *New York Times*, May 1, 1873.

1 Mark Twain, *Autobiography of Mark Twain*, Vol. 1 (Berkeley: University of California Press, 2010), 364.

2 *New York World*, December 3, 1892.

3 Henry Davenport Northrop, *Life and Achievements of Jay Gould, the Wizard of Wall Street* (Philadelphia: The S. M. Southard Publishing Co., 1892).

4 David Freeman Hawke, *John D: The Founding Father of the Rockefellers* (New York: Harper & Row, 1980), 189.

5 *New York Tribune*, December 14, 1892.

6 *New York Times*, May 20, 1887.

7 *USA Today*, April 16, 2019.

8 https://founders.archives.gov/documents/Franklin/01-41-02-0391.

9 https://archive.vcu.edu/english/engweb/transcendentalism/authors/emerson/essays/wealth.html.

10 https://www.digitalhistory.uh.edu/disp_textbook.cfm?smtID=2&psid=3122.

11 https://henrygeorgethestandard.org/volume-1-may-14-1887/.

Chapter One: School Days

1 Abel Crosby to Helen Gould, May 20, 1897, Helen Miller Gould Shepard Papers, New York Historical Society.

2 Murat Halstead, *Life of Jay Gould: How He Made His Millions* (Philadelphia: Edgewood Publishing, 1892), 46.

3 John Burroughs, *My Boyhood* (Garden City, NY: Doubleday, Page, 1922), 68.

4 Robert Irving Warshow, *Jay Gould: The Story of a Fortune* (New York: Greenberg Publisher Inc., 1928), 22.

5 Report of the Committee of the Senate upon the Relations Between Labor and Capital, Senate Hearings, 41st Congress, Vol. 28 (Washington, DC), 1:1063.

6 Ibid.

7 *Angell v. Gould*. New York Public Library, 163.

8 Polly Gould to Sarah Gould Northrop, August 2, 1854, Helen Miller Gould Shepard Papers.

9 *Angell v. Gould*, 456.

10 Ibid., 641.

11 Ibid., 767.

12 J. W. McLaury, "Reminiscences Composed for Miss Helen Gould," Helen Miller Gould Shepard Papers.

Chapter Two: The Seduction of Zadock Pratt

1 J. W. McLaury, "Reminiscences Composed for Miss Helen Gould," Helen Miller Gould Shepard Papers.

2 Alf Evers, *The Catskills: From Wilderness to Woodstock* (Woodstock, NY: Overlook Press, 1982), 342.

3 Ibid. 346.

4 Nahum Capen, *Biography of Zadock Pratt* (Prattsville, NY, 1852), 52.

5 Jay Gould to Zadock Pratt, September 5, 1856. Boston: Boston University Ralph Ingersoll collection.

6 Gould to Pratt, August 15, 1857. Ralph Ingersoll collection.

7 Gould to Pratt, December 11, 1857. Ralph Ingersoll collection.

8 Gould to Pratt, February 3, 1857. Ralph Ingersoll collection.

9 Gould to Pratt, December 24, 1856. Ralph Ingersoll collection.

10 Gould to Pratt, October 12, 1857. Ralph Ingersoll collection.

11 Jay Gould to Hamilton Burhans, September 9, 1857, Helen Miller Gould Shepard Papers.

12 Ibid.

13 Jay Gould to John Burr Gould, August 7, 1857, Helen Miller Gould Shepard Papers.

Chapter Three: Tanners War

1 *New York Herald*, October 7, 1859.

2 *New York Herald*, March 16, 1860.

3 Ibid.
4 Ibid.
5 Jay Gould to James Oliver, November 5, 1860, Helen Miller Gould Shepard Papers.

Chapter Four: This Thing Ambition

1 Edwin G. Burrows and Mike Wallace, *Gotham: A History of New York City to 1898* (New York: Oxford University Press, 1999), 865.
2 Ibid., 864.
3 Ibid., 865.
4 *Fraser's Magazine*, May 1869.
5 R.G. Dun & Company collection. Baker Library, Harvard Graduate School of Business Administration. 201:204, quoted in Edward J. Renehan, Jr., *Dark Genius of Wall Street* (New York: Basic Books, 2005), 80.
6 Elizabeth Gould Palen to Anna Palen, March 25, 1893, Helen Miller Gould Shepard Papers.
7 *Angell v. Gould*, 300.
8 Jay Gould to Helen Miller Gould, January 27, 1864, Jay Gould Papers, Library of Congress.
9 Jay Gould to James Oliver, September 2, 1865, Kansas Historical Society, quoted in Renehan, *Dark Genius of Wall Street*, 88.

Chapter Five: Influencers

1 William Augustus Croffut, *The Vanderbilts and the Story of Their Fortune* (Chicago: Belford, Clake & Co, 1886), 33.
2 Wheaton J. Lane, *Commodore Vanderbilt. An Epic of the Steam Age* (New York: Alfred A Knopf, 1942), 207.
3 *New York Times*, January 5, 1877.
4 William Worthington Fowler. *Ten Years in Wall Street* (Hartford: Worthington, Dustin & Co., 1870), 207.
5 *Harper's Weekly*, July 11, 1863.
6 Ibid.
7 Fowler, *Ten Years in Wall Street,* 127.
8 Henry Clews, *Fifty Years in Wall Street*, Part 1 (New York: Irving Publishing Co., 1908), 116.
9 Croffut, *The Vanderbilts and the Story of Their Fortune*, 79.

Chapter Six: Erie

1 Edith Wharton, *The Age of Innocence*, Book 1, Chapter 9.
2 Report of the Committee of the Senate upon the Relations Between Labor and Capital, Senate Hearings, 41st Congress, Vol. 28, 1064.
3 William Augustus Croffut, *An American Procession* (New York: 1931), 281.
4 *Fraser's Magazine*, May 1869.
5 William Augustus Croffut, *The Vanderbilts* (New York: Belford, Clark & Co., 1886), 83.
6 T. J. Stiles, *The First Tycoon: The Epic Life of Cornelius Vanderbilt* (New York: Alfred A. Knopf, 2009), 453.
7 R. W. McAlpine, *The Life and Times of Colonel Jim Fisk, Jr.* (New York: New York Times Book Co., 1872), 52.
8 Alexander B. Callow, Jr., *The Tweed Ring* (London: Oxford University Press, 1965), 136.

Chapter Seven: Sardines

1 Robert H. Fuller, *Jubilee Jim, reproduction* (London: Texere, 2001), 17.
2 Fowler, *Ten Years in Wall Street*, 501.
3 McAlpine, *The Life and Times of Col. James Fisk, Jr.*, 46.
4 Robert Sobel, *Panic on Wall Street* (New York: E. P. Dutton, 1988), 127.
5 Fowler, *Ten Years in Wall Street*, 483.
6 *New York Herald*, March 6, 1868.
7 Clews, *Fifty Years in Wall Street*, 139.
8 Fowler, *Ten Years in Wall Street*, 500.
9 Ibid.
10 Fowler, *Ten Years in Wall Street,* 501.

Chapter Eight: The Flight

1 Clara Morris, *Life on the Stage* (New York: McClure, Philips: 1901), 308.
2 *New York Herald*, January 18, 1871.
3 Ibid.
4 *New York Herald*, March 12, 1868.
5 *New York Herald*, March 28, 1868
6 Ibid., April 15, 1868.
7 Fowler, *Ten Years in Wall Street*, 504.
8 Ibid., 505.
9 Clews, *Fifty Years in Wall Street*, 138.

Chapter Nine: Peculiar Affairs

1 Edward Harold Mott, *Between the Ocean and the Lakes: The Story of Erie* (New York: Ticker Publishing Co., 1908), 161.
2 W. A. Swanberg, *Jim Fisk* (New York: Charles Scribner's Sons, 1959), 74.
3 Ibid., 74.
4 Alexander B. Callow, Jr., *The Tweed Ring*, 166.
5 *New York Times*, October 24, 1868.
6 Ibid., November 4, 1868.
7 Ibid., November 5, 1868.
8 Ibid., November 10, 1868.
9 *New York Times*, November 15, 1868.
10 Edward Harold Mott, *Between the Ocean and the Lakes*, 165.
11 Ibid., 165.
12 Clews, *Fifty Years in Wall Street*, 119.

Chapter Ten: Good Morning, Commodore

1 https://oll.libertyfund.org/title/earth-hunger-and-other-essays-1913.
2 *New York Herald*, November 19, 1868.
3 Mott, *Between The Ocean and the Lakes*, 171.

Chapter Eleven: Prophet of Regulation

1 Edward Chase Kirkland, *Charles Francis Adams Jr.* (Cambridge, MA: Harvard University Press, 1965), 41.
2 Ibid., 95.
3 Ibid., 35.
4 Charles Francis Adams, Jr., *Chapters of Erie* (Prospect Heights, IL: Waveland Press, 2002), 1.
5 Ibid., 48.
6 Ibid., 56.
7 Ibid., 98.
8 https://whitmanarchive.org/published/periodical/journalism/tei/per.00398.html.
9 Burroughs, *My Boyhood*, 38.
10 Henry Adams, "The New York Gold Conspiracy," in Charles Francis Adams, *Chapters of Erie*, 106.

Chapter Twelve: Gold

1 Fowler, *Ten Years in Wall Street*, 527.

2 *New York World*, December 3, 1892.

3 Kenneth D. Ackerman, *The Gold Ring* (Falls Church VA: Viral History Press, 2011), 46.

4 George Boutwell, *Reminicenses of Sixty Years in Public Affairs: Volume 2*, Reproduction (Frankfurt Am Main, Germany: Outlook Verlag, 2020), 112.

5 *New York Times*, March 12, 1869.

6 Ibid.

7 https://www2.illinois.gov/alplm/xxmuseum/Education/Documents/Ulysses%20 Grant%20Inaugural%20Addresses.pdf.

8 Fowler, *Ten Years in Wall Street*, 516.

9 Henry Adams, "The New York Gold Conspiracy," 114.

10 Investigation into Causes of the Gold Panic, House Report, No. 31, 41st Congress, 2nd Session, 314.

11 Trumbull White, *The Wizard of Wall Street and His Wealth* (Philadelphia: John C. Yorkston & Co., 1893), 92.

Chapter Thirteen: The Plot

1 New York *Sun*, October 4, 1869.

2 *Angell v. Gould*, New York Public Library, 480.

3 *New York Times*, August 25, 1869.

4 Investigation into Causes of the Gold Panic, House Report, No. 31, 314.

5 Ibid., 31, 163.

6 Ibid., 31, 136.

7 *New York Times*, January 1, 1870.

8 Investigation into Causes of the Gold Panic, House Report, No. 31, 172.

9 Ibid., 171.

Chapter Fourteen: The Mix-up

1 Investigation into Causes of the Gold Panic, House Report, No. 31, 174.

2 Ibid., 9.

3 Fuller, *Jubilee Jim*, 347.

4 Letter from Fahnestock to Cooke, September 17, 1869, Cooke Papers, Philadelphia Historical Society, quoted in Ackerman, *The Gold Ring*, 130.

5 Investigation into Causes of the Gold Panic, House Report, No. 31, 186.

6 Ibid., 251.

Chapter Fifteen: Pump and Dump

1 Investigation into Causes of the Gold Panic, House Report, No. 31, 205.
2 Ibid., 256.
3 Clarence Stedman, *The New York Stock Exchange* (New York: New York Stock Exchange Historical Company, 1905), 223.
4 *New York Times*, September 24, 1869.
5 *New York Tribune*, October 1, 1869
6 *New York Times*, September 24, 1869.
7 *New York Tribune*, October 1, 1869.
8 Investigation into Causes of the Gold Panic, House Report, No. 31, 142.
9 *New York Times*, September 24, 1869.

Chapter Sixteen: Black Friday

1 *New York Times*, September 24, 1869.
2 Investigation into Causes of the Gold Panic, House Report, No. 31, 65.
3 Ackerman, *The Gold Ring*, 196.
4 Ibid, 197.
5 *New York Times*, October 25, 1869.
6 Investigation into Causes of the Gold Panic, House Report, No. 31, 65.
7 Matthew Josephson, *Edison* (New York: John Wiley & Sons, 1992), 77.
8 *New York Times*, October 25, 1869.
9 *New York Times*, January 24, 1870.
10 Ibid.
11 Investigation into Causes of the Gold Panic, House Report, No. 31, 202.
12 Ibid., 203.

Chapter Seventeen: The Day After

1 New York *Sun*, September 27, 1869.
2 *New York World*, September 26, 1869.
3 Fowler, *Ten Years in Wall Street,* 526.
4 Investigation into Causes of the Gold Panic, House Report, No. 31, 67.
5 Ibid., 68.

Chapter Eighteen: The Reckoning

1 *New York Herald*, October 8, 1869.
2 New York *Sun*, October 23, 1869.
3 Investigation into Causes of the Gold Panic, House Report, No. 31, 136.

4 Ibid., 139.

5 Ibid., 166.

6 New York *Sun*, October 8, 1869.

7 Investigation into Causes of the Gold Panic, House Report, No. 31, 170.

8 Ibid., 302.

9 Ibid., 101.

10 Ibid., 142.

11 Ibid., 14.

12 Northrop, *Life and Achievements of Jay Gould,* 326.

13 Investigation into Causes of the Gold Panic, House Report, No. 31, 135.

Chapter Nineteen: Fisk's Reward

1 *New York Herald*, April 12, 1870.

2 Meyer Berger, *The Story of the New York Times* (New York: Simon & Schuster, 1951), 48.

3 Denis T. Lynch, *Boss Tweed: The Story of a Grim Generation* (New York: Boni & Liveright, 1927), 382.

4 Edward Harold Mott, *Between the Ocean and the Lakes*, 180.

5 *New York Times*, January 7, 1872.

6 *New York Herald*, January 8, 1872.

7 Edward Harold Mott, *Between the Ocean and the Lakes*, 187.

8 *New York Herald*, March 11, 1872.

9 Edward Harold Mott, *Between the Ocean and the Lakes*, 189.

10 New York *Sun*, March 12, 1872.

11 Ibid.

Chapter Twenty: Cows in the Moonlight

1 Northrop, *Life and Achievements of Jay Gould*, 307.

2 *New York Herald*, September 27, 1872.

3 Edward Harold Mott, *Between the Ocean and the Lakes*, 210.

4 Northrop, *Life and Achievements of Jay Gould*, 85.

5 Edward Harold Mott, *Between the Ocean and the Lakes*, 212.

6 *New York Times*, December 13, 1872.

7 *New York Commercial Advertiser*, November 26, 1872.

8 Maury Klein, *The Life and Legend of Jay Gould* (Baltimore: John Hopkins University Press, 1986), 97.

9 New York *Sun*, November 27, 1872.

Chapter Twenty-one: Union Pacific

1 *New York World*, July 2, 1887.
2 *Commercial and Financial Chronicle*, October 19, 1872.
3 Stedman, *The New York Stock Exchange*, 261.
4 J. John Lubetkin, *Jay Cooke's Gamble* (Norman: University of Oklahoma Press, 2006), 287.
5 https://www.thevintagenews.com/2019/10/20/sitting-bull-speech/.
6 *New York Herald*, September 19, 1873.
7 Richard White, *The Republic for Which It Stands* (New York: Oxford University Press, 2017), 266.
8 United States Pacific Railway Commission, Testimony, Executive Document No. 51, Senate, 50th Congress, 1st Session, 1887, 446.
9 Klein, *The Life and Legend of Jay Gould*, 221.
10 Ibid., 140.
11 Alice Northrop Snow and Helen Nicholas Snow, *The Story of Helen Gould, Daughter of Jay Gould* (Madison, Wisconsin: F.H. Revell, 1943), 67.
12 Murat Halstead, *Life of Jay Gould: How He Made His Millions* (Philadelphia: Edgewood Publishing, 1892), 1180.
13 *New York Tribune*, May 6, 1874.
14 Gould to Clark, September 5, 1874, Kingdon Gould Papers, quoted in Klein, *The Life and Legend of Jay Gould*, 149.
15 Gould to Dillon, September 12, 1875, Jay Gould Papers, quoted in Renehan, *Dark Genius of Wall Street*, 230.
16 Gould to Rollins, quoted in Klein, *The Life and Legend of Jay Gould*, 150.
17 *Philadelphia North American*, March 5, 1875, quoted in Julius Grodinsky, *Jay Gould: His Business Career* (Philadelphia: University of Pennsylvania Press, 1957), 127.
18 *New York Times*, August 1, 1875.

Chapter Twenty-two: Edison

1 Josephson, *Edison*, 116.
2 *New York Times*, December 4, 1892.
3 Josephson, *Edison*, 120.
4 Ibid., 47.
5 Ibid., 81.
6 Ibid., 126.

7 *New York Times*, January 5, 1877.

8 Arthur T. Vanderbilt II, *Fortune's Children* (New York: HarperCollins, 1989), 70.

9 T. J. Stiles, *The First Tycoon* (New York: Alfred A. Knopf, 2009), 152.

10 Croffut, *The Vanderbilts and the Story of Their Fortune*, 259.

11 Josephson, *Edison*, 126.

12 Ibid.

13 *New York Times*, August 3, 1877.

Chapter Twenty-three: Dirty Tricks

1 Klein, *The Life and Legend of Jay Gould*, 183.

Chapter Twenty-four: In Gould's Grip

1 *New York Times*, January 30, 1879.

2 Pacific Railway Commission, Klein, *The Life and Legend of Jay Gould*, 247.

3 Northrop, *Life and Achievements of Jay Gould*, 144.

4 Ibid., 193.

5 Pacific Railway Commission, 450.

6 Ibid., 482.

7 Ibid., 510.

8 Klein, *The Life and Legend of Jay Gould*, 247.

Chapter Twenty-five: Acquisitions

1 New York *Sun*, February 9, 1880.

2 *New York Tribune*, January 4, 1881.

3 *Railroad Gazette*, March 26, 1880.

4 Klein, *The Life and Legend of Jay Gould*, 244.

5 Ibid., 253.

6 Ibid., 268.

7 Gould to William Hart, June 27, 1865, Jay Gould Papers. Library of Congress.

Chapter Twenty-six: Western Union

1 Klein, *The Life and Legend of Jay Gould*, 280.

Chapter Twenty-seven: Elevated

1 https://www.newyorker.com/magazine/2009/11/16/hosed.

2 *New York Times*, December 27, 1881.

3 Ibid.

Chapter Twenty-eight: Wares at a Bazaar

1 Edwin Hoyt, *The Goulds* (New York: Weybright & Talley, 1969), 65.
2 *New York Tribune*, May 1, 1873.
3 Kirkland, *Charles Francis Adams*, 60.
4 Ibid., 57.
5 *Boston Advertiser*, December 27, 1881.

Chapter Twenty-nine: Terror

1 Ron Chernow, *Grant* (New York: Penguin, 2017), 922.
2 *New York Times*, May 15, 1884.
3 Ibid.
4 Alexandra Villard de Borchgrave and John Cullen, *Villard: The Life and Times of an American Titan* (New York: Nan A. Talese, 2001), 339.
5 Klein, *The Life and Legend of Jay Gould*, 327.
6 *New York Herald*, June 11, 1884.
7 *New York Tribune*, July 5, 1886.

Chapter Thirty: The Strike

1 *New York Times*, March 31, 1886.
2 Craig Phelan, *Grand Master Workman: Terence Powderly and the Knights of Labor* (Westport, CT: Praeger, 2000), 161.
3 Ibid., 160.
4 Theresa Case, *The Great Southwest Railroad Strike and Free Labor* (College Station: Texas A&M University Press, 2010), 175.
5 *St. Louis Post-Dispatch*, March 8, 1886.
6 https://en.wikipedia.org/wiki/Thomas_A._Scott#:~:text=Scott%2C%20 often%20referred%20to%20as,federal%20troops%20to%20end%20the.
7 Phelan, *Grand Master Workman*, 181.
8 *New York Times*, March 29, 1886.
9 Ibid.
10 *New York Sun*, March 29, 1886.
11 Klein, *The Life and Legend of Jay Gould*, 362.
12 *New York Times*, April 7, 1886.
13 Ibid.
14 Trumbull White, *The Wizard of Wall Street and His Wealth* (Philadelphia: John C. Yorkston & Co., 1893), 150.
15 Halstead, *Life of Jay Gould*, 82.

16 Erik Loomis, *A History of American in Ten Strikes* (New York: The New Press, 2018), 61.

17 *New York Times*, April 10, 1886.

18 *New York Times*, April 11, 1886.

19 *St. Louis Post-Dispatch*, April 7, 1886.

20 Terence V. Powderly, *The Path I Trod: Autobiography of Terence V. Powderly* (New York: Columbia University Press, 1940), 135.

21 Klein, *The Life and Legend of Jay Gould*, 227.

22 Edward Bok, *The Americanization of Edward Bok* (Chicago: Lakeside Press, 2000), 104.

Chapter Thirty-one: A Gould Wedding

1 Snow and Snow, *The Story of Helen Gould*, 354.

2 Renehan, *Dark Genius of Wall Street*, 283.

3 *New York Tribune*, June 14, 1887.

4 "Memphis Under Quarantine," *Frank Leslie's Illustrated Paper*, September 20, 1879.

5 Northrop, *Life and Achievements of Jay Gould,* 480.

6 Ibid.

Chapter Thirty-two: In the Dark

1 *New York Times*, May 7, 1887.

2 *New York Times*, May 18, 1887.

3 Ibid.

4 Ibid.

Chapter Thirty-three: Bad News

1 *New York Herald*, October 30, 1887.

2 Ibid.

3 Northrop, *Life and Achievements of Jay Gould*, 233.

4 *New York Herald*, February 28, 1881.

5 Ibid., March 27, 1888.

6 *New York Herald,* April 1, 1888.

7 Klein, *The Life and Legend of Jay Gould,* 409.

8 Northrop, *Life and Achievements of Jay Gould*, 307.

9 Ibid., 204.

Chapter Thirty-four: Morgan

1 Kirkland, *Charles Francis Adams,* 120.
2 Klein, *The Life and Legend of Jay Gould*, 438.
3 John K. Winkler, *Morgan the Magnificent* (Garden City, NY: Doubleday, Doran & Co, 1932), 111.
4 Ibid., 112.
5 Ibid.
6 Ibid.
7 Kirkland, *Charles Francis Adams*, 119.
8 Ibid.
9 Jean Strouse, *Morgan* (New York: Random House, 1999), 306.
10 Gould to Clark, February 6, 1890, quoted in Klein, *The Life and Legend of Jay Gould*, 440.

Chapter Thirty-five: Change at the Top

1 *New York Times*, April 13, 1890.
2 Report of the Committee of the Senate upon the Relations Between Labor and Capital, Senate Hearings. 41st Congress, Vol. 26, 962–64.
3 Kirkland, *Charles Francis Adams*, 123.
4 Ibid.
5 Ibid. 93.
6 Ibid., 94.
7 Ibid., 125.
8 Snow and Snow, *The Story of Helen Gould*. 188.
9 *New York Herald*, November 7, 1890.
10 Kirkland, *Charles Francis Adams*, 126.
11 Ibid., 125.
12 Ibid.
13 Ibid., 126.
14 Ibid., 127.
15 *New York World*, November 27, 1890.

Chapter Thirty-six: Woodlawn

1 *New York Times*, October 2, 1891.
2 Ibid.
3 Ibid.
4 Northrop, *Life and Achievements of Jay Gould*, 296.
5 Snow and Snow, *The Story of Helen Gould*, 193.

Chapter Thirty-seven: An Appraisal

1 Twain, *Autobiography*, 364.
2 Elizabeth Warren, "Here's How We Can Break Up Big Tech," March 8, 2019, https://2020.elizabethwarren.com/toolkit/break-up-big-tech.
3 Paul Krugman, "For Richer," *New York Times Magazine*, October 20, 2002.
4 Julius Grodinsky, *Jay Gould: His Business Career* (Philadelphia: University of Pennsylvania Press, 1957), 595.
5 Sinclair Lewis, *Babbitt* (New York: Harcourt, Brace & World, 1950), 101.

INDEX

Index

Index

ABOUT THE AUTHOR

GREG STEINMETZ is a partner with a New York money management firm. Before moving to finance, he was a journalist and served as London bureau chief for *The Wall Street Journal*. He lives in Larchmont, New York.